The Federalist Literary Mind

The Federalist
Literary Mind

Selections from the
Monthly Anthology and Boston Review, 1803–1811,
Including Documents Relating to the Boston Athenaeum

Edited by Lewis P. Simpson

Louisiana State University Press

Copyright 1962 by
Louisiana State University Press
Library of Congress Catalogue Card Number: 61–13013
Manufactured in the United States of America by
J. H. Furst Co., Baltimore, Maryland

To My Mother
and to the memory of
My Father

Acknowledgments

IN THE COMPLETION of this volume I have incurred a good many debts. Only a few can be acknowledged here. To the John Simon Guggenheim Memorial Foundation I owe a very special debt for having made it possible for me to take a year's leave of absence from teaching to undertake a broad research project having to do with the history of literary order. This book represents the completion of a phase of this project. I am indebted to the Research Council of Louisiana State University for additional financial assistance in support of my research. Also, I am under obligation to the office of the Graduate School of Louisiana State University for aid in typing the manuscript of this volume.

Librarians of the libraries at Louisiana State University, the University of Texas, and Duke University have been helpful to me. I must express my particular appreciation to Walter Muir Whitehill, the director of the Boston Athenaeum, for his interest in my work, for reading it in manuscript, and for allowing me to reproduce the portraits of various members of the Anthology Society which are in the Athenaeum collection.

Others who have been interested in this undertaking and who have looked at it in whole or in part include Theodore Hornberger, Henry Nash Smith, John Paul Pritchard, and Harry H. Warfel. I am grateful to them, as I am to several other persons who have had a less direct hand in the book, but who have encouraged me in my studies. These include Thomas A. Kirby, Arlin Turner, Gordon Mills, Darwin Shrell, Otis Wheeler, Leo Levy, and my sister, Miss Betty Simpson. Finally, I should like to thank my wife for her constant and patient helpfulness.

The first two sections of the Introduction are adapted from essays which originally appeared in the *Emerson Society Quarterly* and the *New England Quarterly* respectively. I appreciate the kind permission of the editors of these journals to make this use of my essays.

L. P. S.

Contents

ix

THE IMAGE OF THE MAN OF LETTERS

FROM BOEOTIA TO ATTICA

Illustrations

Introduction

This Society shall meet on the Thursday evening of every week at 7 o'clock P. M. from the autumnal to the vernal & at 8 o'clock P. M. from the vernal to the autumnal equinox.

> —Article Eighth of the Constitution of the Anthology Society (1805)

Every judicious effort to promote the love of Letters and Arts is entitled to countenance, for this, among other reasons, . . . that a progress in letters and arts corresponds to the progress of society in other respects in our country.

> —Editors' Address, *Monthly Anthology*, IV (January, 1807)

IN. MEMORIAM

ARTHUR MAYNARD WALTER:

BONI ;

JURIS, AC OMNIUM

RERUM,

LITERIS ATTINENTIUM,

SUPRA SUAM ÆTATEM,

VALDE PERITI.

ANNO DOMINI

MILLESIMO OCTINGENTESIMO SEPTIMO;

ÆTATIS SUÆ

VICESIMO SEXTO ;

JANUARII

DIE SECUNDO,

SPLENDIDIOREM INIRE,

HANC VITAM RELIQUIT.

,,,,,,,,,

Eheu, vos charum tam perdere sanguine junctos !
Eheu, vos comites miseros tam perdere fidum !
Eheu, vos Musas tristes tam perdere amicum !
Eheu, mundum infelicem tam perdere rectum !
Tristes dilectum sobolem plorate Camænæ !
Occidis infelix puer, ah ! memorande per ævum,
Nulla tuam poterit virtutem abolere vetustas.

Memorial to ARTHUR MAYNARD WALTER from the
Monthly Anthology

The Myth
of New England's Intellectual Lapse

THIS VOLUME HAS two purposes. One is to afford a history in some detail of the publication and editing of the *Monthly Anthology and Boston Review, Containing Sketches and Reports of Philosophy, Religion, History, Arts, and Manners* (1803–1811). The second, and primary, intention is to illustrate the Federalist literary mind, as it existed in early nineteenth-century Boston, through an organized selection of extracts from the miscellaneous contents of this pioneer American magazine.

From the standpoint of American literary history, the *Monthly Anthology*, edited by a "Society of Gentlemen" known as the Anthology Society, was a more important literary journal than has been generally recognized. Its major contemporary, Philadelphia's *Port Folio*, was more widely read and is today better known to students of the literary culture of the early American Republic. The *Port Folio*'s reputation was generated and has been sustained by the fame of its founder and first editor, Joseph Dennie. One of the nation's first professional men of letters, Dennie was not only a talented editor and critic but a literary personality as well. Yet, it may be argued, the magazine he created, in spite of its relatively long existence, was more an end than a beginning. Its historical context is the decline of Philadelphia as the literary hope of the new nation. The *Anthology* was a beginning. Its history is a part of the origins of mid-nineteenth-century Boston's wide-ranging literary influence.

The various circumstances which conspired to reduce the literary quality of Philadelphia cannot be elaborated here. Possibly, however, Philadelphia's literary aspirations were always more apparent than real. The social, and until 1800, the political, capital of the Republic, the city had, in addition to belles-lettres, elegance, politics, and science. It may have had too much of these

for the sake of literature, especially too much science. Philadelphia's intellectual life was dominated by the "American Philosophical Society, held at Philadelphia for promoting useful
Knowledge." In the city of Dr. Benjamin Rush, Charles Willson
Peale, and Benjamin Smith Barton—the inheritors of Franklin's
scientific pursuits and the philosophical allies of Jefferson—intellectual interests were more cogently expressed in the pages of
the *Transactions of the American Philosophical Society* than in
Dennie's Addisonian *Port Folio*. Surely this is one reason why
Philadelphia did not develop a serious humanistic literary culture,
even though it did become a leading publishing center.[1]

In Boston a different and essentially more promising literary
situation existed. Hoping New Englanders would emulate the
American Philosophical Society, John Adams founded the American Academy of Arts and Sciences in Boston in 1780. Its success
was limited. Although the Bostonians were not in general an-
tagonistic to science, they tended to subordinate it to a complex
religious and humanistic heritage. This heritage, questing after
new directions in the days of the Anthology Society and the
Anthology, fulfilled its destiny in the mid-century renaissance.
In this age the literary power exercised by Boston spread from
New England over the new nation.

Still, in spite of the fact that Boston's literary authority is one
of the leading features of the literary history of the United States
during the nineteenth century, little attention has been given
to the initial shaping of this authority during the Federalist period.
(More attention has been paid to the decline of Boston's literary
dominance in the late nineteenth and early twentieth centuries,
a subject of delight in some quarters.) For the neglect of the
time of the *Anthology* there is one obvious, and from certain
points of view, overwhelming, reason: this era is barren of
any literary work now remembered for its intrinsic excellence.
A less obvious, but perhaps more significant, reason, lies in what
may be called "the myth of New England's intellectual lapse."

---

[1] For a somewhat different attitude toward the literary quality of Boston,
see William Charvat's interesting study entitled *Literary Publishing in
America, 1790-1850* (Philadelphia, 1959), 27-37.

A brief inquiry into the origin and perpetuation of this myth is illuminating.

If it can be traced to a single source, the myth of New England's intellectual lapse can be said to have originated in Ralph Waldo Emerson's scorn for his father's generation.

Emerson first suggested it in a letter to his brother William in 1850, subsequently made it as a dogmatic statement in an entry in his *Journals* in 1852, and eventually generalized it in his vivid " Historic Notes of Life and Letters in New England." In the letter to his brother, he expresses his embarrassment over requests for a biographical sketch of their father, the Reverend William Emerson, whose career as a Boston minister and man of letters was ended by his early death in 1811. One request had come from that venerable worthy Josiah Quincy, who was at work on his *History of the Boston Athenaeum* (1851), another from the Reverend William B. Sprague, who was compiling his multi-volumed *Annals of the American Pulpit* (1857–1869), and still another from the Reverend William Ware, who was engaged in editing his comprehensive *American Unitarian Biography* (1851). Why Emerson was doubtful about assisting in this series of tributes to his father's literary and religious significance is partly to be explained simply by the fact that his recollection of him was faint. But the primary reason was that the writings of his father seemed to him commonplace, imitative, and docile. The literary relics of the Reverend William Emerson, his son judged, were the pallid mirror of his age, " that early ignorant & transitional *Month-of-March*, in our New England culture." [2]

Emerson concludes the letter, to be sure, with a more positive interpretation of his father's significance. " His literary merits really are that he fostered the Anthology & the Athenaeum." [3] These early growths " ripened into " Joseph Stevens Buckminster, William Ellery Channing, and Edward Everett. From the standpoint of historical accuracy, this is, of course, an inexact metaphor. Buckminster (1784–1812), the brightest ornament of the Boston pulpit in his brief day, lived hardly more than long enough to

[2] Ralph Waldo Emerson to William Emerson, *Letters of Ralph Waldo Emerson*, ed. Ralph L. Rusk (New York, 1939), IV, 179.
[3] *Ibid*.

preach William Emerson's funeral sermon; and William Ellery
Channing (1780–1842) had been in the pulpit almost a decade
when Emerson's father died. Both were contemporary with the
Anthology Society and the founding of the Boston Athenaeum.
In the case of Edward Everett (1794–1865), Emerson's metaphor
is more apt; for in a very real sense he was a product of the
cultural aspiration embodied in such ventures as the *Anthology*
and the Athenaeum, which grew out of the Anthology Reading
Room set up in 1806.

New England's intellectual history—or the lack of it—during
the generation preceding his own continued to interest Emerson.
Two years after his letter to his brother, he confided to his
Journals a more explicit and more unsympathetic reading of its
quality: " To write a history of Massachusetts, I confess, is not
inviting to an expansive thinker. . . . [*sic*] Since, from 1790 to
1820, there was not a book, a speech, a conversation, or a thought
in the State. About 1820, the Channing, Webster, and Everett
era begun, and we have been bookish and poetical and cogitative
since." [4] This statement represents an intensification of the attitude expressed earlier in the letter to his brother. " About 1820 "
a new literary and intellectual era suddenly commenced in New
England. No allowance is made for a transition, even a raw
March of incipient growth. One notes, incidentally, that Emerson has replaced Buckminster with Daniel Webster in his trinity
of literary inaugurators. This hardly lessens the confusion.
Webster was born two years after Channing and, like him, was
largely moulded in the century's first decade.

After the Civil War, when Emerson put together his comments
entitled " Historic Notes of Life and Letters in New England,"
he stated his rejection of his father's world in terms of a comprehensive theory of history: " There are always two parties, the
party of the Past and the party of the Future; the Establishment
and the Movement. At times the resistance is reanimated, the
schism runs under the world and appears in Literature, Philosophy, Church, State, and social customs. It is not easy to date
these eras of activity with any precision, but in this region one

[4] *Journals of Ralph Waldo Emerson*, ed. Edward Waldo Emerson and
Waldo Emerson Forbes (Boston and New York, 1909–1914), VIII, 339.

made itself remarked, say in 1820 and the twenty years following." [5] Obviously this concept of a clash between the Establishment and the Movement allows for a broader and more discerning
treatment of New England's intellectual history than does either
the Month-of-March idea or the theory of a complete lapse of
intellect between 1790 and 1820. The implication is that the
years preceding 1820 represent a period of domination by the
Establishment; no longer are they merely a crude transition or
merely a blank. Yet this is only by implication. The essay is
devoted to characterizing the Movement, and develops no image
of the Establishment. The "Historic Notes," consequently, does
little to modify Emerson's idea of an intellectual and literary
hiatus in New England for a period of thirty years.

Emerson's rejection of his father's generation should be placed
in two contexts: one, the mid-century sense of achievement,
and, two, Emerson's complete refusal of the eighteenth-century
rationalistic heritage. By the 1850's, Perry Miller observes, Emerson not only felt a conviction of personal accomplishment but
shared with his contemporaries the feeling that in their time
New England had come of age. At "the moment of adult
health, the culmination of power," the era of the *Anthology*
and William Emerson seemed remote and bleak. The significance of the other context, Emerson's attitude toward the
eighteenth century, is suggested by Sherman Paul when he points
out how early nineteenth-century New Englanders, in their
dedication to the "Lockean understanding," took "from the
manifold riches of the eighteenth century those elements of
method and philosophy which, in terms of their spiritual needs,
were showing the most effects of hardening and inutility." [6]
Similarly, one may add, they tended to take the literary theories
and techniques of the age of Pope and Johnson which, in terms
of the requirements of literary originality, were the least promising. The result was an inhibiting formalism and imitativeness

[5] *Complete Works of Ralph Waldo Emerson*, ed. Edward Waldo Emerson
(Boston and New York, 1904), X, 325.
[6] See *The Transcendentalists*, ed. Miller (Cambridge, Mass., 1950), 16;
Paul, *Emerson's Angle of Vision* (Cambridge, Mass., 1952), 13-14. Cf.
Emerson's "Plato; or the Philosopher," *Works*, IV, 46-47.

which Emerson cast off in its entirety. His letter to William, his comment in his *Journals*, and his remarks in the "Historic Notes" are brief, revealing glimpses into some of the intimacies of his rejection of the past, the negative counterpart of his affirmation of self-reliance. His concept of New England's intellectual lapse was not the result of historical scrutiny—he is elsewhere, as a matter of fact, an advocate of the coherence of New England culture—but a necessity of his transcendental vision.[7]

In the present century, however, Emerson's notion was to gain wide currency through Vernon L. Parrington's great, highly influential, thesis-ridden *Main Currents in American Thought*. Parrington employs Emerson's cold dictum to the effect that from 1790 to 1820 not a book, speech, conversation, or thought graced Massachusetts as the major text of a very emotional chapter on the New England Renaissance. After quoting Emerson's assertion, Parrington argues eloquently that " in its contemptuous dismissal of the age of Fisher Ames and Robert Treat Paine " the statement is " scarcely unjust." " The utter sterility of those old times," he says, " Emerson understood only too well." The New England Renaissance, Parrington contends, was a total revolt against a constricting parochialism which had delayed the flowering for a whole generation. The sources of this revolt lay in the romantic revolution and in " a sudden reawakening of the ethical passion of Puritanism . . . ; a vision of a new heaven and a new earth that it proposed to take by storm." Parrington sees a hybrid liberalism—compounded of French rationalism, New England mysticism, German metaphysics, and literary romanticism—assuming the role of hero and savior, awakening the slumbering New England mind from "the nightmare dreams of Calvinism that debased human nature, and the counting house dreams of Federalism that conceived of man as an exploitative animal." Thus Parrington's zealous imagination, working out to its own satisfaction the implications of Emerson's attitude toward the Federalist age, created a myth that has undoubtedly had a controlling influence on the historical attitude assumed toward Federalist New England—or, more particularly, toward its cultural capital, " the

---

[7] See Emerson's essay entitled "Boston," *Works*, XII, 183-211.

complacent little Boston of Fisher Ames and Robert Treat Paine," as Parrington calls it.[8]

It is possible, however, to construct another image of Federalist New England and of Boston's place in it. The general outline of this image was suggested some sixty-five years ago by Henry Adams in his classic *History of the United States, 1801–1817*. Adams accepts the time of William Emerson and Joseph Stevens Buckminster on its own terms; he sees the limitations placed on its intellect by conservative forces, but at the same time suggests its renascent quality and its relation to the future, urging upon the reader the spirit of intellectual aspiration and literary ambition in the Boston of the early 1800's.

It was the ambition, the determination to be literary, as Adams saw it, that counted.[9] " In the usual course of national aggrandizement," Buckminster said before a Phi Beta Kappa audience in 1809, " it is almost certain, that those of you, who shall attain to old age, will find yourselves citizens of an empire unparalleled in extent; but is it probable, that you will have the honor of belonging to a nation of men of letters? " [10] The response to this challenge was a quest to establish the fraternity and authority of the vocation of mind amid the conditions of the new national existence. It was a response made in various ways all over the infant Republic; nowhere, though, more insistently than in the Boston of William Emerson. His personal response had already been made in 1804, when to his burden of clerical and civic duties he had added the editorship of the fledgling *Anthology*, a deserted offspring of literary ambition early frustrated.

[8] *Main Currents in American Thought* (New York, 1927, 1930), II, 317, 273, 296.

[9] See Henry Adams, *History of the United States, 1801–1817* (New York, 1889–1891), IX, 201-208.

[10] " On the Dangers and Duties of Men of Letters," *Anthology*, VII (September, 1809), 146.

The Anthology Society
and the Monthly Anthology

THE "ANTHOLOGY" FIRST appeared in November, 1803, as
The Monthly Anthology, or Magazine of Polite Literature. Its
publisher was E. Lincoln in Water Street; its editor was " Sylvanus
Per-Se," a pseudonym (suggested by " Sylvanus Urban " of the
Gentleman's Magazine) masking the identity of a Boston schoolmaster, David Phineas Adams, Harvard, class of 1801. Adams,
hoping possibly to imitate Joseph Dennie or Charles Brockden
Brown, had determined to make a professional literary career
for himself. Had he succeeded he would be remembered among
Boston's first professional men of letters; but within six months,
unable to lure either subscribers or contributors in sufficient
numbers, he relinquished his editorship and with it his intended
profession. His failure may have been partly due to his obscure
origin. A poor farmer's son from Lexington, Massachusetts, he
had little to recommend him to the Bostonians save a Harvard
degree.[11]

What the moribund *Anthology* needed, the ambitious young
printing firm of Munroe and Francis decided, was an editor of
established reputation. So Munroe and Francis took over the
publication in 1804 and persuaded the busy pastor of Boston's
First Church, William Emerson, to assume the editorship. Well
known in the Boston community for his literary interests, Emerson induced various friends to aid him in his new enterprise:

[11] See Josiah Quincy, *History of the Boston Athenaeum, with Biographical
Notices of Its Deceased Founders* (Cambridge, Mass., 1851), 1-2 n. (The
appended biographical notices are paginated separately.) Also, see *Journal
of the Proceedings of the Society Which Conducts the Monthly Anthology
& Boston Review, October 3, 1805, to July 2, 1811*, ed. M. A. DeWolfe
Howe (Boston, 1910), 4. (Hereinafter references to the *Journal* will be
incorporated in the text and indicated by the abbreviation *J.*)

among others, the Reverend John Sylvester John Gardiner, pastor of Trinity Church, Samuel Cooper Thacher, later pastor of the New South Church, and William Smith Shaw, lawyer by profession, antiquarian and bibliophile by avocation. All three later became prominent members of the Anthology Society. When the second volume of the *Anthology* got underway, contributors multiplied and Emerson's scheme began to look promising.[12]

It looked still better some eight months later when a group of Boston men of letters—all of them of the Federalist persuasion—formally established the Anthology Society. Earlier they had appointed Buckminster, newest occupant of the pulpit of the Brattle Street Church, Arthur Maynard Walter, Boston lawyer, and the enterprising Shaw to draw up a constitution for their proposed club. One afternoon in October, 1805, the charter members of the Anthology Society gathered at Gardiner's home to approve the constitution and to elect officers. They made an interesting group, including besides those already mentioned: William Tudor, Jr., first editor of the *North American Review*; Edmund Trowbridge Dana, brother of R. H. Dana, Sr.; William Wells, bookseller and classicist, later of the firm of Wells and Lilly, publishers; Peter Oxenbridge Thacher, brother of S. C. Thacher and judge of Boston's Municipal Court; Joseph Tuckerman, Unitarian minister and humanitarian; Thomas Gray, long-time minister of the Third Church in Roxbury; and two promising young physicians, Drs. James Collins Warren and James Jackson.

This body had strong resources in youth, intellect, and aspiration. Of the fourteen original members, the majority were in their twenties in 1805, and the oldest, Gardiner, who was chosen president, was only forty-one. Emerson and Wells were in their thirties. All the Anthologists, by the standards of the day, were well educated in books, and several were versed in European travel, or soon would be. All were eager to be men of letters, and some supported their ardor with diligence. As Henry Adams says, the *Anthology*'s editorial resources were " greatly superior " to those ordinarily existing in the early Republic.[13] By organizing their varied capabilities and interests, the Anthologists could func-

---

[12] See Quincy, *History of the Boston Athenaeum*, 2-3.
[13] *History of the United States*, IX, 202.

tion as a board of specialists in several fields of knowledge. To illustrate, when they voted to prepare a retrospect of literature in the United States for the first six months of 1806, they divided the labors as follows: classic literature, Gardiner; poetry and belles-lettres, Dana and S. C. Thacher; law, P. O. Thacher; politics and history, Shaw and Walter; medicine, chemistry, and so forth, Warren and Jackson; theology, Emerson, Buckminster, Gray, and Tuckerman (see *J*, 43-44). Here was the Republic of Letters in provincial microcosm. Oliver Wendell Holmes justifiably remarks, " There was no more brilliant circle than this in any of our cities." [14]

In editing and supplying the *Anthology*, however, their brilliance proved to be an inconstant resource. At their commencement the Anthologists made the error common to literary projectors of the early Republic. They aspired to do more than their circumstances would permit. Not only was the *Anthology* to be " versed in almost every art and science," it was to have " a general acquaintance with the great affairs of the political world." In addition, it was to serve as an American review, offering a candid opinion on all " important literary productions " published in America.[15]

Turning through the files of the *Anthology*, one cannot fail to remark that the Anthologists were not altogether unsuccessful in pursuing these goals. In the miscellaneous section of their magazine they published essays on subjects ranging from the necessity of revelation to the purring of cats; they presented travel letters from New Englanders in several countries abroad, including England, France, Italy, and Spain; and they exhibited a considerable volume of poetry, mostly well forgotten, in both Latin and English. Particular selections cannot be discussed, but special attention may be called to " The Remarker," a periodical essay series running to forty-five numbers; " Silva," a department

[14] *Works*, (Boston and New York, 1892), XI, 22. Henry Adams gives a misleading impression of the Anthology Society when he says that it was made up chiefly of clergymen. Of the original fourteen members, six were clergymen. Of the twenty-eight members who belonged to the society from its inception until its disbanding, only seven were ministers.

[15] William Emerson, " Preface," *Anthology*, I, i-iii.

of literary gleanings and anecdotes which appeared seventy-six times; "The Botanist," a pioneer series of lectures on American botany by Benjamin Waterhouse (incorporated in his book, *The Botanist*, 1811); "Letters from an American Traveller," thirty-one letters from Europe by John Lowell; and poems by John Quincy Adams and Washington Allston.

For their review department, which Henry Adams judges "far surpassed any literary standards then existing in the United States, and was not much inferior to any in England . . . ," [16] the Anthologists deserve stronger recognition. The most extensive yet attempted by an American periodical, it noticed many "very trifling" books simply because they were products of America.[17] But if they at times dealt in the ephemeral, the Anthologists knew it and had a way of saying so. They maintained their critical clearing house on high, if narrow, standards; and by the very bulk of their transactions gave a certain weight and significance to American letters in an unpropitious era. Nor should it be forgotten that they maintained a monthly catalogue of books published in America which is still useful. In addition to its regular review department, moreover, the *Anthology* displayed in its last five volumes a series of forty-one articles on "American ancient works." This series, known as "Retrospective Notices of American Literature," was sponsored by Buckminster and was based on his desire to provide a body of materials for the future historian of American life and letters.

Still, the Anthologists might well have followed the advice of some of their critics and limited the character of their publication either to that of a review or a miscellany. Thereby they could have expended their talents more economically and more forcefully. Instead, compelled by the eighteenth-century emphasis upon breadth and variety, they demanded of themselves an effort they did not have the capacity to make. And in time the symptoms of their incapacity became obvious in their ill-defined

---

[16] *History of the United States*, IX, 201.

[17] See Buckminster to Shaw, no date cited, Eliza Buckminster Lee, *Memoirs of Rev. Joseph Buckminster, D. D., and of His Son, Rev. Joseph Stevens Buckminster* (Boston, 1849), 235. Hereinafter cited as *Memoirs of the Buckminsters*.

conception of editorial responsibility, their difficulties in main-
taining an effective organization, and their inability to provide a
reliable supply of original material for the *Anthology*.

Throughout its career the *Anthology* was edited in piecemeal
fashion, with the agreement among the editors " that no individual
was the responsible director of the publication " (*J*, 54). The
society's constitution provides for an editor who shall be elected
annually and " shall have a general power of preparing & superintending " the magazine. Specifically, his duties are defined as
reading proofs, handling correspondence, and other mundane
editing chores. By implication he is denied authority to approve
material for publication. On the other hand, in the constitution
the society imposes upon itself only a limited collective editorial
task. Book reviews are to be read to the group and approved
before publication (see *J*, 31). Who, then, is obligated for the
miscellany? This problem was never met forthright. When
President Gardiner urged its importance, " no particular determination took place." Buckminster proposed an awkward plan
whereby the editor would state in each issue " what the S. considered themselves responsible for " (*J*, 47). As a compromise
the gentlemen agreed to hear each number of " The Remarker "
(and later each article for " Silva ") before publication. From
time to time they also listened to other items offered for the
miscellany, though never assuming a consistent responsibility for
doing so.

The loose manner in which the *Anthology* was edited shielded
individual Anthologists from injured readers, especially after the
editor was made into the " Superintending Committee." (S. C.
Thacher, the editor, composed the committee. See *J*, 54) But
it blocked a clear-cut exploration of the society's editing problems
and obligations; and it increased the difficulty of supervising the
magazine, a problem which became pressing when Thacher's
departure for Europe in 1806 deprived the *Anthology* of his
editorial experience. Two solutions suggested themselves. One
was to expand the editorial committe, an expedient adopted about
a year after Shaw replaced Thacher as editor (see *J*, 123). But
reinforcing the Superintending Committee was hardly a cure for
patchy editing. The *Anthology* needed a full-time editor. Though

this fact must have been apparent from the beginning, the Anthologists, reluctant probably to violate their amateur status, sought to hire an editor only at the eleventh hour, when Andrews Norton was offered the position. His demand for a salary of five hundred dollars per year and a percentage of the income seems to have effectively squelched the proposition (see *J*, 245-47).

The inability or unwillingness of the Anthology Society to formulate an efficient editorial scheme is related to the fact that their membership was not sufficiently continuous to insure their adequacy as a board of writers and editors. Of the original fourteen members, in fact, half left the group permanently before 1811, and nearly all the others absented themselves from it for long periods. Business requirements, travel abroad, professional duties, and death—these were the chief reasons for the depletion of the society's membership. Within two years after the club's organization, P. O. Thacher asked, for business reasons, to be excused except for one meeting a month, William Tudor embarked for the West Indies as his brother Frederic's agent in an abortive effort to establish the later famous ice trade, Buckminster and Thacher sailed for a prolonged European tour, and Drs. Jackson and Warren, finding their medical skills more in demand than their literary talents, became completely inactive in the society. A devoted and productive Anthologist, A. M. Walter, died in the same period. Afterwards E. T. Dana withdrew, William Emerson resigned, and Gardiner left the club.

During its existence the society elected at least fourteen members to fill vacancies in its ranks and to increase its strength. Of these no more than six retained their seats from their election until the club disbanded. Among the first to be elected were Benjamin Welles, a young lawyer, and Robert Field, the miniature painter and engraver. Attracted by other interests, one supposes, they deserted. An entry in the *Journal* records that " only M^r McKean, Mr Field & Mr B. Welles [were] absent, of whom the two last have long appeared obliti nostrorum, and our own pride forces us to add obliviscendi et nobis " (*J*, 136-37). Staunchly faithful were James Savage and two other young recruits, George Ticknor and Jacob Bigelow, who enlivened the society's twilight days. Also a sound Anthologist among the members elected subsequently was the Reverend John Thornton Kirkland, who became president of the society in 1810, the same year he was made president of Harvard. Other members must be passed over (see *J*, 297-301).

The unsettled state of the group's membership is reflected in the variable attendance at its weekly suppers, where most of the editorial work on the *Anthology* was done. A full session was " an event of almost as rare occurrence and portending perhaps as much as any prodigy of Livy"; and at many meetings the "number of the faithful" was hardly sufficient to conduct the business of the *Anthology* with assurance. Some meetings were held with no more than three persons present; and at least one did not even materialize (see *J*, 231, 227, 254). Evidently the average meeting saw about half the members appear. Formality, incidentally, did not discourage attendance. The gentlemen came and went as they desired. "Mr Emerson," the minutes report in one instance, "as usual, went away early, on which Mr Dana remarked, that he was, like Mercutio, always killed in the second act" (*J*, 139).

Perhaps more than a casual reason for the inconsistent attendance at the meetings, though it added variety and fun to them, was the society's insecure, peripatetic supper table. Initially, the weekly suppers were held in the homes of members, with William Emerson, for a reason not altogether clear, committed to receive his fellows once each month. When this proved to be too demanding on the pastor's household, he frankly "brought on the subject of suppers at his house once a month, which he stated as being too frequent & as inconvenient & disagreeable . . ." (*J*, 46). His complaint was a bad omen. From this time on the *Journal* frequently refers to the society's gastronomic difficulties. Eventually the Anthologists hired a caterer, James Cooper, the clerk of Trinity Church, who served them in Robert Field's quarters, with the understanding that the gentlemen "should supply themselves with wine & segars . . ." (*J*, 82). Later they moved to Cooper's house and were left homeless when Cooper moved. Once again they took refuge in the homes of members, until President Gardiner located a new caterer. On an inglorious evening, "through a thick fog and much mud," they attempted to find his house, only to find that the president had directed them to the wrong place. They finally reached their goal, a Mr. Sanger's in Milk Street, where "the beef was good and the wine bad" (*J*, 127-28). When Cooper reinstituted his services to the society in 1808, the gentlemen were pleased "with a very fine supper," provoking the secretary to remark cynically of the next gathering: "The club was very well attended, the last supper having diffused its scent widely" (*J*, 156-57). A few months later the society pursued Cooper to still another house, where they met in an attic room; and still later they took up their headquarters in "the attick story of Minot's house," the scene of their final days. Cooper appears to have continued as their caterer until the end. Merely a shadow in the pages of the *Journal*, he was, one senses, a vital part of the *Anthology*'s existence.

Possibly one may correlate the gastronomic insecurity the Anthologists periodically experienced and their delinquency as contributors to their magazine. Original contributions to the *Anthology* came from four sources: the members of the society; nonmembers who were invited to contribute; nonmembers who sent in unsolicited offerings; and, after 1809, corresponding members elected by the society. Of these the last three were never fruitful. The *Anthology* generously invited "the learned of our country, in all arts and sciences, . . . to give immortality to its pages by a liberal communication of their speculations." [18] But the response was not as overwhelming as the invitation. Oftentimes, moreover, the Anthologists were dubious about the kind of immortality those who did respond would confer on the *Anthology*. "Something about Atheists was rejected half read," the secretary laments once. "In our misfortunes every Ass seems to kick at us" (*J*, 140). Hoping to increase its supply of material for the *Anthology*—and obviously to bolster its patronage and prestige—the society provided in 1809 for corresponding memberships. In this way they added to their list of prospective contributors several prominent men, including Benjamin Silliman

[18] Note prefixed to an article on "Independence of the Judiciary" by Chief Justice Dana, *Anthology*, IV (January, 1807), 20.

and James Luce Kingsley of Yale and Chancellor James Kent of New York. Silliman and Kingsley contributed one article each, Kent nothing. More prolific were lesser known corresponding members like Charles Stewart Davies of Portland, Maine, and Paul Allen of Providence, Rhode Island.

Yet the *Anthology*'s chief source of material was the Anthologists themselves. For a time after the magazine got underway they contributed plentifully. But within a year enthusiasm cooled. Soon there came an occasion when the secretary called for the reading of reviews previously assigned and got no response at all. At a later meeting he noted after reading the review roll, "Some of the Gentlemen seriously promised to do the duties assigned to them, & others faintly apologized for their neglect" (*J*, 50, 78). The efforts the Anthologists made to remedy their habitual delinquency were largely ineffectual, and at times embarrassing. A few examples will suffice. When Shaw proposed the distinguished Dr. Kirkland for membership, Walter seconded the motion "on condition that Dr K. should first be requested to give an explicit promise" that he would perform his writing duties (*J*, 92). At another meeting, after the gentlemen had bound themselves by an elaborate plan to furnish the *Anthology* (see *J*, 109-10), James Savage, backed by S. C. Thacher, scored his colleagues for neglecting their commitments, asserting neither he nor Thacher would continue to fulfill their writing obligations unless supported by their fellows (see *J*, 123-24). Later on, Savage, a systematic, prudent, and literal young man, moved "that every member of this Society furnish two pages of his own composition for the Anth. of each month; & that for every deficiency of one page he shall pay to the Treasurer the sum of one Dollar." Before making this motion, during "a long and very terrible discussion," he detailed each member's contributions for the past year (*J*, 171). Shunted to a committee, his motion was never acted upon. Savage, who served as secretary from Walter's death in 1807 until he was elected vice president in 1811, took what satisfaction he could in periodically asking each member what he would contribute to the next issue, then noting his answer in order to check the pledge against the performance. "M^r [John] Stickney," he records in one instance,

" is punctual at supper but brings nothing for the Anthology "
(*J*, 210, 229).

Underlying the problems of editing and supplying the *Anthology* is a vagueness the Anthologists felt about the purpose
of their association. Were they a club of editors or a club of
friends? Did they meet primarily to work, or to eat, drink, and
talk? Ideally, of course, they thought to join intellectual and
social pleasures in the eighteenth-century manner, all being in
Dr. Johnson's terminology, " clubbable " gentlemen. Thus they
sought to adhere to the formula for an Anthology evening suggested by one entry in the *Journal*: " After supper wit and
burgundy came in abundance, but our duties were not forgotten "
(*J*, 122). Though this recipe was followed at a majority of the
meetings, the *Journal* is spiced with entries like these:

Augt 7, 1806

No business of any kind was transacted by the Society of
Gentlemen, who conduct the Monthly Anthology & Boston
Review.

N. B. Supper of woodcock. [*J*, 83]

May 7, 1807

At this meeting no business, except eating, drinking, and
smoking, was attended to. [*J*, 113]

May 29, 1810

We had a meeting sufficiently pleasant, though no business
was done. The Vice president [Kirkland] had the chair. M^r
Savage offerred [*sic*] to read something for Silva, but was not
allowed to. [*J*, 230]

Although such entries by no means predominate, do they not
suggest a tension typical of the literary club? It is represented
on the one side by the conscientious Savage trying to save the
Anthology and, on the other, by the sociable Kirkland en-
deavoring to save the evening. On the whole, the Anthologists
leaned strongly toward elevating excellence in friendship and
conviviality above editorial excellence. In his letters to Shaw
from Europe, Buckminster indicates this tendency clearly. He

bemoans his absence from "the circle of the beloved acquaintance in Boston" to which he is bound "by that holy affection in which Cicero has written that golden treatise on Friendship. . . ." He admonishes Shaw: "Be careful, I beseech you, about admitting new members. I am very much afraid, that, during my absence, you will metamorphose it from a club of friends into a club of editors." [19]

The problems of editing and supplying the *Anthology* were aggravated by its precarious financial history, which affords an interesting commentary upon the economics of literature in the Boston of the early 1800's.

During its brief day the *Anthology* was issued by no fewer than five different printing concerns. To each it was a losing venture. E. Lincoln gave it up when David Phineas Adams despaired as editor, and, as has been explained, Munroe and Francis hopefully took over the nearly stillborn periodical, and engaged William Emerson to quicken it. The terms of Emerson's connection are not known; neither are the exact terms of several contracts the Anthology Society later signed with Munroe and Francis. Evidently these were not carefully detailed statements of the relationship between the society and the printers, but were chiefly agreements whereby Munroe and Francis agreed to pay the Anthologists for their labor in conducting the magazine.

In any event, before long the gentlemen of the society were unhappy with their publishers; and the publishers were hardly pleased with their editors. If the society complained about the "negligence and niggardliness" of Munroe and Francis in turning over money due it, the printers wondered why the *Anthology* had only 440 subscribers, while Charles Brockden Brown's *Literary Messenger* had 600 and Joseph Dennie's *Port Folio* boasted 1,500.[20] Furthermore, Munroe and Francis pointed out, the comparatively few subscribers the *Anthology* did have were

[19] Buckminster to Shaw, June, 1806, Quincy, *History of the Boston Athenaeum*, 51; Buckminster to Shaw, no date cited, Lee, *Memoirs of the Buckminsters*, 236. Cf. A. M. Walter's comments on the "Classick Club," *Anthology*, III (November, 1806), 578.

[20] See an account of a letter from Munroe and Francis to Shaw, July 16, 1806, Joseph B. Felt, *Memorials of William Smith Shaw* (Boston, 1852), 215.

lax in their payments; in 1808 they were over eight hundred dollars in arrears (see *J*, 136). A darker source of bitterness between the Anthologists and Munroe and Francis seems to have been the question of whether or not the printers had a right of property in the *Anthology* (see *J*, 81). This issue is obscure, but obviously the society successfully maintained its proprietary control of the *Anthology*. For after two years of periodic quarreling with Munroe and Francis, the Anthologists began seeking a new printer. At this critical point Shaw happily reported to his colleagues a joint proposal by two Boston printing firms not only to publish the *Anthology* but to pay its editors the magnificent remuneration of one thousand dollars a year.

Pursuing this happy delusion, the Anthologists prepared to settle their affairs with Munroe and Francis and requested the *Anthology*'s subscription list. Only, the publishers countered, if they received twelve hundred dollars from the society "in full of all demands" (*J*, 140). These demands presumably represented the amount claimed by Munroe and Francis in unpaid subscriptions and unsold copies of the *Anthology*. "With fear and trembling" Savage undertook to study the situation for his associates (*J*, 141). After he had reported to them, a committee empowered to institute legal proceedings if necessary was appointed. But ultimately such a course was deemed unfeasible; and at a special meeting in April, 1808, Shaw moved that the *Anthology* be temporarily suspended. Buckminster hopefully called for the society to make a final appeal to Munroe and Francis for the subscription list, and Shaw dramatically rushed out of the meeting to parley with the recalcitrant printers. Even though he returned without the list, the *Anthology* survived. Warmed by the perversity of Munroe and Francis, the gentlemen took heart, agreed to continue, and issued an appeal for their subscribers to identify themselves (see *J*, 142-43).

Thereupon the Anthologists entered into a joint agreement with the two firms which had approached them earlier, Snelling and Simons, and Hastings, Etheridge, and Bliss. Within a short time Snelling and Simons withdrew, and in 1809 Hastings, Etheridge, and Bliss, after signing a bond guaranteeing to pay five hundred dollars annually for three years to the society, became its sole printer. When they received the first installment for 1809, the gentlemen experienced " a glow of self complacency and hope " (*J*, 184). But only a few months later they " assembled under much anxiety, owing to the insolvency of Hastings, Etheridge & Bliss " (*J*, 202). Somehow the *Anthology* was saved once again. Thomas B. Wait and Company took it over temporarily, and later offered to publish the magazine for five years, paying four hundred and fifty dollars for the first three years and five hundred the last two. Their proposition was accepted (see *J*, 217). For the final time the illusion of hope glossed over the *Anthology*'s devious struggle for existence. At the beginning of the year 1810, the customary " Address of the Editors " included a well-earned tribute to themselves:

We have completed the seventh volume; a great age among the literary ephemera of this country. Having arrived at this degree of maturity, in spite of innumerable predictions to the contrary, we almost begin to flatter ourselves, that our constitution and temperament are more vigorous, than those of most others in the class to which we belong; and that this uncommon duration is not accidental or artificial, but is the evidence of something sound in our stamina, and pertinacious in our structure. Still the wonder and mystery of our existence, more extraordinary to us than it can be to the world, was so impressed on our minds, that when we have been confidently told we were speedily destined to perish, we have assented to the declaration with almost as much humility and conviction, as we should to the same truth, when applied to us more seriously as individuals. Yet after acquiescing in these predictions of the certitude of our fate, the elasticity of hope, or the force of vanity has made us the next moment exclaim, to compare small things with great, like Galileo rising from his recantation before the tribunal of the holy inquisition, *però se muove*.[21]

Yet the time when the *Anthology* would cease to survive through the " elasticity of hope, or the force of vanity " was inevitably coming. Though a few months passed without further financial crises, by April, 1811, the Anthologists were listening to a familiar report: the printers could not pay their quarterly

[21] VIII (January, 1810), 3. By William Tudor, Jr.

installment (see *J*, 252). But now the spirit to persist was gone. As early as January, 1811, as a matter of fact, the gentlemen seem to have at last yielded, withal cheerfully, to a sense of doom (see *J*, 247-48). A compromise was worked out with Wait and Company to continue publication of the *Anthology* without paying any salary to the society until Volume X should be completed (see *J*, 253).[22]

Is it not conceivable in the light of its several resuscitations that the *Anthology* could once again have been saved? Six months before its termination, the Anthologists " thought that the Anthology might stop where it was, or might be continued, if adequate exertions were made in a short time " (*J*, 247). Those made were insufficient, hardly, it appears, more than nominal. The society, more or less deliberately, chose to let the *Anthology* die and, though this was not an absolute consequence, to perish with it. This choice was dictated not only by the circumstances which have been sketched; it had something to do with a more subtle vexation, a progressive loss of the sense of fraternity animating the faithful. On June 11, 1811, S. C. Thacher read before the society a valedictory to be included in the *Anthology*'s final issue. In the course of his remarks Thacher enumerates various reasons for the periodical's end. Summing up, he says, " Upon the whole, too, the Anthology has perhaps lived long enough, and its future existence, at least for the present, would be forced and unnatural." Why " forced and unnatural " ? Financially its career had always been so, and the future could hardly have been more arbitrary in this respect than the past. Thacher seems to have had in mind the society's flagging *esprit de corps*. No longer, he implies, could they face the public as they had some four years earlier: " Doubtless many men of sense ascribe to us a species of fanaticism, as the spring of that propensity we discover to enlighten, improve, and entertain a publick, which gives us for our pains neither fame nor money. We suggest to them a solution of our conduct, which does not assign us a place greatly below or above the standard of human nature. We are exposed

---

[22] The fiscal history of the Anthology Society may be studied further in the *Journal*. For example, it sustained itself in its most difficult periods by assessments upon the members.

to the influence of that " Esprit de corps," which animates literary association." [23] When the Anthologists lost this spirit, they had arrived at the ultimate vexation. They had lost the solidarity which had sustained their hope and pride, and, consequently, their necessary reason for being.

Why did their " clubbability " disintegrate? Changing times is the basic reason. It is mirrored in the Reverend J. S. J. Gardiner's break with the society.

The young Anthologists who elected and re-elected Gardiner their president considered him the embodiment of the literary tradition to which they subscribed. He was perhaps Boston's most eminent man of letters, its Dr. Samuel Johnson or, more aptly, its Dr. Samuel Parr, "England's best and perhaps vainest classical scholar," in George Ticknor's opinion.[24] The circumstances of Gardiner's education had a great deal to do with this fame. Although he had begun his schooling in Boston, at the commencement of the Revolution he had been sent to England, where for six formative years he attended Parr's well-known school for boys. Following his return to Boston, he studied for the bar, practiced law briefly in Boston, then sought ordination in the Episcopal church. In 1792 he became assistant minister at Trinity Church, Boston, and in 1805, the rector. Forced to supplement his income after he married in 1794, Gardiner established in Boston a sizable classical school modelled on Parr's. During the ten or twelve years he conducted this school, he did much to rejuvenate the traditions of classical discipline revolutionary Boston had allowed to lapse. Even after he abandoned his school, moreover, he continued to prepare selected pupils for Harvard. Meanwhile, he became known as a pulpit orator, a conversationalist, a literary, and even a theatrical critic, a periodical essayist, and a political controversialist. In the records of his time, one sees him variously: presiding at small literary suppers in his home ("little *symposia*," Ticknor remembered

[23] Thacher, "Address of the Editors," *Anthology*, X (June, 1811), 364; Joseph Thornton Kirkland, "Address of the Editors," *ibid.*, IV (January, 1807), 3.

[24] Ticknor to Thomas Jefferson, March 15, 1816, *Collections of the Massachusetts Historical Society*, LXI, 254.

them, " full of fun and wit, and always rich in literary culture ");
holding "a long literary conversation" with A. M. Walter in
the Boston bookshop of Francis Nichols; perusing Latin poetry
submitted for the *Anthology* and happily discovering a young
Bostonian " turning his attention to ancient literature ";[25] sitting
sturdily in his chair at the Anthology table outsmoking midnight,
his " canonical hour," with his hardier companions (*J*, 153).

Gardiner's most ambitious literary project was a continuation
of Johnson's *Lives of the Poets* in a series of critical essays. He
got no further than six pieces on Charles Churchill. Virtually
all that Gardiner derived from Johnson or his Whig imitator
Parr was their manner, pompous and rough. He was form without substance. Narrow in his learning, believing High Church
doctrine, the Federalist creed according to Fisher Ames, and a
decadent neoclassic authority to be civilization's unalterable
values, he was redeemed from his deadly absolutism by his
sociability. But this could not entirely obscure his lack of identity
with those Anthologists who were disturbed by strong, if ill-
defined, aspirations toward the future. The result was the creation in the Anthology Society of a discernible tension. The
consequences can be seen in Gardiner's relations with his colleagues.

In December, 1810, the society's caterer informed the gentlemen that their " Revd President had withdrawn his name from
the Society " (*J*, 244). For this cold leave-taking the *Journal*
records no reason; probably the Anthologists needed none. Earlier
they had made " some oblique observations . . . on the absence
and neglect of the President, who has appeared but twice at
club for more than four months and has not afforded a line for
nine months " (*J*, 226). And somewhat later they had reached
the conclusion that Gardiner had " abdicated " (*J*, 230). Behind
his action lies a story of growing disaffection rooted in both
literary and religious dissensions.

It began with a literary quarrel between Gardiner and Buck-

[25] *Life, Letters, and Journals of George Ticknor*, ed. G. S. Hillard, Mrs.
Anna Ticknor, and Miss Anna Eliot Ticknor (Boston, 1876), I, 9; Walter
to Shaw, May, 1800, Felt, *Memorials of Shaw*, 111; Gardiner to Shaw,
February 14, 1807, *ibid*., 238.

minster. The dispute centered upon Thomas Gray's poetic merits; the issue involved was the nature of taste and genius. As a literary stunt Gardiner published imitations of Gray's " Ode to Summer " and " Ode to Winter " in the *Anthology*. Following Johnsonian precedent, he intended to prove that Gray " is altogether a mechanical poet, and that any scholar, who has the command of poetical language, can write as well." Buckminster took up the defense of Gray and published an essay in the *Anthology* asserting Gray is among the English poets who have retrieved the lyric powers of the language and saved English poetry " from the elegant perfection of the school of Boileau. . . ." In his argument he refers to a " higher species of poetry, than the mere language of reason." To Gardiner this was manifest heresy. He replied in an essay suggesting his fellow Anthologist employ his time " more usefully, than in the defence of absurdity." When Buckminster continued the exchange with still another essay, Gardiner seems to have written a still more trenchant reply. This he tore up at a society meeting after Buckminster objected to a sentence in it, thereby ending the controversy (see *J*, 159). But his action implies a certain imperious condescension. A breach had been created, one thereafter widened and deepened by religious differences.[26]

Gardiner's leading fellow Anthologists—Emerson, Buckminster, and Thacher—were religious liberals, who more than once used the *Anthology* to promote their cause in the increasingly bitter conflict between the liberal and orthodox factions of the New England Congregationalists. Indeed, the *Anthology*, which took a decided stand in the fight over the Reverend Henry Ware's appointment to the Hollis Professorship of Divinity at Harvard, became identified in conservative minds with the " Boston religion." At first Gardiner seems to have played at least a passive rôle in the *Anthology*'s advocacy of the liberal cause. There is no indication that he objected to polemical statements published

---

[26] For the exchange between Gardiner and Buckminster see the following in the *Anthology*: Gardiner—" Silva, No. 36," V (February, 1808), 100-101; " Silva, No. 41," V (July, 1808), 357; " The Remarker, No. 35," V (August, 1808), 416-19; " Silva, No. 43," V (September, 1808), 495-97; Buckminster— " The Remarker, No. 34," V (July, 1808), 367-72; " To the Author of the 35th Remarker," V (September, 1808), 484-86.

in it, notably S. C. Thacher's attack on "the Jesuit's College at Andover" (*J*, 160). This internecine fight among the Congregationalists, he may well have confided to himself, would do him no harm and might well enhance the Episcopal establishment in New England. Soon, however, disturbing implications for Christianity, literature, and social order began to appear in the growing struggle. Especially obvious was the liberal tendency toward out and out Unitarianism. Before long Gardiner assumed a religious stand as inflexible as his literary doctrine. What is more, he equated his religious with his literary orthodoxy.

In 1810 he attacked the Unitarians and warned against their success in America in *A Preservative Against Unitarianism*. The analogies he draws among politics, religion, and literature are interesting, if hardly subtle:

The candor of a Unitarian resembles the humanity of a revolutionary Frenchman. It is entirely confined to words; and I will venture to affirm that no greater outrages against good manners can be found than in the writings of their leaders, Wakefield, Belsham, and Priestley. But let them measure their own moderate stature with the gigantic dimensions of a Bacon, a Milton, and a Johnson, and perhaps they will be candid enough to allow that all genius and knowledge are not confined to Unitarians, and that a man may be a Trinitarian without being necessarily either a blockhead or a hypocrite.[27]

The following year Gardiner employed this strategy at greater length, when he preached and published another discourse relating literature and religion. Its title affords an adequate commentary on it: *A Sermon Preached on Trinity Sunday, at Trinity Church . . . in Which Is Proved That the Greatest Writers in the English Language Have Borne Testimony to Their Faith in the Trinity, viz. Lord Bacon, Tucker, Jenyns, Johnson, Sir William Jones, Edmund Burke, Milton, Dryden, Pope, Young, Cowper.*[28] In

---

[27] Quoted in James Spear Loring, *The Hundred Boston Orators Appointed by the Municipal Authorities and other Public Bodies from 1770 to 1852* (Boston, 1852), 171-72.

[28] Cf. a review of another discourse by Gardiner, *A Sermon, Delivered at Trinity Church, Christmas Day, December 25, 1810, on the Divinity of Jesus Christ* (Boston, 1811). The Anthologists secured this review from a

the light of the literary and religious opinions he proclaimed during the latter days of the Anthology Society, there can be little doubt why Gardiner withdrew his name from it. Nor can there be much doubt that his thinly disguised attacks on them were painful to men like Buckminster and Thacher, who had looked to Gardiner as a symbol of literary tradition. It seems necessary to modify the genteel legend about Gardiner passed on by Oliver Wendell Holmes: "Mild Orthodoxy ripened in Unitarian sunshine, is a very agreeable aspect of Christianity, and none was readier than Dr. Gardiner . . . to fraternize with his brothers of the liberal persuasion, and to make common cause with them in all that related to the interests of learning." [29] Even during the brief span of the Anthology Society, the world changed. How much so is indicated simply but graphically by the fact that there came a time when it was no longer possible for Gardiner and his young cohorts to make common cause in letters and learning—even over "a mongrel goose of surpassing beauty" (J, 243).

The Anthology Society
and the Boston Athenaeum

MEANWHILE, THE ANTHOLOGISTS had made a permanent contribution to the literary life of the new nation by supporting the establishment of the Boston Athenaeum. This project was foreshadowed at a meeting of the society in October, 1805, when William Emerson made a motion, seconded by William Smith Shaw, "that a LIBRARY of periodical publications be instituted for the use of the Society" (J, 41). After several Anthologists

liberal sympathizer outside the intimate circle, John Lovejoy Abbot. "There is too liberal a use of some opprobrious epithets in this sermon," Lovejoy says. *Anthology*, X (March, 1811), 184.

[29] *Works*, XI, 22.

offered to present their personal collections of such magazines as the *Gentleman's Magazine*, the *European Magazine*, and the *Mercure de France* to the proposed library, the society authorized its Standing Committee to draw up regulations for its use; and the Anthologists thus added the maintenance of a library to their writing and editorial duties. Several months later, after a good deal of talk had gone on about it, Shaw moved the appointment of a committee to consider setting up a reading room. This was done. A prospectus was drawn up and, later, as arrangements proceeded, the society placed the direction of the reading room under a board of five elected trustees. Subsequently, the gentlemen of the society, led by Shaw, agreed to the transformation of the Anthology Reading Room into an institution to be known as the Boston Athenaeum. The Athenaeum was chartered by the legislature of Massachusetts on February 13, 1807.[30]

The Anthology Society hoped to devote the profits from its magazine to the Athenaeum. But, as the discussion of the financial history of the *Anthology* has shown, this publishing venture was something less than an economic success. The Anthologists, however, found other ways to help the newly founded library.

One of the most important of these has never been sufficiently recognized and might well be emphasized here. This was the purchase of books for the Athenaeum by Anthologists who traveled abroad during the infant years of the library. Shaw, the leading spirit of the early Athenaeum, commissioned anyone he could who was going to Europe to act as a voluntary agent of the project. His most important agent was Buckminster, who left America in May, 1806, the month in which the Anthology Reading Room was established, and who returned some six or seven months after the Athenaeum had been formally constituted. Although he went abroad in an effort to remedy his precarious health, he was pursued by letters from Shaw, inquiring, directing, and exhorting on behalf of the library. And Buckminster responded faithfully. As soon as he arrived in Liverpool, in fact, he secured a copy of the regulations of the Liverpool Athenaeum for immediate transmittal to Shaw, who used them as the basis

[30] See Quincy, *History of the Boston Athenaeum*, 18-22.

for setting up the government of the Boston Athenaeum. The fulfillment of one request immediately led to others from Shaw:

I pray you to make it an object to collect as much information as will be in your power respecting all literary societies, catalogues of their libraries, their laws, &c., &c. They will be pleasant to have in our reading-room at least, and they may be made useful in America, to stimulate our countrymen to some important mental exertions. I wish you could be prevailed upon to avail yourself of the advantages your residence in London this winter will afford you, to collect information relative to the literature of England, their colleges, their schools, their scientific institutions, their literary men, &c. &c., and publish a series of papers in our dearly cherished *Anthology* on the present state of English literature. . . . Write a series of letters from England to us in America, as Laharpe wrote from Paris to the Emperor Paul the First, of Russia.[31]

If Buckminster did not find time to turn out another *Correspondance Littéraire*, he did carry out a charge in the same letter from his friend to purchase five hundred dollars worth of books for the Anthology Reading Room. This became the nucleus of the Athenaeum collection, one that within forty years numbered 37,000 volumes.[32] A major reason for the success of the Athenaeum was the willingness of Shaw and Buckminster to spend money first for the popular and the useful in order to lure a full complement of subscribers as soon as possible. Buckminster was perhaps the steadier of the two. For example, when Shaw proposed that they acquire the transactions of the various English learned societies, Buckminster reluctantly refused. " We must, at least for some time, think of popularity, and I know of no method so likely to procure it, as to keep our rooms furnished with abundance of magazines, pamphlets, and new books." Buckminster advocated laying " slowly and diligently the foundation

[31] Shaw to Buckminster, December 1, 1806, Lee, *Memoirs of the Buckminsters*, 395.

[32] See C. K. Bolton, " The First One Hundred Years of Athenaeum History," in Bolton ed., *The Influence and History of the Boston Athenaeum* (Boston, 1907), 15-56.

of a permanent library of works difficult to be procured in America." [33]

In April, 1807, he concluded the bulk of his purchasing for the Athenaeum. The books were insured by Francis Williams and placed aboard the *Amelia*, a vessel belonging to Samuel Welles, who kindly carried "the precious deposit" to Boston without charge.[34]

The actual purchases which Buckminster sent to Boston were not so significant as the spadework he did in studying the European book markets, becoming acquainted with booksellers, making arrangements with them for future deliveries, and compiling lists of works for Shaw to order from different cities on the Continent. In the years that followed Buckminster's return, other Bostonians, their pockets crammed with catalogues and commissions from Shaw, searched the bookshops of England and the Continent for opportune buys, schemed to secure more rapid delivery of newspapers and periodicals across the embattled Atlantic, and sought the good will of men of wealth and learning abroad toward the Athenaeum.

The Anthology *as a "Progress Piece"*

TWO LEADING FEATURES of the *Anthology* are discouraging to an editor seeking, by means of a group of selections from it, to represent its essential character to the modern reader. One is its style, which for the most part never rises above the standards of second-rate neoclassic prose. The second is its catch-all appearance—its clumsy amalgam of literary curiosities and hopefully serious essays, its haphazard mixture of borrowed and original materials. An editor, of course, can do nothing about

[33] Buckminster to Shaw, April 3, 1807, Lee, *Memoirs of the Buckminsters,* 409.

[34] See *ibid.,* 410.

the style. A little of it goes a long way with the present-day reader. But if an editor does not demand that the Anthologists be something other than what they were, and if he approaches their magazine with historical imagination, he can reduce its miscellaneous contents to a significant order based on (1) the *Anthology's* inquiry into political, economic, and social conditions; (2) its effort to define the vocation of the man of letters; and (3) its attempt to encourage the development of literary culture and to establish critical standards. In accordance with this scheme, the selections from the *Anthology* which appear in this volume are arranged in three general divisions entitled as follows: " Of Democracy and Money "; The Image of the Man of Letters "; and " From Boeotia to Attica."

In the editing of *The Federalist Literary Mind* an over-all— it may be said poetic or metaphysical—theme has been kept in mind. This is the theme or concept of " the progress of letters."

There is no essay in the *Anthology* explicating this concept; its appearance in the magazine, in fact, is random. But its persistence, explicit or implicit, indicates the presence of an idea which the Anthologists assumed as a major theme of their cultural heritage. With it they axiomatically identified their literary ambitions and endeavors, feeling no reason to justify it or to examine it critically, employing it in diverse and even contradictory ways, yet being directed by it to seek the fulfillment of a powerful, complex cultural quest.

Generally speaking, in the theme of " the progress of letters " as it appears in the *Anthology* three motives may be discerned. One may be called the " transferential motive," another the " redemptive motive," and still another the " improvement motive."

The transferential motive belongs to the idea of the *translatio studii*, the transfer of letters from ancient times to the present in a progress from East to West. Enunciated as early as the ninth century, the *translatio studii*, George H. Williams has brilliantly shown, was clearly present in the early history of Harvard, whose founders and perpetuators were motivated in part by their vision of Harvard's place in the epic succession of knowledge, theological and humanistic, to the New World under God's Providence.[35] For over 170 years at the time the Anthology Society was organized, Harvard, a New England version of the *studium generale*, had fostered a sense of the continuity and community of letters and learning. Nowhere in New England was this sensibility more vividly felt than in the immediate area of Harvard, the small Boston-Cambridge world.

In the seventeenth century the concept of the transfer of knowledge became the basis of a literary genre, the " progress piece." Although the genre soon deviated widely from its inspiration, in its most legitimate manifestations it expressed the feeling of cultural continuity to be seen in Sir John Denham's " The Progress of Learning" or in Sir William Temple's " Essay Upon Ancient and Modern Learning." Temple observes:

Science and Arts have run their circles, and had their periods in the several Parts of the World. They are generally agreed to have held their course from *East* to *West*, to have begun in *Chaldaea* and *Egypt*, to have been transplanted from thence to *Greece*, from *Greece* to *Rome*, to have sunk there, and after many Ages to have revived from those Ashes, and to have sprung up again, both in *Italy* and other more *Western* Provinces of *Europe*. When *Chaldaea* and *Egypt* were Learned and Civil, *Greece* and *Rome* were as rude and barbarous as all *Egypt* and *Syria* now are and have been long. When *Greece* and *Rome* were at their heights in Arts and Science, *Gaul*, *Germany*, *Britain* were as ignorant and barbarous as any Parts of *Greece* or *Turkey* can be now.[36]

As the eighteenth century dawned and the possibilities of life in America more and more engaged the European imagination, the old idea of the westering course of letters and arts gained in strength. Bishop Berkeley, combining the historic concepts of *translatio studii* and *translatio imperii*, that is, the inevitable westward progression of empires, composed his famous poem " On the Prospect of Planting Arts and Learning in America ":

---

[35] See George H. Williams, " Church, Commonwealth, and College," in *The Harvard Divinity School*, ed. George H. Williams (Boston, 1954), 298 *et passim*.

[36] "An Essay Upon Ancient and Modern Learning," in *Critical Essays of the Seventeenth Century*, ed. J. E. Spingarn (Oxford, 1909), I, 50-51.

There shall be sung another golden age,
   The rise of empire and of arts,
The good and great inspiring epic rage,
   The wisest heads and noblest hearts.

Not such as Europe breeds in her decay;
   Such as she bred when fresh and young,
When heavenly flame did animate her clay,
   By future poets shall be sung.

Westward the course of empire takes its way;
   The four first acts already past,
A fifth shall close the drama with the day;
   Time's noblest offspring is the last.[37]

A little later St. Jean de Crèvecoeur was writing in his *Letters from an American Farmer*, "Americans are the western pilgrims, who are carrying along with them that great mass of arts, sciences, vigour, and industry which began long since in the east; they will finish the great circle." And Horace Walpole was saying, "The next Augustan age will dawn on the other side of the Atlantic." American colonials sounded the progress theme numerous times in one way or another, growing more vehement as the Revolution came on. John Adams documents the state of mind in eighteenth-century America solidly: "There is nothing, in my little reading, more ancient in my memory than the observation that arts, sciences, and empire had traveled westward; and in conversation it was always added since I was a child, that their next leap would be over the Atlantic into America." [38] Still later, in the Napoleonic age, this theory of history seemed to be coming true, at least to some observers like an anonymous contributor to an English publication called *Aikin's Annual*

---

[37] *Works of George Berkeley*, ed. Alexander Campbell Fraser (Oxford, 1901), IV, 366.

[38] *Letters from an American Farmer* (New York, 1904), 55. Walpole's observation occurs in a letter to Sir Horace Mann, 1774, which is quoted in Rexmond C. Cochrane, "Bishop Berkeley and the Progress of Arts and Learning: Notes on a Literary Convention," *Huntington Library Quarterly*, XVII (May, 1954), 245. A discussion of the progress idea in colonial America may be found in Benjamin T. Spencer, *The Quest for Nationality* (Syracuse, 1957), 22-24, from which the remark by John Adams is quoted.

Review. In 1805 he commented on Samuel Miller's *A Brief Retrospect of the Eighteenth Century* (New York, 1803), as follows:

> We are glad to observe that the new world sets out with so few of the prejudices of the old; and that one of the most opportune books, which American literature has yet added to the stock of English reading, should precisely have been consecrated to the history of human improvement. In this retrospect of the eighteenth century we seek in vain for the pedigrees of kings, and the carnage of warfare; we hear of no revolutions but those in the theory of science, of no achievements but those in literature and art. Happy the people to whose peaceful leisure such contemplations are chiefly dear: their emulation will be directed to the discovery of truth, to the production of beauty, to the realization of improvement; they will seek wealth from industry, not from pillage; fame from mental, not corporeal vehemence; and happiness from the diffusion of comfort, not from the agitations of hostility. While Europe re-barbarizes under her Fredericks and her Bonapartes, America may beckon to securer shores the trembling virtues, the patient industries, the curious researches, and the forsaken muses.

" Zealous at all times for the honour of our country " and " anxious to fulfill the prophecies respecting our literary advancement," the Anthologists prefixed this comment by the English reviewer to Theodore Dehon's " The Importance of Literature to Our Country." [39]

A second motive in the idea of the progress of letters is the theme of the saving or redemptive power of letters and the arts. Its sources lie in that complex of humanistic attitudes which insist on the integral relation between virtue and learning and the correspondence between the state of letters and arts and the moral fiber of a nation, in particular a nation threatened by the growth of luxury. Although this theme appears in several selections in the *Anthology*, it is probably stated in its purest form in John Thornton Kirkland's preface to the fourth volume:

---

[39] *Anthology,* IV (September, 1807), 465.

Every judicious effort to promote the love of Letters and Arts is entitled to countenance, for this, among other reasons, that a progress in letters and arts corresponds to the progress of society in other respects in our country. We are becoming familiar with wealth. Out of wealth grows luxury. If those enjoyments that flow from literature and taste are not emulated, we shall be exposed to that enervating and debasing luxury, the object of which is sensual indulgence, its immediate effect, vice, and its ultimate issue, publick degradation and ruin.[40]

The Anthologists also paid allegiance to a third motive in the theme of "the progress of letters." This involves the question of whether or not learning and the arts have actually improved in the course of history. Emerging from the quarrel between the ancients and the moderns in the seventeenth century—a quarrel each age repeats in one way or another—the improvement motive appeared first in full-bodied form in the thinking of Fontenelle and became a part of the complex of ideas which made up the eighteenth-century metaphysic of linear progress. It was a confused motive, for obviously a distinction must be made between accumulative knowledge and transcendent artistic achievement. But this distinction was seldom clearly drawn, partly because the fragmenting process of specialization had not yet begun. Consequently, the intellectual was likely to accept the improvement motive without worrying about its inner logic. How the *Anthology* reflects this tendency may be seen in an extract from its celebration of the history of libraries:

Among the many literary and scientifick establishments, which have been thought worthy of the patronage of influence and wealth, that of large repositories of books has justly been considered as most illustrious for its dignity, its importance, and its pleasures. The history of learned libraries is the history of power consecrated to learning. It celebrates the patronage of monarchs, the munificence of a splendid nobility, the support of a lettered clergy, and the liberality of cultivated gentlemen. This generous aid of rank, opulence, and influence proceeds from the intrinsick excellence of the subject. Whatever is intellectual is a portion of the supreme reason, and proportionally as it is free from cor-

[40] *Ibid.*, (January, 1807), 4.

ruption, approaches nearer the fountain. The operations of this principle are recorded in volumes. The earliest of these is almost coeval with the primary institutions of society, and from that period to the present the mass of human knowledge, notwithstanding the diminutions it has suffered, and the obstructions it has encountered, has accumulated from age to age, and has descended from generation to generation, till its present possessors are captivated in admiring the variety of its parts, the beauty of its materials, or are lost in contemplating its extensive magnitude, its diversified splendour, and its irresistible power.[41]

This is part of an appeal for the support of the Boston Athenaeum, which, according to the Anthologists, will become an instrument of the chronological, accumulative progress of learning. Joined to the transferential motive, the improvement motive created a dynamic vision of the future of the intellect in the New World.

Still, the vision was not altogether clear, even to the most resolute and optimistic of the Anthologists. For gazing at the attractive prospect of the transfer of letters and the arts to America, they were forced to contemplate the possibility that in America another kind of progress would occur, one of cultural decline and decay. In other words, the possibility that in America the *translatio studii* would find not its fulfillment but its ultimate frustration in conflict with the progress of a new barbarism that would conquer America as well as Europe.

Like their optimism, the pessimism of the Anthologists had its roots in their eighteenth-century heritage. In his distinguished explication of Alexander Pope's *The Dunciad*, Aubrey L. Williams has shown how this complicated satire documents not just an age of literary quarrels but a conviction of cultural peril. Reversing the *translatio studii*, Pope creates an ironic vision of " a *translatio stultitiae*, a transplantation of the rule of Dulness to one country after another." By means of this device, he dramatizes the relentless power of aggressive ignorance, what he called " duncery," to create disorder in the realm of letters and learning, to corrupt the creative power of words, and finally to bring about cultural chaos.

[41] *Ibid.*, IV (November, 1807), 600.

> Lo! thy dread Empire, CHAOS! is restor'd;
> Light dies before thy uncreating word:
> Thy hand, great Anarch! lets the curtain fall;
> And Universal Darkness buries All.[42]

Pope's poem is a study of the literary situation of his time and a defense of literary values in the face of the revolutionary economic, political, and technological conditions of literary creation which arose in the eighteenth century. These conditions, operating to create an ever increasing multiplicity of books and writers, became more pronounced as the century continued; and Pope's sense of progressive disorder haunted those who shared the temper of the Augustan mind with its strong feeling for structure and propriety and for the humanistic community of literature.

In post-revolutionary America the pessimistic temper was encouraged in patrician minds by the apparent institutional uncertainty in a new nation verging on democracy and developing a highly speculative economy.

Would the perpetuation of learning and the arts be likely in the United States, where, according to one *Anthology* writer, everyone is a politician and, according to another, the national maxim is " Get money "? " In such a country," the latter said, " genius is like the mistletoe on the rock; it seems to exist upon the barren and unyielding surface only by its own resources, and the nourishment it receives from the dews of heaven. The progress of literature has therefore been very slow. . . ." [43] Theodore Dehon foresaw the fateful possibility of the " republic of letters " progressing downward in America into a " democracy of letters," thereby foreboding a basic conflict in the history of American literary culture.[44] Fisher Ames, the gloomy prophet of New England Federalism, comprehended the whole situation by pro-

[42] See Aubrey L. Williams, *Pope's Dunciad* (Baton Rouge, 1955), 42-48, 153-54.

[43] Benjamin Welles, "Colloquial Politicks," *Anthology*, IV (October, 1807), 542-43; Winthrop Sargent, "Letters to Leinwha," *ibid.*, II (January, 1805), 16.

[44] See "The Importance of Literature to Our Country," *Anthology*, IV (September, 1807), 472.

claiming a general and inevitable "progress of licentiousness" in the United States. In his desperate dialectic, democracy progressed to chaos and thence to despotism, following the pattern he believed France exemplified. If one accepted Ames's view, he could have little hope for cultural progress of any kind.[45]

Actually, as the reader can see in the selections included in this volume, few of the Anthologists took the bleak path into the ultimate reaches of Amesian pessimism. For some of them anxiety was more a convention than a reality; for others, although real enough, it was not their fundamental mood. It was, however, a restraining force, and the reader of the *Anthology* is always aware that the ambiguous dimensions of fear confined the minds of the Anthologists. A passage from the first selection in this edition, Arthur Maynard Walter's review of a new edition of *Discourses on Davila* by John Adams, is instructive:

In this situation of human affairs it becomes the duty of everyone to exert his talents for the preservation of what exists, and the renewal of what is past. This can be effected only by a steady, sober, and religious application of our minds to the development and settling of first principles in morals and politicks. Much, perhaps most, of the excellence of the past century, arose from the writings of Locke, Montesquieu, Vattel, Burlamaqui, and other national writers, whose noble views and enlarged speculations extended round the horizon, and took in the whole nature of man. It is true indeed that Voltaire, Priestley, Condorcet, and the bloody banditti of atheists, almost obliterated the benignant influence of the former class; yet wisdom and energy may still support the falling ruin, and perhaps may add some goodly stones to the foundation.[46]

If this is pessimism, it is not the desperate pessimism of a Fisher Ames. ("We are sliding down into the mire of a democracy, which pollutes the morals of the citizens before it swallows up their liberties.") It allows for the patriotic, energetic efforts of young Bostonians like Walter, Buckminster, and Shaw to extend the possibilities of literary and intellectual life in the United States. But the action, or reaction, Walter advocates—"the preser-

[45] See Adams, *History of the United States*, I, 88.
[46] *Anthology*, II (April, 1805), 200.

vation of what exists, and the renewal of what is past"—would
consolidate history, putting an end to all kinds of progress, good
and bad. From the more limited point of view of literary history,
this desire to withdraw from history can be seen in Buckminster's
highly prescriptive theory of literary polity. (See pp. 176-82.)

If the foregoing remarks are reasonably apt, they may suggest
to the reader that an illuminating, figurative way to consider
the *Anthology* is as a commentary on the progress theme, a kind
of miscellaneous "progress piece." The progress metaphor, in
both its affirmative and negative versions, inspired, and inhibited,
the endeavors of the Anthologists. They sought, in other words,
to mediate for the new nation between two visions of its cultural
fate: a vision of the progress of letters in America and a prospect
of the barbarization of letters in America. Their effort was
clumsy, confused, even naïve, but they made a more determined
and a more coherent attempt than any other literary group in
America to assimilate the humanistic tradition to the cultural
conditions of the early Republic. In so doing they shaped an
environment of literary aspiration. And they determined the
dominant mode of nineteenth-century New England letters, the
academic manner of the Brahmins, with their sense of the social
and institutional nature of literature and their strong feeling for
the continuity of letters in Western civilization. Out of the
Boston of the Anthologists emerged the Boston of Longfellow,
Holmes, Lowell, and the later Emerson, the Boston of the *North
American Review*, the Athenaeum, the Saturday Club, and the
Atlantic Monthly, the Boston called the "American Athens,"
the only compelling symbolic literary center America has ever
had. William Dean Howells doubted "if anywhere in the world
there was ever so much taste and feeling for literature as there
was in that Boston." John Jay Chapman, who saw it in its latter
days, remembered it as "the first living civilization which I
knew." [47] For the first and last time, it is hardly an exaggeration
to say, this Boston made the "literary life" as a "way of life"
seem truly believable in the United States.

[47] Howells, "American Literary Centres," in *Literature and Life* (New
York, 1902), 184; Chapman as quoted in *The Shock of Recognition*, ed.
Edmund Wilson (New York, 1943), 596.

To its contemporaries it seemed a long distance away from the Boston of the early part of the nineteenth century. But in both its chief virtue—respect for the vocation of intellect—and its chief limitation—a tendency toward an introverted over-refinement—the Boston of mid-century represented the historical fulfillment of the literary sensibility descended from the Federalist literary mind as this was expressed by the *Anthology* and the Anthology Society.

Editorial Note

THE EDITING OF this volume has been rather drastic—but, it is hoped, imaginative. Titles of selections have been cut, altered, or in some cases, supplied. Various selections have been abridged. The eighteenth-century punctuation has been modified to some extent, especially when its logic seemed meaningless to a modern reader. Since there is no point in repeating them, several typographical errors have been corrected. To preserve something of the flavor of the period, however, eighteenth-century peculiarities in spelling and diction have been retained. To make it easy for a reader to consult the original of a selection, its location in the *Anthology* is cited at its conclusion.

The ascription of authorship is based on the list of contributors supplied in the appendix to the *Journal of the Anthology Society*. (See a further note on this which prefaces " Contributors to the *Anthology* " at the end of this book.) The notes are something more than occasional but considerably less than exhaustive. Most of the names and titles mentioned incidentally in the selections can be found easily in standard reference sources.

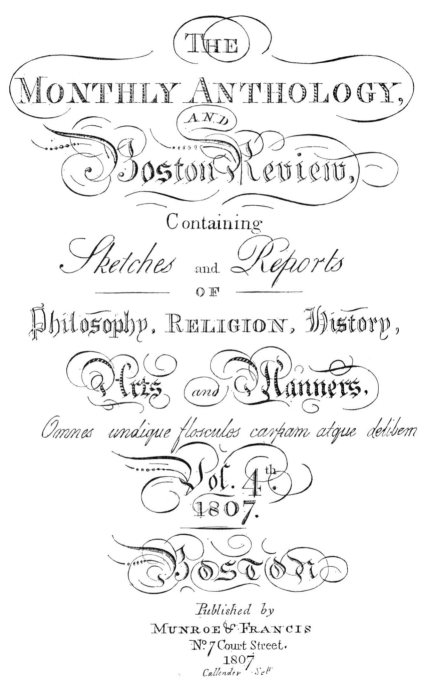

The Monthly Anthology, and Boston Review,

Containing

Sketches and Reports

OF

Philosophy, Religion, History,

Arts and Manners,

Omnes undique flosculos carpam atque delibem

Vol. 4th.
1807.

Boston

Published by
Munroe & Francis
N.o 7 Court Street.
1807
Callender Sculp

Title Page from the *Monthly Anthology*

Of Democracy and Money

We are sliding down into the mire
of a democracy, which pollutes the
morals of the citizens before it
swallows up their liberties.

—Fisher Ames (1805)

We may say that we have spice
ships at the Philippines, and that
our cannon has echoed among ice
islands at either pole. This is honourable . . . but. . . for myself I
think we ought to have produced
a few scholars. . . .

—Arthur Maynard Walter
(1806)

Preface

THIS SECTION OPENS with Arthur Maynard Walter's appraisal of the revolutionary character of the eighteenth century—an
appraisal which suggests how William Smith Shaw, in the second
selection, might well encourage readers of the *Anthology* to
study "the morals of a degenerate age" as depicted in the
writings of Tacitus.

These selections are followed by various examples of the *Anthology*'s indictment of democracy and materialism in America.
All of them may be read merely as symptoms of Federalist
indigestion; but they foreshadow the Transcendental indictment
of American society and, in a broader sense, represent a pioneer
stage of the self-conscious criticism of American culture which
has been one of the major traditions of American letters. It is
interesting, moving far down the years, to compare laments about
American civilization, or the lack of it, uttered by young Federalist intellectuals in the early nineteenth century with complaints
registered in the twentieth century; for instance, those voiced in
Civilization in America, the famous collection of essays edited by
the once-notorious expatriate Harold Stearns in the early 1920's;
or those expressed in the writings of the Fugitive-Agrarian group
in the 1920's and 1930's; or those set forth in the works of a
number of American writers in the 1950's and 1960's. If the
differences among them are great, one similarity is striking: the
feeling that life in America is frustrating to talent and genius.

Save for the artist Washington Allston, however, no member
of the *Anthology* group went to Europe to live. Expatriation
came later. No less than half of the original members of the
Anthology Society traveled abroad, but they came back home,
seeking, as Walter said, "a pathway open in this country to a
goodly land." *

* See Lewis P. Simpson, "Not Men, But Books," *Boston Public Library
Quarterly*, IV (October, 1952), 167-84.

A Century of Literature and Revolutions

ARTHUR MAYNARD WALTER

THE EIGHTEENTH CENTURY was remarkable for its literature and revolutions. It contributed more than the preceding to the development of general truth, and though the tremendous destruction of royalty and religion in France will mark it with an horrible blot, its various excellencies will forever excite gratitude and admiration. During that period the condition of the human race was not only improved, but it was tending as rapidly to a high degree of perfection, as the weakness and wickedness of man will allow.

In Europe we more particularly discovered the good effects of the last century. Every empire, kingdom, and republick seemed to have acquired a great degree of happiness in the course of a few years, rather by some sudden impulses than by a laborious accumulation of ordinary improvements. This is a fact, which the nations knew to be true, though their writers have taken little pains in explaining its causes and tendency. In some of the states liberty was enjoyed in as great a degree as is consistent with order; and where this great blessing was little known, the nations derived much happiness from their immemorial customs and usages, which were gaining the certainty of law; from the extension of knowledge, which teaches us the supply of our wants; from the dignity, splendour, charity, and munificence of their princes, aristocracy, and clergy, who corrected what they could not reform; and from the great revolution which was taking place in the breast of sovereigns, who began to perceive and to feel that their power was commensurate with the prosperity of the nation.

This progress towards national felicity was fatally arrested by the French revolution. Advocates are indeed found who represent this event as the most glorious in the history of the world; and who endeavour to establish its necessity from a survey of the previous system of European politicks; and to seek its beneficial effects in the delivery of France from feudal and ecclesiastical tyranny, and in its restoration to a due preponderance in the balance of power. But this on examination is found to be false and hollow. The revolution was not justified by necessity; and its happy results are less than vanity compared with its horrours and crimes. Besides the introduction of an atheistical rebellious philosophy, the transfer of the sceptre from the house of Bourbon to that of Bonaparte with all its effects, either consequential or collateral, will have finally operated such changes as a century will not be able to remedy.

In this situation of human affairs it becomes the duty of every one to exert his talents for the preservation of what exists, and the renewal of what is past. This can be effected only by a steady, sober, and religious application of our minds to the development and settling of first principles in morals and politicks. Much, perhaps most, of the excellence of the past century arose from the writings of Locke, Montesquieu, Vattel, Burlamaqui, and other national writers, whose noble views and enlarged speculations extended round the horizon and took in the whole nature of man. It is true indeed that Voltaire, Priestley, Condorcet, and the bloody banditti of atheists, almost obliterated the benignant influence of the former class; yet wisdom and energy may still support the falling ruin, and perhaps may add some goodly stones to the foundation.

In America, where great happiness is the portion of every one, writers have not been regardless of their high duty in fixing fundamental principles. If they have not discoursed much on oecumenical politicks, they have illustrated the nature of our different constitutions, and have thereby thrown much light on the nature and condition of man. In this class are particularly to be mentioned Adams on the American constitutions, the Federalist by Hamilton, and to these we now add with pleasure the author of *Discourses on Davila.* . . .[1]

—II (April, 1805), 199-200

[1] John Adam's *Discourses on Davila* were first published serially in Philadelphia's *Gazette of the United States* in 1790. In 1805 the papers were collected and published in Boston by Russell and Cutler. The preface to this edition is by an unknown hand, although Adams supplied the motto for it. Henrico Caterino Davila was the author of *Dell' Istoria delle Guerre civili de Francia.*

The Age of Tacitus

WILLIAM SMITH SHAW

THE WRITINGS OF Tacitus display the weakness of a falling empire and the morals of a degenerate age. The period in which he lived was favourable to the exercise of writing; and under the auspices of Trajan he was not restrained from painting strongly what he had ardently conceived. His genius was energetick and penetrating. In the horrours of the years which preceded the reign of Vespasian he finds an ample subject for the workings of his mind, and in his reflections on the corruptions of manners and the state of society he discovers the most profound knowledge of our nature. Accordingly his writings by the scholars in Europe have been studied diligently as a regular task. They form the subject of deep meditation for all statesmen who wish to raise their country to glory; to continue it in power, or preserve it from ruin. Time has destroyed that part of the history which depictured the virtues of Titus, Nerva, and Trajan; but as if to show how vile our nature can be, has left almost untouched the lives of Tiberius and his successors to the accession of Vespasian. The mutilations have, however, been almost restored through the patronage of princes, the industry and erudition of successive editors and commentators; so that the world is now presented, as by a wild Salvator Rosa, with a faithful picture of the miseries and crimes of the Roman empire from the death of Augustus to the assassination of Vitellius. Perhaps this series of time was as fertile in crimes as the dark ages. Before these, mankind had become inured to misery. No one knew what was liberty, and very few had even heard of it. Of course, their situation was not materially worse during the centuries that followed. But previously to the commencement of the empire, even in the days of Marius, and Sylla, and Pompey, and Caesar, there was some reverence for ancient laws and institutions. Freedom was not entirely forgotten, and where real felicity was wanting, there was a false, alluring, mock-sun glory, which attracted, illuminated, and deceived. The knowledge of this was in the remembrance of the slaves of Tiberius, and fathers had told it to their children, so that both realised the miseries of the times—rendered more excruciating from the recollection of the tales of the victories of Caesar and the splendour of Augustus. The causes which led to the downfall of this mighty empire are highly worthy of the consideration of every statesman and scholar; and no where can they be studied with more pleasure and profit than in the writings of Tacitus.[2]

—IV (July, 1807), 368.

The Mire of Democracy

FISHER AMES

IT HAS BEEN said that every man may be flattered. A fine understanding may make its possessor shrewd to detect the flatterer's art, and great experience in the world may place suspicion as a sentinel at one's door. All this may increase the difficulty of finding access to a man's vanity, but still it is not inaccessible. There are opinions which every man wishes every other man to entertain of his merit, temper, or capacity, and he is sure to be pleased when he discovers that his skilful flatterer really entertains them. He indulges a complacency and kindess towards him who puts him at peace and in good humor with himself. But to flatter the ignorant and inexperienced requires no skill, it scarcely requires any thing more than a disposition to flatter; for with that class of people the very disposition is

[2] This note on Tacitus suggests the appeal he had for the young Federalist. Arthur Maynard Walter at one time set out to write an ambitious series of essays on Tacitus. See "Proem to Thoughts on Tacitus," *Anthology*, II (October, 1805), 514-17.

accepted as an evidence of kindness. It is still easier to make
flattery grateful to a multitude, and especially an assembled multitude of such men. No arts are too gross, no topicks of praise
disgusting. Popular vanity comes hungry to an election ground,
and claims flattery as its proper food. In democracies the people
are the depositaries of political power. It is impossible they should
exercise it themselves. In such states therefore it is a thing
inevitable that the people should be beset by unworthy flatterers
and intoxicated with their philtres. Sudden, blind, and violent
in all their impulses, they cannot heap power enough on their
favourites, nor make their vengeance as prompt and terrible as
their wrath against those whom genius and virtue have qualified
to be their friends and unfitted to be their flatterers. The most
skilful sort of flattery is that which exalts a man in his own
estimation by ascribing to his character those qualities which he
is most solicitous to be thought to possess. He mellows into
complacency when he finds that his pretensions are rightly understood and cheerfully admitted. As nothing so conspicuously lifts
one man above every other man in society as power, of course
it is of all topicks of praise the most fascinating and irresistible.
When therefore a demagogue invites the ignorant multitude to
dwell on the contemplation of their sovereignty, to consider
princes as their equals, their own magistrates as their servants and
their flatterers, however otherwise distinguished in the world as
their slaves, is it to be supposed that aristocratick good sense will
be permitted to disturb their feast or to dishonour their triumph?
Accordingly we know from history, and we might know if we
would from scrutiny into the human heart, that every democracy,
in the very infancy of its vicious and troubed life, is delivered
bound hand and foot into the keeping of ambitious demagogues.
Their ambition will soon make them rivals, and their bloody dis-
cords will surely make one of them a tyrant.

But the fate of democracies, which every man of sense will
deem irreversibly fixed, is not so much the object of these remarks
as the complexion of popular opinions while they last.

They will all be such as the multitude have an interest, or
which is the same thing, a pleasure in believing. Of these, one of
the dearest and most delusive is that the power of the people is

their liberty. Yet they can have no liberty without many strong and obnoxious restraints upon their power.

To break down these restraints, to remove these courts and judges, these senates and constitutions, which are insolently as well as artfully raised above the people's heads to keep them out of their reach, will always be the interested counsel of demagogues and the welcome labour of the multitude. The actual state of popular opinion will be ever hostile to the real and efficient securities of the publick liberty. The spirit of '76 is yet invoked by the democrats, because they, erroneously enough, understand it as a spirit to subvert an old government, and not to preserve old rights. Of all flattery, the grossest (gross indeed to blasphemy) is that the voice of the people is the voice of God; that the opinion of a majority, like that of the Pope, is infallible. Hence it is that the publick tranquillity has, and the democrats say ought to have, no more stable basis than popular caprice; hence compacts and constitutions are deemed binding only so long as they are liked by a majority. The temple of the publick liberty has no better foundation than the shifting sands of the desert. It is apparent then that pleasing delusions must become popular creeds. After habit has made praise one of the wants of vanity, it cannot be expected that reproof will be sought or endured; a stomach spoiled by sweets will loathe its medicines. Prudence and duty will be silent.

An individual rarely passes unpunished who forms and prosecutes his plan of life under a great mistake of his own qualifications and character. And shall a democracy, which is sure to over-stretch its rights, to despise its duties, to entrust its traitors and persecute its patriots, to demolish its own bulwarks and invite the host of its assailants to come in, shall such a system last long, or enjoy any degree of tranquillity while it lasts? It is impossible.

Nevertheless, it is assumed as a position of uncontested authority that the discontents of the people never ripen into resistance and revolution unless from the oppression and vices of their government. The people are alleged to be always innocent when they refuse evidence, the government is almost always culpable when it exacts it. It may be admitted that no ordinary pressure of grievances would impel a people to rise against government, when that government is possessed of great strength and is administered with vigour. It cannot be supposed that men conscious of their weakness will attack a superiour power. Yet oppression may at length make a whole nation mad, and when it is perceived that the physical strength is all on one side the political authority will inspire no terror.

But surely there is no analogy between such a government and a democracy. As the force of this latter depends on opinion, and that opinion shifts with every current of caprice, it will not be pretended that the propensity to change is produced only by the vices of the magistrates or the rigour of the laws, that the people can do no wrong when they respect no right, and that the authority of their doings, whether they act for good cause or no cause at all but their own arbitrary pleasure, is a new foundation of right, the more sacred for being new.

To guard against this experienced and always fatal propensity of republicks to change and destroy, our sages in the great Convention devised the best distribution of power into separate departments that circumstances permitted them to select. They intended our government should be a *republick*, which differs more widely from a democracy than a democracy from a despotism. The rigours of a despotism often, perhaps most frequently, oppress only a few, but it is of the very essence and nature of a democracy for a faction claiming to be a majority to oppress a minority, and that minority the chief owners of property and the truest lovers of their country. Already the views of the framers of the Constitution are disappointed. The Judiciary is prostrate. Amendments are familiarly resorted to for the purpose of an election, or to wreak the vengeance of an angry demagogue upon the senate. We are sliding down into the mire of a democracy, which pollutes the morals of the citizens before it swallows up their liberties. Our vanity is the parent of our errors, and these, now grown vices, will be the artificers of our fate.[3]

—II (November, 1805), 563-66

[3] The views of Fisher Ames were not accepted uncritically by the Anthologists. Apparently it is this essay on democracy which the *Journal* refers to under an entry dated October 23, 1805: "Mr. B. [Buckminster] then read a political piece from Mr. Ames of Dedham. The Society thought it a poor thing, but as Mr. Ames was the author & as we had solicited his assistance, it was voted to be accepted" (J, 39).

Political Methodism

BENJAMIN WELLES

"I saw a smith stand with his hammer thus,
The whilst his iron did on the anvil cool,
With open mouth swallowing a tailor's news!"

COLLOQUIAL POLITICKS, BY which I mean the slang of citizens about the evolutions of the world and the manoeuvres of their own government and country, have made with us thousands of blockheads, and crammed the heads of men of good sense with more stuff than ever a quack packed into the stomach of a sick man. This delightful liberty of speech and liberty of the press make up a great part of . . . "Hail, Columbia." We are all politicians, from a senator to a tailor, and all senators, from a tailor to the gentlemanly learned. But what national dignity can be expected from a country, where there are so many hundreds of political methodists canting about universal liberty, promiscuous equality; and preaching about political milleniums, the new light of reason, republican purity, and the diffusion of knowledge throughout the country? How happy and peculiar is our state that Colin Clout can spell out a long-winded newspaper column, stale from the head of a printer's devil, into the ear of Blouzilinda, while she is scouring her milk-pails! What can be more absurd than this diffusion of Dilworth learning to clowns, who ought to be brightening their plowshares instead of dog-earing their spelling-book. From this, we see postmen drawing the latchet of a log-house, and leaving the "print" for its gaunt and poverty-struck tenant to labour through by the light of a pine-knot flambeau. How improving to the morals, when the landlord of a village-tavern, mounted in his bar, and showing through the casement a huge ruby face, which looks very like his demijean of brandy,

begins to flame at the mouth with a political harangue, and when
the point is finally to be settled, at the hazard of some dozen
knips of sling and *quarts of black strap.*

Our cities are not less infected with this political virus than
our villages. A whining town-meeting orator is in the same ratio
of noise and disturbance with the Boniface described. Our caucus,
instead of being the Caucasus of old, where the Gods met together
to decide on the affairs of this world, is now the aldermens' hall,
whose walls are stained with the smoke of roast beef and "smell
woundedly" of the breath of fat and greasy citizens. You cannot,
in these political days, set at table to your wine a minute before
a heavy pair of lungs roar on your ear a patriotic toast, and then
comes a song, or rather an ode for the occasion, from the nose of
a twanging psalm singer; in the midst of which you are forced
up from your seat to the ardour of the times and of a sudden
find your hand frying in the greasy palm of a patriot citizen.
If we are destined always to such a yankee-doodle state of things,
what wise man would wish to exclaim, with father Paul, for his
country, *esto perpetua?*

–IV (October, 1807), 542-43

Tom Moore on American Democracy

ANDREWS NORTON

AMONG THE REMAINING poems,[4] there is none better than
that in which the author takes leave of our country . . . , from
which the following is an extract:

Farewel to the few I have left with regret;
May they sometimes recall, what I cannot forget,

---

[4] Tom Moore's *Epistles, Odes, and Other Poems* was published in Philadelphia in 1806. The volume is made up mostly of poems written during
his American tour in 1804.

That communion of heart and that parley of soul,
Which have lengthened our nights and illumin'd our bowl,
When they've asked me the manners, the mind or the mien
Of some bard I had known, or some chief I had seen,
Whose glory, though distant, they long had ador'd,
Whose name often hallowed the juice of their board!
And still as, with sympathy humble but true,
I told them each luminous trait that I knew,
They have listen'd, and sigh'd that the powerful stream
Of America's empire should pass, like a dream,
Without leaving one fragment of genius, to say
How sublime was the tide which had vanish'd away!

In his censures upon our country Mr. Moore, in some of his
epistles, has been not a little severe. We do not mean to contro-
vert their justness. We know that in this land, where the spirit
of democracy is every where diffused, we are exposed, as it were,
to a poisonous atmosphere, which blasts everything beautiful in
nature and corrodes every thing elegant in art; we know that
with us the "rose-leaves fall ungathered"; and we believe that
there is little to praise and nothing to admire in most of the
objects which would first present themselves to the view of a
stranger. We have the same feeling with Mr. Moore for that
miserable love of power of popularity,

> Which courts the rabble's smile, the rabble's nod,
> And makes, like Egypt, every beast its God;

and we know that our country must improve much before she
can hope to

> . . . see her poets flash the fires of song
> To light her warriors' thunderbolts along.

But there are very few passages in these epistles which are of equal
merit with the two which we have just quoted. The weapon
of satire is unwieldy in the hands of their author. His indignation is impotent; his invective is frequently little more than low
expressions, coarsely applied. . . .

—IV (January, 1807), 43-44

The Discoveries of Captain Lewis

JOHN QUINCY ADAMS

Good people, listen to my tale,[5]
'Tis nothing but what true is;
I'll tell you of the mighty deeds
Atchiev'd by Captain Lewis—
How starting from the Atlantick shore
By fair and easy motion,

---

[5] "Gentlemen: The following 'elegant and glowing stanzas' are not from
the pen of Mr. Barlow; nor were they recited by Mr. Beckley at the
'elegant dinner,' given by the Citizens of Washington to Captain Lewis.
See *National Intelligencer*, 16 January, 1807."—Prefatory note by Adams.

In his *The Connecticut Wits* (Chicago, 1943), Leon Howard points out
that Barlow's "On the Discoveries of Captain Lewis" was considered an
important poem by the author, for underlying it were two of his persistent
hopes: "the peaceful union of his country and the development of its
internal resources." Barlow envisioned the Potomac, the Ohio, and Missouri
rivers being supplemented by the Columbia, which he would call the
"Lewis," so that together they made a system of waterways extending
east and west across the continent (see *The Connecticut Wits*, 331). Barlow
enclosed his poem, Howard says, in a letter to Jefferson, and the poem
exists in manuscript in the Henley-Smith Papers in the Library of Congress.
(See *ibid.*, 423) Howard apparently did not discover the occasion of Barlow's
poem, nor that it was printed in the *National Intelligencer*, together with an
account of the dinner given in honor of Lewis.

Below is Barlow's poem as it is found in the *National Intelligencer*. It is
prefaced by the following remark: "At an early period of the entertainment, the following elegant stanzas, from the pen of MR. BARLOW, were
recited by Mr. Beckley."

ON THE DISCOVERIES OF CAPTAIN LEWIS

Let the Nile cloak his head in the clouds, and defy
The researches of science and time;
Let the Niger escape the keen traveller's eye,
By plunging, or changing his clime.
Columbus! not so shall thy boundless domain
Defraud thy brave sons of their right:

He journied, *all the way by land,*
  Until he met the ocean.

Heroick, sure, the toil must be
  To travel through the woods, sir;
And never meet a foe, yet save
  His person and his goods, sir!
What marvels on the way he found
  He'll tell you, if inclin'd, sir—
But I shall only now disclose
  The things he did not find, sir.

He never with a Mammoth met,
  However you may wonder;

Streams, midlands and shorelands illude us in vain,
  We shall drag their dark regions to light.
Look down, sainted sage, from thy synod of Gods;
  See, inspired by thy venturous soul,
Mackensie roll northward his earth-draining floods,
  And surge the broad waves to the pole.
With the same roaring genius thy Lewis ascends,
  And, seizing the car of the sun,
O'er the sky-propping hills and high waters he bounds,
  And gives the proud earth a new zone.
Potowmak, Ohio, Missouri had felt
  Half her globe in their cincture comprest;
His long carving course has completed the belt,
  And tamed the last tide of the west.
Then hear the loud voice of the nation proclaim,
  And all ages resound the decree:
Let our Occident stream bear the young hero's name
  Who taught him his path to the sea.
These four brother floods, like a garland of flowers,
  Shall entwine all our states in a band,
Conform and confederate their wide-spreading powers,
  And their wealth and their wisdom expand.
From Darien to Davis one garden shall bloom,
  Where war's wearied banners are furl'd;
And the far-scenting breezes that waft its perfumes,
  Shall settle the storms of the world.
Then hear the loud voice of the nation proclaim,
  And all ages resound the decree:
Let our Occident stream bear the young hero's name,
  Who taught him his path to the sea.

Nor even with a Mammoth's bone,
    Above the ground or under—
And, spite of all the pains he took
    The animal to track, sir,
He never could o'ertake the hog
    With navel on his back, sir.

And from the day his course began,
    Till even it was ended,
He never found an Indian tribe
    From Welchmen straight descended:
Nor, much as of Philosophers
    The fancies it might tickle;
To season his adventures, met
    A Mountain, sous'd in pickle.

He never left this nether world—
    For still he had his reason—
Nor once the waggon of the sun
    Attempted he to seize on.
To bind a *Zone* about the earth
    He knew he was not able—
They say he did—but, ask himself,
    He'll tell you 'tis a fable.

He never dreamt of taming *tides*,
    Like monkeys or like bears, sir—
A *school*, for teaching floods to flow,
    Was not among his cares, sir—
Had rivers ask'd of him their path,
    They had but mov'd his laughter—
They knew their courses, all, as well
    Before he came as after.

And must we then resign the hope
    These Elements of changing?
And must we still, alas! be told
    That after all his ranging,
The Captain could discover nought
    But Water in the Fountains?

Must Forests still be form'd of Trees?
  Of rugged Rocks the Mountains?

We never will be so fubb'd off,
  As sure as I'm a sinner!
Come—let us all subscribe, and ask
  The Hero to a Dinner—
And Barlow stanzas shall indite—
  A Bard, the tide who tames, sir—
And if we cannot alter *things*,
  By G—, we'll change their *names*, sir!

Let old Columbus be once more
  Degraded from his glory;
And not a river by his name
  Remember him in story—
For what is *old* Discovery
  Compar'd to that which new is?
Strike—strike *Columbia* river out,
  And put in—*river Lewis*!

Let dusky Sally henceforth bear
  The name of Isabella;
And let the mountain, all of salt,
  Be christen'd Monticella—
The hog with navel on his back
  Tom Pain may be when drunk, sir—
And *Joel* call the Prairie-dog,
  Which once was call'd a Skunk, sir.

And when the wilderness shall yield
  To bumpers, bravely brimming,
A nobler victory than men;—
  While all our heads are swimming,
We'll dash the bottle on the wall
  And name (the thing's agreed on)
Our first-rate-ship United States,
  The flying frigate *Fredon*.

True—Tom and Joel now, no more
  Can overturn a nation;

And work by butchery and blood,
  A great regeneration;—
Yet, still we can turn inside out
  Old Nature's Constitution,
And bring a Babel back of *names—*
  Huzza! for REVOLUTION!

—IV (March, 1807), 143-44

Baron Von Hartzensleigzenstoffendahl Views America

WILLIAM TUDOR, JR.

GENTLEMEN,

Being in possession of the following letter, which appears by the date to have been recently written, I have thought proper to send it to you, and to leave it at your disposal.

A Correspondent.

Translation of a letter from the Baron Von Hartzensleigzen-stoffendahl, to the Countess Amelia de C..............at Vienna.

Boston, ...1808

The last letter which I wrote to my adorable, my inconceivable Amelia! was dated from a port, where our inimitable language is spoken.—Alas! I now never hear its accents, except from my faithful Spongler! When will my ear again catch its variegated sweetness from those coral lips, the very remembrance of whose humid, pouting expression often suffuses my eyes with tears!

Poor Spongler is quite happy here—he finds tobacco so cheap that it seems to console him for being an exile!—While I am perpetually giving way to a sensibility too powerful to restrain!

and yet I meet with no sympathy.—The other evening, while meditating on the old world—a propos to that, my dear madam, I like every thing young, but a nation,—and puffing the pipe which my dear Prince Ernest gave to me as a parting token, my eyes filled with tears!—delicious tears! !—my mistress of the house happening to come into the room at the time, as she must have often remarked by this appearance of sensibility—stupidly said, " she wondered why I smoked, when it made my eyes water so." I made her no answer—In a strange country, after so many tossings and tumblings—so many fair winds and so many foul winds!—the sea and sky, both so blue!—the dangers I might have encountered—the misfortunes that happen to travellers— the harshness of this foreign language—Alas! dearest Amelia, when shall we meet again!—

How shocking it is that wherever we meet humanity, we encounter inhumanity!—Very soon after my arrival here, I was struck with the truth of this sentiment. It was during the very first week, that they had oysters for supper at the house where I lodge. The practice is not peculiar to this people, but our inland situation prevents its being so common with us.—Only think of men and women sitting down at a round or square table indifferently—a square table to sup on, is detestable!—and cheerfully devouring live fish—yes! actually swallowing one after another living oysters!—Everything contributes to promote this unnatural repast—even the fellow who sells them has, by much custom, acquired an inhuman quickness and skill in separating their shells—no one appeared to be affected at it, so completely may our feelings be blunted!—I was persuaded to taste of them— found them delicious—eat only a dozen the first evening—but I have supped on them ever since, eating sometimes half a bushel, and I have experienced no inconvenience, having never rested better.

These people are eminent eaters. All their societies, charitable, learned, or political—all dine—A dinner celebrates a victory— a dinner consoles for a defeat—They have indeed no fancy in their festivals—eating hot or cold forms the only variety. They have disused the Christmas holidays, common to all the nations of Europe, when the era of hope to mankind becomes the season

of gaiety and rejoicing—when children return from school—
when the poor receive charities, and the rich congratulations;
when dressing the houses with branches of evergreens, an affecting
event is commemorated, and a pleasing contrast within made
to a dreary season without. This festival they have discarded,
but they have a day for giving thanks, which is rendered remarkable by the incredible quantities of meat and pastry that are
eaten! [6] I have been assured by a well-informed citizen, that
it has been ascertained after very accurate calculations, that a
greater quantity of poultry is devoured at this period, than has
ever been known to be consumed by any people of modern
times—

I have not seen much of private society here, and the few
traits of character which I have been able to glean since my
arrival to amuse my dearest C. de C. are drawn from public
exhibitions or assemblies. Although they have so little of the
vivacity or naïveté of our dear Germans, I have met with some
things that have mightily pleased me. Being at the theatre to see
The Stranger performed, translated, though the title is changed,
from a play of our divine Kotzebue, I was affected to admiration
at the gentleness and amiableness of this people.[7] In one of the
remote parts of the house were some of those wretched females
of the most abandoned sort, which are to be found in all cities—
their conduct was of the most outrageous, indecent, disgusting
kind, but the audience submitted to it without a murmur, as I am
told they always do—even parents with their daughters who were
present, made no opposition to it! What gentle toleration—What
amiable tenderness for misfortune!—What humane indulgence for
the wretched—To suffer two or three miserable beings, as some
alleviation of their abandonment, to offer the most indecent

---

[6] The observance of Christmas was restrained in New England even much
later than the time of the Anthology Society. Probably Tudor's family,
cosmopolitan and Anglican, were more festive at Christmas time than their
neighbors. The Anthologists did not meet on Christmas Day. "Last
evening being Christmas," the *Journal* notes on December 26, 1810, "the
club was adjourned to tonight" (*J*, 245).

[7] Tudor refers to a play by August von Kotzebue (1761–1819). Its original
title was *Menschenhass und Reue*. A sentimental tragedy, it enjoyed a long
vogue in England and America in translation.

insults to a whole audience! Candour obliges me to add, that I do not believe any other nation would be capable of such magnanimity! such generosity!

I have been present at one or two sittings of the legislature of this state, who are now in session. The lower house is a very numerous body, and appeared to me very much like a collection of the better sort of buyers and sellers at one of our fairs. To me who neither understood their language, nor their movements, the scene seemed as much confused as do the ropes of a ship, or the streets of a city to a villager. I should make one general remark, if I were going to describe them physically; they are all ruminating animals, they all chew the cud. I was assured however, that they transact a great deal of business, though it principally consists in regulating the militia, which, like a lady's watch, is always out of order, and in enacting laws respecting the taking of *old wives* by the citizens!—[8] These people have some odd materials in their composition—What can be the reason of so much solicitude in this case?—Perhaps, like the celebrated Sterne, they think that no woman ought to marry after *Wilke's first number*, though a man should be allowed to at what age he pleased.—I need not quote his reason—Still I should think they would be much more attentive to the taking young wives, as it is the general practice to marry very early, which is probably owing to the embarrassments attending the former kind of wives—What strange vagaries human nature runs into—What unexpected and singular customs—This I have just been mentioning has never occurred in any other nation—This people are destined to be remarkable!

I am quite impatient to leave this part of the United States; and I hope soon to be in Philadelphia, which is the capital of Pennsylvania, by far the most interesting state in the union. There, the quick intelligence and lofty views of the descendants of Germans, have an universal influence. It is even said that they will not elect any person for a legislator who does not speak broken English, either with a German, French, or Irish accent;

[8] "Ignorance of a language and the hurry of a traveller have seldom led to a more whimsical mistake."—Tudor's note. The reference is obviously to a law regulating the catching of ale wives."

and I am assured that the consequences are felt in all the acts
and in the whole character of the government—How I long to
be among my countrymen, or at least among those who speak
its language—the very knowledge of which qualifies a man for
overcoming difficulties.

From Philadelphia—I shall go to Washington, to be presented
at court, and to see the national government which is assembled
at Washington and Georgetown—I have already a pretty good
notion of these cities, as they were described by a French lady—
" Washington and Georgetown," said she, " are two very curious
cities; one is composed of streets without houses, and the other
of houses without streets."—But houses and streets are not my
object; it is man in his sublimest form—the legislators of a nation!
From what I have heard, I am all eagerness—The proud, mag-
nanimous spirit of liberty and independence will be shewn in all
their deliberations—The deputies from the southern states, I am
told, possess this spirit in a much higher degree, than those from
the northward, whose blood is chilled and sluggish in its circulation—The former too are uncontaminated by any intercourse
with, or knowledge of the world—They rise like meteors out of
the swamps and forests they inhabit; and, such is the force of their
genius, trample on those who have been long accustomed to the
meditations of statesmen, and boldly dictate measures that are to
influence the intercourse of nations!—Their talents have been most
conspicuous on all commercial questions. Unfettered by any
concern in the object, and unprejudiced by an local or minute
acquaintance with its operations, they have decided upon it with
as much wisdom as we could display in the interior of Germany.

—Surrounded by their slaves, the love of liberty is sublimated
to a passion—and they go to the capitol with a zest for personal
independence, that is whetted by the continual sight of the
miseries of slavery, and which by the force of habit spurns all
the frigid ceremonies and decencies to which the rest of the
world are subject—They follow an argument with a blow, and
are ready to fight as well as reason—Only conceive, my dear
friend, how strong an interest must be excited by one of these
orators, whose genius is not frittered away by any of the childish
rules of rhetorick—To behold him declaiming to the representatives of the nation! and if his arguments do not reach their head—

you perceive the pistol in his pocket, whose ball will reach their heart!—Yet this is not occasioned by their love of fighting, as they generally attempt to provoke those whose principles are opposed to private combat—They will sometimes take a beating from a man whom they are sure will fight, because his character is ascertained—There seems to be great refinement and self-denial of glory in their conduct; they seem rather to wish to extend the practice than to increase the victims—I am told that most of them have red hair, and wear red pantaloons! How picturesque! How I long to behold them!

Dearest Amelia! I abandon my pen—my paper—my ink—every thing but the thoughts of thee—I am stupefied in this uninteresting country. I must see a group of Germans—I must hear their well-known tones before I have the courage to write to thee again—When surrounded by all that is brilliant in Vienna, wandering in our magnificent promenades on the banks of the Danube—look into its stream—and think of the rivers of tears I have shed—Dearest lady! I cannot bear to conclude—I tear myself away!—Adieu!—[9]

—VIII (February, 1810), 89-94

The National Maxim

WINTHROP SARGENT

I AM EVERY day more and more convinced, that men labour after calamity, whilst happiness is within their reach. Unwilling to be only happy, they seek for something more; and the brief candle of existence goes out, before they find that the world

[9] Tudor's satire on the German language and the German people follows an established convention. He attempted another effort in the same vein in "Secret Causes of the American and French Revolutions," which can be found in his *Miscellanies* (Boston, 1821), 112-25. Meanwhile, the prejudice against German culture was being broken down by Madame de Staël and others. By 1815 George Ticknor and Edward Everett were on their way to study in Germany.

is too narrow for such enjoyments. How hard it is to discover truth! how easy to be deceived! I have actually changed my opinion more than an hundred times respecting this nation within the short space of thirteen days.[10] Their ignorance has yielded to their wisdom, and their wisdom has been eclipsed by their cunning. What was at first artifice, I afterwards thought ingenuousness; but this was only affability made subservient to interest; and I now find that interest governs all, and for this they labour and are exhausted. They have a national maxim which the infant is taught to lisp in its nurse's arms; it is very long, and I do not recollect it; but I know it is equivalent to " *get money* "; and I believe this useful lesson is never taught in vain. The chief men have grown old in its practice; and still hobble out, with all their infirmities to the place of traffick, when they should be at home in their mansions waiting the call of death. With us, you know, there is content and thankfulness with a little: labour ceases with the vigour of manhood, and age sits down to enjoy what it has acquired in the days of industry and youth. . . .

When this is the predominant passion of a nation, nothing can be expected but its concomitant evils. The gentler virtues are unknown, and charity is driven into exile. Science is confined to the rules of commerce, and commerce erects an idol before which all are prostrate. The social principle is lost in its contemplation; love and friendship are diverted to its worship; and honesty is dazzled with its golden splendour. In such a country, genius is like the mistletoe on the rock; it seems to exist upon the barren and unyielding surface only by its own resources, and the nourishment it receives from the dews of heaven. The progress of literature has therefore been very slow; it seems just emerging from the clouds of ignorance, and its lustre is yet too feeble to be seen by the eye alone. . . .

—II (January, 1805), 15-16

[10] This is an extract from one of Sargent's periodical essays entitled " Letters from Leinwha, Teacher of Morality in the Recesses of Latinguin . . . from a Wanderer in the West." Sargent follows the convention established by Montesquieu's *Lettres Persanes* and imitated by Goldsmith's *The Citizen of the World*.

A Wide African Sand Garden

ARTHUR MAYNARD WALTER

Surely the descendants of Englishmen in America are not absolutely degenerate. The mother country is proud of her bench of learned bishops, of her retired scholars, and illustrious professors in both universities. But when they ask us, why do you not do something to spread the glory of the English language, we are silent, like slaves. We may say that we have spice ships at the Philippines, and that our cannon has echoed among ice islands at either pole. This is honourable and tells our enterprise; but here the story ends, nor will I busily ask if there are no spots and stains on our flag which the waters of the oceans we traverse could not efface. For myself, I think we ought to have produced a few scholars; in this opinion, however, all are not unanimous, but if they agree that poetry is natural to any country, we must be ashamed of our own. We boast of no epick, tragedy, comedy, elegies, poems, pastoral or amatory, but this field is all desert, a wide African sand garden, showing brambles, and rushes, and reeds.

—III (November, 1806), 579

The Multiplicity of Our Literary Institutions

ROBERT H. GARDINER

THE RAPID GROWTH and population of the United States have excited the wonder and astonishment of Europe. While many countries of the old world have been retrograding from their former prosperity, and while the most flourishing have advanced with slow and painful steps to their present importance, America seems to have been exempted from the common lot of nations, and to have risen in the short period of thirty years to a distinguished rank in the world. The Grecian colonies proceeded, like Minerva, from their parent at the full period of maturity, and then slowly advanced or declined with the nations around them. The United States, on the contrary, deprived in early infancy of a mother's fostering care, had long to struggle for independence; but, from the moment that was obtained, she has surpassed the sanguine expectations of ideal calculations, and has increased beyond any former example in numbers, strength, and riches, and we might add learning, were an opinion to be formed from the number of her literary institutions. While the growing political importance of the United States is acknowledged by every one, it may be useful to inquire how far her numerous schools, academies, and colleges entitle her to the character of being really learned.

New England, with less than double the population of either London or Paris, can boast of possessing more universities than either England or France.

Academies are established in every part of the country, and not a village, but has its schools. Indeed strangers might reasonably expect to find learning possessed here by every peasant, to see numbers in every village familiar with the writings of the ancients, or who had explored the deepest recesses of science;

and that her universities would annually produce numbers who by their taste and erudition might enlighten their own age and advance the rising generation. It is true that information is more generally possessed in New England than in almost any other country in the world; that there are few who are unacquainted with the first rudiments of learning; that a competent knowledge of mechanicks, but more particularly of geography, is generally diffused through the country; but in politicks, to which every one thinks himself competent, the people are the dupes of every designing knave; while the higher branches of learning, those which elevate the soul, and teach man the use of his noble faculties, droop for want of culture. The tree puts forth leaves most luxuriantly, but the fruit is without flavour. Our colleges are careful to exhibit catalogues of the numbers whose brows they have encircled with the laurel wreath, but more care is taken to enrol their names than to store their minds. . . .

Many, at the moment of receiving their degree, could not pass the examination by which they gained admittance. Indeed not only are the students allowed to neglect the studies of the college; but those studies are inadequate to the formation of a finished scholar. Nor do the colleges afford the proper means of instruction, either in classick literature or abstruse science. . . .

Vain would be the attempt to improve the internal regulations without a radical reform in the whole system. Upon the present weak pillars the cumbersome superstructure could not be supported, but must speedily fall to the ground; the inadequate compensation of its officers is a defect which pervades every branch of our government, and prevents its commanding the first talents for any situation. An office without allowing its possessor a proper support holds him as a mark for envy and discontent to shoot at. Indeed a man of abilities must possess uncommon ambition or uncommon patriotism who accepts an office either in the state or college. The teachers of our schools are those who will serve cheapest, not those who know their duty best. An instructor at an academy may hope to obtain the wages of a day labourer, and a tutor at college generally receives as much as a mechanick can earn by the sweat of his brow. At the same time our democratick ideas would lead us to divide these paltry stipends among a still larger number of institutions; for every one supposes himself injured by the establishment of any institution nearer to his neighbour than to himself. We have not, it is true, travelling colleges or travelling academies; but as we have in some states travelling legislatures and, in our own, travelling law courts, we may still hope for this further improvement.

The multiplicity of colleges may tend to the diffusion of knowledge; but it likewise tends to disperse the rays. Collected into one focus, they might kindle some happy luminaries to give light and warmth to an age, but now, dispersed, are lost on too wide a surface. The same funds, which now faintly move through the veins of our numerous colleges, would give life and animation to one university, and excite an impulse that would bring every dormant faculty into operation.

—IV (March, 1807), 113-15

The Patronage of Letters and National Prosperity

JAMES SAVAGE

THE ENCOURAGEMENT OF learning and the patronage of genius are subjects of which, though we hear much in our country, we have not yet a perfect understanding. From the records of our state legislature we may ascertain how often they have voted, and how little they have done for our university; how liberal they have been in acts of incorporation to inferiour schools, and how sparing of grants to maintain them. They would have never dared to pay from the treasury a sum sufficient to erect a college or endow a professorship; but they have most liberally empowered trustees at different times to pursue a system of gaming that is forbidden by law to a single subject, and have assessed taxes in the shape of lotteries, whose effect has been little more than to compensate the labours of the managers and corrupt the morals of the publick. Some of the most important studies are therefore faintly pursued, because the oldest and most respectable literary institution in America wants competent funds to support instructors, and a dancing-master is better paid than a tutor.

If however the government has been niggardly, we may well boast, that the munificence of individuals has been applied to increase the utility of our establishments and to assist the talents of the studious. The liberality of our merchants is as well known at home, as their enterprise abroad. . . .

To learn how intimate is the connexion between the state of knowledge in any country and its prosperity, we need only compare the present condition of parts of Europe with that of the feudal ages of darkness. The fetters of papal supremacy restrained the exertions of science, and the barbarity of monarchs and of subjects, varying less in reality than in mode, gave no encouragement to art. Of the history of such times the mind rests on but few portions with delight. It resembles an extensive coast, enveloped in mist, where, though a few eminences are enlightened, the greater part appears dark, barren, and wearisome. Great minds are hardly distinguished in the ignoble herd of their countrymen. Like the companions of Aeneas after the tempest, *apparent rari nantes in gurgite vasto.*

They rarely from the dark abyss emerge.

Of the nations of moden Europe, Italy, which was first in the race of civilization has long given up the hope of victory. Art and science were there resuscitated, but have long since been overpowered by lethargy. Statuary has indeed asserted her ancient honours; but how long can she contend with domestick poverty and foreign domination? The masterpieces of antiquity, and the rival vouchers of modern genius are transported beyond the Alps. The immortal city has no longer the club of Hercules to defend her; her Apollo is torn away to grace the palace of the Tuileries; the thunder-bolt of Jupiter is wielded in a foreign country. The old ceremony of *evocation* has been performed by the French commanders; the gods of Rome have deserted to the enemy.

In Switzerland moral causes cannot counteract the designs of nature, who said at the creation, here shall the inhabitants labour for a scanty subsistence and enjoy liberty, though debased by ignorance. Their mountains and vallies, deformed with rocks or buried in snow, seem destined to be the cradle of genius; but the poverty of the country will not support his manhood. No other nymph than she whom Gessner courted, who seems to delight in mountain air, can live in so bleak an abode.

Spain, from her happy climate, and luxuriant soil, ought to be the elysium of Europe, and the genius of her natives might vie with that of Greece. But ecclesiastical bigotry there sways a sceptre more powerful than the wand of Mercury, which drove only the shades of departed mortals, while the inquisition constrains the spirits of the living.

The causes of the decline of Holland may be estimated variously by different politicians; but all will allow that one, not the least efficient, was the neglect of learning by her citizens, and the universal pursuit of wealth. The mighty mass of matter, in the composition of a Dutchman, was moved only by the competition for gain.

Between France and England, the contention for excellence in arts has been as animated as for superiority in power. Learning has, in each country, been the subject of their highest pride. In the land of our forefathers, the Cam and the Isis are more reverenced than all the rivers of the East, " whose foam is amber, and their gravel gold." In all the liberal arts, except poetry, France has, perhaps, the advantage; but the free spirit of Englishmen vindicates their superiority in abstract science.

If we are not the spurious offspring of our fathers, if we have not degenerated by transplantation, we ought, in no distant time, to rival England in learning, as in commerce. As we are in our infancy, perhaps attention is due rather to institutions than to individuals; and literary societies and projects deserve encouragement, before solitary genius can be patronised. To such plans every man, however inferiour in station or wealth, may be invited to contribute, though he should modestly shrink from the honours of Mecaenas or Lorenzo.

—IV (May, 1807), 243-45

The Image of the Man of Letters

In the usual course of national aggrandizement, it is almost certain, that those of you, who shall attain to old age, will find yourselves citizens of an empire unparalleled in extent; but is it probable, that you will have the honor of belonging to a nation of men of letters?

—Joseph Stevens Buckminster (1809)

Preface

THE WRITINGS IN this section express the attempts the Anthologists made to project a satisfactory image of the man of letters and to define the nature of the literary vocation. As the reader can see, their efforts were uncertain and surely at times misguided.

Their unfortunate tendency to take refuge in the sterile dilettantism that is one strain of the humanistic tradition is obvious in Buckminster's depiction of the Anthologists in the role of "gentle knights" defending their snug literary citadel against the "paynim host," and in other examples of excessive refinement—some have thought it to be endemic in Boston—here and there throughout the *Anthology* and the records of the Anthology Society. Indeed their cozy posturing tends to mask the intensity and firmness of the Anthologists' literary aspirations and to obscure their quest for a vision of a literary existence commensurate with their ambition.

A more compelling vision of the literary vocation gleams in Walter's somewhat tortured exposition of Dr. Johnson's status in "the empire of morals." It is realized to a fuller extent in Buckminster's Phi Beta Kappa address on the "Dangers and Duties of Men of Letters," a pronouncement acclaimed with the enthusiasm a later generation was to express for Emerson's Phi Beta Kappa oration on "The American Scholar." Buckminster concerned himself with the same basic question which prompted Emerson: What are the responsibilities of the man of letters and learning? Their answers differed greatly, but their broad cultural context was the same ancient problem, the relation of thought to action. Emerson's spoke for a radical rejection of tradition and a way of looking at thought as action. Buckminster's answer was one sanctioned by tradition and symbolized for him and his audience by the contrast he draws between Atticus, who dwelled in "the quiet of his library," and Cicero, who went through "the regular course of public honours and services." Buckminster, in other words, solves the problem of "inactive versus active learning" by appealing to the Roman and Renaissance ideal of the *doctus orator*, in whom virtue, wisdom, and eloquence join in the leadership of the commonwealth.

Such a solution was highly appealing to the Anthologists, for it answered one of their most urgent needs, the reconciliation of the political and the literary vocations in "a day of peril and depravity." "The Society spent a very pleasant evening & talked much upon politics & literature," one entry in the *Journal* reads (J, 70). Yet, more often than not the Anthologists tended to take the simpler, and more strategic, position handed down from aristocratic humanism that literature and politics are opposed areas of existence. Thus, for example, when John Quincy Adams, while serving as the first Boylston Professor of Rhetoric and Oratory at Harvard, became an apostate from the Federalist cause, the Anthologists attacked him not for having betrayed the Ciceronian ideal but for having deserted literature for the cause of political faction. The "gentle knights" cast him out into the night to roam with the "paynim host."

The Architecture of a Great Mind

JAMES SAVAGE (?)

THE OFFICE OF biography is to teach by examples. It then only fully attains its end when the incidents which form or illustrate character and conduct are so selected and disposed as to leave just, deep, and well defined impressions upon the mind. If it be the felicity of the biographer to light upon some rare individual, the ornament of his age, or of his nature, his task is indeed delightful, but it is high and difficult. A great mind is like some august temple, the slow work of labour and genius. It has effect as a whole. It has symmetry among its parts. Its proportions are well preserved. Its foundations are laid among and with materials of a gross and earthy nature. Its sublime top vaults toward heaven. If such an object be presented for the contemplation of the publick, we have a right to expect that all of these characteristick harmonies should be noticed; and that our attention should be directed to each distinct excellence. Nothing which contributes to its beauty or utility can be omitted in a just delineation. Nothing which had an influence on its commencement or progress can be superfluous in its true history. Thus far the analogy holds. But moral, mental structures have uses and relations higher and infinitely more numerous, as well as more important, than fabricks of wood, of brick, or of marble. These are objects of emulation, and give hints for architectural improvement to one or two monarchs, or nations in an age. Whereas those are examples of the progress of an individual towards the perfection of his nature and are the best inheritance of the whole human race, because they are sensible standards of moral and intellectual power by which every man may measure the stature of his own attainment. Like the works of the ancient masters in painting and sculpture, they contain outlines of general beauty, which all may lawfully copy; and exemplify eternal rules of thought and action by which it is the duty of each individual, making just allowance for situation and condition, to model and perfect himself.

These considerations impose a high class of duties on him who undertakes to write the life of an eminent man. He is not to content himself with meagre diaries, or with transcripts from occasional correspondences, however elegant or interesting. His labours ought not to cease so long as any source of information remains unexplored. If the object of research have been cotemporary, much light may be gathered from the companions of his early youth, or the friends of his manhood; from those who feared, and those who envied him; from patrons and rivals; from all who had occasion to observe, and capacity to mark with a distinguishing eye, his course and conduct. Out of this mass of materials it is the duty of the biographer to select the discriminating attributes of character; to seize upon them; and, tracing them through the various stages of existence, to show their origin, their growth, and the utmost limits of their expansion. Nor should he neglect to describe the obstacles which thwarted his advancement; as also the means by which he was enabled to surmount them. . . .

A noble plan of biography seems to be imperiously requisite when the character to be described is of an extraordinary cast; uniting excellencies, rare either for their number, nature, or combination; when labour is found associated with genius; high mental, with high moral, attainments; great strength of intellect with refined delicacy of feelings; and those splendid talents which make men admired and conspicuous on the great theatre of the world are seen united, not obscuring, but adding lustre to those qualities which make men lovely and amiable in the small circles and among the common relations of private life. Undoubtedly, Sir William Jones was a character of this class. We regret, therefore, that in these memoirs of his life we do not find a plan, conformable to our general notions of an excellent biography. If ever a character required the hand of a master to do justice to its beauties, to discriminate them, to give relief to its great, and throw a strong light on its delicate parts, it is that of this excellent, we may justly add, this wonderful man. Lord Teignmouth does not aspire to an high rank among biographers. His work is indeed worthy to be perused, and even studied, by all; particularly by the young. The path he has taken is easy and pleasant, fascinating both to the author and reader, but less elevated and less luminous than a genius like Sir William Jones has a right to claim, and will, certainly, in time command. . . .[1]

—II (July, 1805) 370-71

The Scholar and the Gentleman United

JOHN SYLVESTER JOHN GARDINER

EDUCATION HAS BEEN greatly improved in this country of late years. But though much has been done, yet much remains to be done. Our literary discipline is well calculated for common purposes, and our professional men are little inferiour to those of other countries in the knowledge of their professions. But here our claims to praise must end. Our lawyers are mere lawyers, our physicians are mere physicians, our divines are mere divines. Everything smells of the shop, and you will, in a few minutes conversation, infallibly detect a man's profession. We seldom meet here with an accomplished character, a young man of fine genius and very general knowledge, the scholar and the gentleman, united. Such a character is not uncommon in Europe, but

[1] Sir William Jones (1746–1794) was one of the famous English men of letters in his day. Although he was a lawyer by profession, his real vocation was the study of the Oriental languages and literatures, and he is remembered as a pioneer Sanskrit scholar. To the young Anthologists he was an ideal image of the man of letters. Savage's remarks come from his review of Lord Teignmouth's *Memoirs of the Life, Writings, and Correspondence of Sir William Jones* (Philadelphia, 1805).

Cf. The admiration Buckminster expresses in his account of "Literary Institutions in Liverpool" (pp. 126-28) for other great literary scholars: William Roscoe (1753–1831), William Shepherd (1768–1847), and Richard Parson (1759–1808).

is here a *rara avis in terris*. Whence proceeds this difference? From the inferiority of education among us. Our schoolmasters receive a mere pittance and are consequently men of inferiour talents. Every man capable of instructing well follows some profession or business able to support him. A preceptor without genius can never inspire a pupil with the love of learning. Instead of reading Virgil and Horace with the enthusiasm of an *amateur*, and of explaining them with the taste and acuteness of a Busby, he will barely require a *verbatim* translation and a knowledge of the rules of grammar.[2] The spirit and beauties of the author remain without notice; and what has never been taught will seldom be discovered. They go to college with but a smattering of learning, and often leave it with still less. For the same system of economy pervades our academick walls, and a college tutor receives rather less than a Boston labourer. Those who are qualified for nothing else consequently become tutors, and our guides to Parnassus are themselves ignorant of the road that leads thither.

The schoolmasters of Europe, particularly of Great-Britain, are amply rewarded for their labours, and generally consist of the best scholars in the kingdom. The employment is honourable and lucrative, and is almost always rewarded with some distinguished ecclesiastical preferment, the preceptors themselves being always clergymen of the established church. I shall close this article with the character of Dr. Sumner, master of Harrow-school, drawn by his pupil, Sir W. Jones, in the preface to his treatise on Persian poetry. The translation of course must be very inferiour to the elegance of the original Latin.

"The reader, I hope will pardon me, if I cannot here resist the temptation of extolling the virtues of this most learned man, who was my intimate friend, and of expressing just sorrow at his lamented death. He was a man of distinguished genius and integrity, of admirable temper, polite manners, and exquisite learning. He possessed, beyond any instructor I ever knew, the faculty of communicating knowledge; and such was the pleasantry of his deportment, that it was difficult to determine, whether he

[2] Richard Busby (1606–1695), a grammarian, was head of the Westminster School.

was more agreeable to his friends, or scholars. In Grecian and Roman literature he was profoundly skilled; and, though like another Socrates, he wrote little himself, no one could more ably detect the faults, or point out the beauties of authors of every description. Had fortune destined him for the bar or senate, and not confined him to the employment of tuition, he would have yielded to no one in eloquence, which is exclusively cultivated in Great Britain. For he possessed, if not in perfection, at least in a very high degree, all the accomplishments commendable in an orator, a musical voice, purity of language, a flowing style, uniting elegance and wit with a most tenacious memory; in a word the eyes, the countenance, the action, not of a player, but of another Demosthenes."

—III (January, 1806), 18-19

Gentle Knights and the Paynim Host

JOSEPH STEVENS BUCKMINSTER

THE FAULTS of our work, of which no one can be more sensible than the editors, result from causes which we can only hope to counteract, but not entirely to remove. The *Anthology* has hitherto been supported by the unpaid and unregulated contributions of a few literary men who are pleased when the publick profits by their reading or shares in their amusements. They have yet had no extraordinary stimulus to write but the friendly curiosity and occasional encomiums of men like themselves. They are not enlisted in the support of any denomination of prejudices; nor are they inspired with the fanaticism of literary crusaders associated to plant their standards on territory recovered from heathens or hereticks. They are satisfied if they in any way contribute to the mild influence of our common Christianity, and to the elegant tranquillity of literary life. They are gentle knights

who wish to guard the seats of taste and morals at home from
the incursions of the "paynim host"; happy if they should now
and then rescue a fair captive from the giants of romance or
dissolve the spell in which many a youthful genius is held by the
enchantments of corrupt literature. If with these objects they
can retain the pleasures of lettered society,

> Mundaeque parvo sub lare pauperum
> Coenae, sine aulaeis et ostro,
> Sollicitam explicuere frontem,

they will try to be as insensible to the neglect or contumely of
the great vulgar and the small as they are to the pelting of the
pitiless storm without when taste and good humour sit round the
fire within.

—VI (January, 1809), 4

The Empire of Morals and Dr. Johnson

ARTHUR MAYNARD WALTER

IN THE SHORT intervals of unmitigated study, or necessary
avocations of ordinary life, my mind delights to dwell on the
severe morality of Johnson. Imagination is sometimes awakened
by the fairy tales of Hawkesworth, and the judgment is closely
exercised by the condensed sense of Lord Verulam. But Johnson
alone confirms the resolutions of virtue and corroborates the
convictions of religion. Whatever may be the pleasure arising
from the perusal of other periodical compositions, the sober
dignity of the *Rambler* alone originates seriousness of thought
and determinations of practical rectitude. In studying the advice
and admiring the sublimity of Johnson's views, I for a moment
at least resolve to forsake the obliquities of pleasure. I then feel
that I am ennobled, I then know that I am immortal, and I conse-

quently promise to pursue a corresponding course of existence. He is the great master of moral painting. His high-wrought designs have all the gigantick fulness of Michael Angelo. The shortness of life, the certainty of death, the folly of pleasure, the inquietude of riches, the fluctuations of popularity, honour, and renown are impressed with such force of sense, such variety of situation, such clearness of figure, combined with such irresistible energy of sentiment and mysterious dictatorial authority of style that we willingly bow to the lawful authority of the master and silently become the disciples of the venerable philosopher.

One grand excellence of Johnson's morals consists in their generality. In his *Idler* indeed there are individuals sketched; and in such a manner that we regret his apparent contempt of such trifling. But regret is vain. The summer house of the Pope could not engage the notice of Buonarotti, whose mind was intent on the swelling vastness of the dome of St. Peter's, and Johnson, who knew that his moral speculations would attend the progress of English conquests in Hindostan, and of English language in America, thought it undignified to dedicate pages to individuals, when his subject was universal man. Therefore all ages, characters, and conditions can draw from this undefiled and exhaustless fountain maxims of general conduct and sentiments of general application. Hence he is every where read with utility, and such is the remarkable nature of his *Rambler* that with inconsiderable difference it affords equal pleasure and enforces equal awfulness on the banks of the Thames, the Ganges, and the Mississippi.

I admire Johnson for his continual propriety. Other writers sometimes relax from rectitude, but he is always consistent. He seems to have abhorred the first appearances of vice in every form and on every occasion. In all social symposia, of which he was the life and leader, he had an intolerable aversion to nonsense; and in his morals he is the uniform and rigid advocate of virtue and religion. He never suffered his speculations to be discordant from rule. *Semper simplex et idem* was his object, and his design he never abandoned; for as he feared no one's frown, so he courted no one's smile, and with independence of sentiment and ponderousness of expression he has censorially chastised the seductive pleasures of life, the effeminate flattery of beauty, the false recommendations of honourable licentiousness, and the imposing confidence of patrician criminality. As a Christian knight, who, in the wars of religion against the Saracenik profanation of the holy city and the awful sepulchre, thought himself unauthorised to hold secret converse or form irreligious convenants with anti-Christian ravagers, so Johnson impressed with the obligations of piety and hallowed in the sanctuaries of the church, disdained a transitory reconciliation with vice; and maintained an unceasing war against the powers and principalities of darkness. In the empire of morals he is at once an officer and a priest; he is girt with the sword of the law and enrobed in the garments of religion. With the authority of a magistrate he enters the midnight haunt and the secret recess; he punishes the perpetrators of crimes, and drives away the votaries of pleasure. With the condescension of a minister at the altar he sometimes furnishes consolation to the trembling diffidence of timorous piety, and sometimes accompanies the blessed aspirations of the fervent enthusiast.

—II (June, 1805), 292-94

Horace Walpole: the Wasted Life

ANONYMOUS

THERE IS NO man, of any rank in literature, who seems to me to have lived more completely in vain, than Lord Orford. He used life, as if he thought it a bauble, which we are to toss about for a few hours, and when we are weary, to resign ourselves to repose, which will never be interrupted. He amused himself, for none of his works have claims to a more dignified character than amusing, with writing " Historick doubts," which have some ingenuity, without either accuracy or utility; a " Catalogue of royal and noble authors," of some value, but of little merit; the " Mysterious Mother " & "Anecdotes of painting," which are said to be his best attempts. Besides these he published some pretty letters and some neglected verses. The rest of his life was wasted in writing a romance, determining the antiquity of a picture, reviving forgotten scandal, or retailing *bon mots*. Such a man as this however did not fear to deride Johnson, dislike Cervantes, and ridicule Christianity.

—II (September, 1805), 460

Milton's Moral and Political Conduct

JOHN SYLVESTER JOHN GARDINER

I HAVE READ Hayley's life of Milton with attention, but am by no means convinced, that he was a man of that amiable character which his biographer fondly attempts to prove. Johnsons' life of him, unfavourable as it is, strikes me, as much more agreeable with truth. Democrats and revolutionists have felt a lively interest in defending the bard, where he is the least defensible, in his moral and political conduct. His opposition to Charles the first might have proceeded from principle; and even his approbation of the illegal trial and murder of that ill fated monarch, may be palliated by the republican enthusiasm of the time. But his gross flatteries of an odious usurper, and his holding an office under him, are stains on the poet's character, which the zeal and ingenuity of his admirers will never be able to wash out. His temper was stern and ferocious, impatient of contradiction, and ill calculated for the enjoyments of social intercourse. As to his genius there can be but one opinion. In sublimity, he exceeds, perhaps, all writers. But his style is often stiff, quaint, and pedantick, from which cause arises the difficulty of reading him. Sheridan, the rhetorician, imagines, that he will be better understood and more relished centuries hence. If English becomes a dead language, and he is studied as ancient, this may possibly be the case, as the imperfections of his style will then be less apparent. Pope's character of *Paradise Lost* is just, and written with his usual elegance.

> Milton's strong pinion now not heav'n can bound;
> Now, serpent-like, in prose he sweeps the ground;
> In quibbles angel and archangel join,
> And God the Father turns a school divine! [3]

—VI (February, 1809), 87-88

Who Gave Up to Party: the Case of John Quincy Adams

SAMUEL COOPER THACHER

WE SHOULD ESTEEM ourselves altogether unworthy the honour to which we aspire of being numbered among the friends of literature, if we could for a moment suffer our judgment of the claims of a man of letters to be influenced by any feelings of political antipathy. It is the delight and charm of literature that it affords us a refuge from the tumults and contentions of active life—a spot, where we may escape from the hot and feverous atmosphere which we are compelled to breathe in the world and enjoy that repose which we find no where else; not always, alas! even in the holy walks of the theological inquiry. We should feel the same sort of repugnance at introducing the

[3] Cf. Buckminster's attack on Milton in "The Dangers and Duties of Men of Letters," p. 96. Later a much more sympathetic and far more influential treatment of Milton was written by William Ellery Channing. Channing's essay provides an interesting contrast to the attitude toward Milton assumed by Gardiner and Buckminster and shows how important Milton actually was to the New England mind.

passions of party into these quiet regions, as at bringing a band of ruffians into the abodes of rural innocence and happiness, to marr their beauty, and violate their peace. At the same time, however, in a country like ours, where politicks possess an interest so overwhelming that he who will not talk of them must be content to pass his days in silence—to say that we have formed no opinion on one who has engaged so much attention as Mr. Adams would be laying claim to a neutrality which it is no part of our ambition to possess. We have indeed no wish to disguise our sentiments on the political career of Mr. Adams. We have on this subject no sympathy with him whatever. We see and lament that the orb of his political glory has become dark—

> Irrecoverably dark, total eclipse:
> Without all hope of day.
>
> SAMSON AGONISTES.

We offer this free expression of our opinions, lest the praise we may be bound in justice to bestow should lose its value by being supposed to proceed from political friends. Having then made this sacrifice to the unhappy temper of the times, we proceed to the examination of the work of this gentleman, whose claims to the name of the best read and most accomplished scholar our country has produced, are, we presume, beyond all dispute.[4]

[4] When John Quincy Adams accepted the appointment to the Boylston Professorship of Rhetoric and Oratory in 1805, he had the full approval of the Anthologists, who spoke publicly in the *Anthology* of "the acknowledged learning, taste, and ability of the Professor elect" (II [July, 1805], 389). Later they printed his inaugural oration with fulsome compliments. (See III [June, 1806], 336; and pp. 162-69.) Even as he settled in Cambridge for his initial lectures, however, Adams seems to have felt a growing sense of alienation from the Federalist political orthodoxy and to have anticipated the condemnation that would eventually descend on him. His subsequent support of certain Jeffersonian policies, especially some relating to the Embargo Act, caused him to be cast out of the Federalist party. He continued to lecture at Harvard until he was appointed ambassador to Russia. His *Lectures on Rhetoric and Oratory* appeared in 1810. When Thacher read his review of this work to the Anthologists, they were divided in their reaction to the polemical introduction and conclusion (see *J*, 225). An account of Adams' career as Boylston Professor at Harvard and of the publication and reception of the *Lectures* will be found in Donald M.

It seems to be generally agreed, that however superiour in philosophy and the exact sciences, the moderns fall far below the ancients in eloquence. The causes usually assigned for this inferiority are examined by Hume in one of his essays, and he pronounces them all to be inadequate and unsatisfactory.[5] There is one reason, however, to which, we conceive, he has not allowed sufficient force. From the changes in our habits, constitution and government, and the more universal diffusion of knowledge, the same effects as formerly cannot now be produced by appeals to the passions. The degree of excellence which any art will attain may be estimated as certainly and exactly by the effects which its perfection will produce, as in commerce the quality of any commodity is regulated by the price which it will command. It is therefore because eloquence has lost so much of its efficacy that it has lost so much of its elevation. If in our courts of jurisprudence the decision of a cause depended on the will of the judges, or if our deliberative assemblies were so constituted that the fate of an empire depended on the passions of a mob, there would be sufficient premium offered to induce men to devote themselves exclusively to the art, and the eloquence of Greece and of Rome would be indubitably rivalled. But, says Hume, "it would be easy to find a Philip in modern times; but where shall we find a Demosthenes?" We reply, show us the country where it depends on the eloquence of a Demosthenes to determine whether to march or not against Philip; and the man will in due time appear, who, like him, will make the chains of the tyrant resound in the ears of his country, till they, like the Athenians, involuntarily start up to oppose him.

We scarcely know whether to consider it as a subject of felicitation or regret that the causes which impede the progress of eloquence are felt less forcibly in our own country than in Europe. Notwithstanding the obstacles which the regular organization of parties, and the superiour diffusion of intelligence, and a spirit of calculation among our common people, oppose to its

---

Goodfellow, "The First Boylston Professor of Rhetoric and Oratory," *New England Quarterly*, XIX (September, 1946), 372-89. This article ignores the political portions of Thacher's review.

[5] The reference is to David Hume's essay entitled "Of Eloquence."

advancement, we believe that greater effects may be produced by it among us than in any nation since the days of antiquity. Nothing, therefore, but inferiority of native genius can prevent this art from regaining something of its ancient pre-eminence. That nature is less liberal of her gifts on one side of the Atlantick than on the other, we presume no one is now child enough to believe. If the opinion were ever seriously entertained by any one, it is now sufficiently refuted by facts. We do not fear to say (and too much nationality is not supposed to be our foible) that the debates on the British treaty and on the judiciary, considered as a whole, afforded a finer specimen of oratorical talents than has been witnessed in any deliberative assembly since the days of the senate of Rome.[6] At the same time, however, we are far from supposing that we have already produced any rivals to the orators of antiquity. With all the vigour and originality which we have seen displayed, there exists a palpable want of that extent and variety of knowledge which regular study alone can supply, and a most deplorable deficiency of that purity of taste which is gained only by long and habitual meditation of the great masters of style. Even in the debate on the judiciary, which however, we admit, produced nothing to rival two or three of the finest speeches on the British treaty, there are very few passages to which we could apply an epithet of higher dignity than that of very eloquent and splendid declamation. Perhaps we might take Mr. Randolph as a pretty fair specimen at once of the excellence and defects of our countrymen. In his vague and often unconsequential reasonings, his coarse invective, and his confused and revolting imagery, we have a striking illustration of our prevailing defects; and in his strong and original conceptions, in the bright and bold flashes of his imagination, and the nervous diction, which he sometimes displays, we have a flattering proof of what our country is capable.

It is the tendency of the remarks we have hazarded to illustrate the necessity of a more regular and scientifick study of rhetorick.

[6] The debates on the British treaty in 1795–1796 were marked by several memorable orations, particularly one by Fisher Ames. In 1799 the debate over the reorganization of the federal judiciary occasioned fervid oratorical displays in Congress.

The establishment of a new professorship of this science at the university of Cambridge we consider as one additional pledge that a spirit of literary improvement has begun its career among us. The book before us, therefore, we take up with singular pleasure, as the first fruits of this establishment; and though we will not say that it is faultless, yet it is certainly in a high degree honourable to the talents and learning of the author, and must be of great and permanent utility. For him, who is desirous of finding a compendium of all the best precepts of the ancient masters of rhetorick, adapted to the state of eloquence in modern times, and the particular circumstances of our own country, we know of no book to which we should so soon refer as to the Lectures of Mr. Adams. . . .

In offering our general opinion on this book, we can say, that after taking into view all its merits, and making every deduction for its defects, its absolute value is great and decided. Its relative rank, compared with the books which are daily issuing from our press, is pre-eminently high. We have pointed out with some freedom what we conceive to be imperfections, because Mr. Adams is one of those writers whose defects are important. He will be widely read and generally admired; and his authority may be sufficient to make his blemishes pass for beauties. It ought not however to be forgotten, that he has been unable to give his work his last revision and corrections; and though his friends, to whom the care of its publication was committed, have doubtless done much, it would have been a task of too much delicacy to have expunged what perhaps after all the author might have valued. The greatest and most permanent merit of this book is the very complete and accurate survey which it gives us of the precepts of antiquity, and the skilful adaptation of them to modern times, and particularly our own country. He has had several predecessors in the view he has taken of his subject; especially Ward, whose track is exactly the same. We have no hesitation however in saying, that Mr. A. is incomparably superiour. Indeed for instruction in what may be called *oral* eloquence, we know not a work of equal value in the language. His book every where displays an affluent mind; enriched however more by reading and study than by original thinking. He has yet higher praise. There runs throughout the book a strain of the most pure and exalted morality, and his morals are always sanctioned and impressed by the authorty of the gospel. The frequent and voluntary tributes of respect and reverence to Christianity are of the more value, coming from a man of his high character, (high, those who differ him in politicks must admit it to be in talents and private virtue) and in a case where none of his prejudices can be supposed to operate. We close the book with sensations of sincere regret that the talents and learning of this gentleman seem now altogether withdrawn from the walks of literature. What nobler object can he propose to his ambition than that which was opened to him in the career in which he was engaged; the glory of forming the minds of youth to moral and intellectual dignity, and contributing to exalt the literary character of his country.

When we contemplate the extent and variety of his acquisitions, and recollect that the kind of learning in which he most excels is so rare in our country as to be almost unknown, we cannot sufficiently lament that he should be willing to abandon the laurels, which he might have gained without a rival, to gather a barren and withering chaplet of political renown. Our opinion of the talents of Mr. A. cannot be better expressed than by applying to him the lines of Goldsmith, with which we close our observations. A man

> . . . . . whose genius is such
> We scarcely can praise it or blame it too much;
> Who, born for the universe, narrows his mind,
> And to party gives up what was meant for mankind.

—VIII (April, 1810), 249-68

The Degeneracy of Modern Scholars

ANONYMOUS

THERE IS HARDLY a surer mark of the degeneracy of modern literature than the inordinate attention which is now paid to bibliography. The knowledge of title pages has succeeded to the knowledge of subjects, and to ascertain the year of an *editio princeps* is now thought of as much importance and divides the learned as seriously as to settle the true year of the birth of Christ. *Scire ubi aliquid posses invenire, magna pars eruditionis est*; but to know *where* a thing may be found is very consistent with ignorance of *what* may be found there. It is well worth inquiry whether the innumerable literary journals of the present age have promoted the cause of real learning. Certain it is that the race of laborious scholars is nearly extinct. Boehart may perhaps be said to have been revived in Bryant; Walton and Castell in Kennicott, Bentley in Wakefield, and more than one scholar of the old school in Sir William Jones. But these men are now dead! Where now are the universal scholars, who can boast of being the legitimate successors of Selden, Grotius, Le Clerc, Vossius, and Bayle? [7] What wonderfully crowded and comprehensive minds! Alas, we are hardly competent to the republications of their works. *Damnosa quid non imminuit dies!*

—III (April, 1806), 175

[7] This is an interesting list, showing as it does the attachment of the Anthologists to the memory of the great legal, philological, and religious scholarship of the seventeenth century. It may well be that Pierre Bayle (1647-1706) was the strongest continuing influence. Buckminster had his complete writings in his library.

The Dangers and Duties of Men of Letters

JOSEPH STEVENS BUCKMINSTER

IN THE USUAL course of national aggrandizement, it is almost certain that those of you who shall attain to old age will find yourselves the citizens of an empire unparalleled in extent; but is it probable that you will have the honour of belonging to a nation of men of letters? The review of our past literary progress does not authorize very lofty expectations, neither does it leave us entirely without hope.[8]

It is our lot to have been born in an age of tremendous revolution; and the world is yet covered with the wrecks of its ancient glory, especially of its literary renown. The fury of that storm, which rose in France, is passed and spent, but its effects have been felt through the whole system of liberal education. The foul spirit of innovation and sophistry has been seen wandering in the very groves of the Lyceum, and is not yet completely exorcised, though the spell is broken. When we look back to the records of our learning before the American revolution, we find, or think we find, (at least in New England) more accomplished scholars than we have since produced; men, who conversed more familiarly than their children with the mighty dead; men, who felt more than we do the charm of classical accomplishments; men, in short, who had not learned to be ashamed of being often found drinking at the wells of antiquity. But so greatly have our habits of thinking been disturbed by the revolutions of the last thirty years, that the progress of our education, and, of course, the

---

[8] Buckminster delivered this address at the annual meeting of the Harvard chapter of the Phi Beta Kappa Society on August 31, 1809. According to John Pierce, it "was received with the utmost attention & approbation." See "Some Notes on the Anniversary Meetings of the Phi Beta Kappa Society," *Proceedings of the Massachusetts Historical Society*, ser. 2, IX, 112-13.

character of our learning have not a little suffered. It is true, we
have shared the detriment with Europe; but the effect upon us,
though perhaps temporary, has been peculiarly extensive and
unfortunate, because our government and our habits were in
some degree unsettled.

In France and in some other countries of Europe, what literature has lost seems to be compensated by the progress of science.
In England the trunk of her national learning was so deeply
rooted, that it has been swayed only, and not injured by this
tempest of reform. It yet retains its vigour, and we doubt not
will entirely recover its former direction. But here, the French
revolution, immediately succeeding our own, found the minds
of men in an unsettled state, and, as you may well imagine, did
not help to compose them. Our forms of education were becoming more popular and superficial; the knowledge of antiquity
began to be despised; and the hard labour of learning to be dis-
pensed with. Soon the ancient strictness of discipline disappeared;
the curriculum of studies was shortened in favour of the im-
patience or the necessities of candidates for literary honours; the
pains of application were derided, and a pernicious notion of
equality was introduced, which has not only tainted our sentiments, but impaired our vigour, and crippled our literary
eminence.

This secret influence of public opinion, though not easily
described, has been felt and lamented by many of us who were
educated in the present generation. We have many steps to
recover; and before we shall travel in the suite of learned in the
old world, we have some long strides to make. Our poets and
historians, our cricks and orators, the men of whom posterity
are to stand in awe and be instructed are yet to appear among us.
The men of letters who are to direct our taste, mould our genius,
and inspire our emulation; the men, in fact, whose writings are
to be the depositories of our national greatness, have not yet
shown themselves to the world. But if we are not mistaken in
the signs of the times, the genius of our literature begins to show
symptoms of vigour, and to meditate a bolder flight; and the
generation which is to succeed us will be formed on better models,
and leave a brighter track. The spirit of criticism begins to plume

itself, and education, as it assumes a more learned form, will take a higher aim. If we are not misled by our hopes, the dream of ignorance is at least disturbed; and there are signs that the period is approaching, in which it will be said of our own country, *tuus jam regnat Apollo.*

You then, my friends, are destined, I hope, to witness the dawn of our Augustan age, and to contribute to its glory. Whatever may be your place in society, I am confident you will not willingly discard the love of virtue and of knowledge; and it is with this confidence that I shall now venture to speak to you of some of THE DANGERS AND DUTIES OF MEN OF LETTERS. The subject is copious; and what will now be offered is a mere essay. If it should be found suitable to this occasion, and to the actual state of our literature, my purpose will be answered.

Every where there are dangers and evils, of which some affect the intellectual improvement, and others are unfavourable to the moral worth of literary men. In this country, especially, it too often happens that the young man, who is to live by his talents, and to make the most of the name of a scholar, is tempted to turn his literary credit to the quickest account by early making himself of consequence to the people, or rather to some of their factions. From the moment that he is found yielding himself up to their service, or hunting after popular favour, his time, his studies, and his powers yet in their bloom, are all lost to learning. Instead of giving his days and nights to the study of the profound masters of political wisdom, instead of patiently receiving the lessons of history and of practical philosophy, he prematurely takes a part in all the dissensions of the day. His leisure is wasted on the profligate productions of demagogues, and his curiosity bent on the minutiae of local politicks. The consequence is that his mind is so much dissipated, or his passions disturbed, that the quiet speculations of the scholar can no longer detain him. He hears at a distance the bustle of the Comitia—He rushes out of the grove of Egeria, and Numa and the Muses call after him in vain. It is, perhaps, one of the incurable evils of our constitution of society that this ambition of immediate notoriety and rapid success is too early excited, and thus the promises of literary excellence are so frequently superseded.

The history of genius is not wanting in examples of powers thus perverted, and passions too early inflamed. If we may go so far back for examples, we find them in Alcibiades and the Gracchi; men educated with all the advantages which Greece and Rome could bestow, and yet lost to every thing but faction. There are no doubt many other instances, but most of them are not now to be recovered from oblivion; for the records of civil dissention, let it be remembered, are not so lasting as those of learning. Here I should be tempted to adduce even the name of Burke, and support myself by the authority of Goldsmith, who ventured early to lament that

——he narrowed his mind,
And to party gave up what was meant for mankind.

But the awful history of our own times has persuaded me to forbear; for of Burke, at least, posterity will never cease to say, *what he gave up to party, he gave to mankind.* The life of Milton, however, is a memorable instance of the temporary degradation of learning. For, notwithstanding the sublime fiction of Gray, that the loss of his sight was occasioned by the brightness of his celestial visions, it is, alas! nothing but a fiction. Those fine orbs were quenched in the service of a vulgar and usurping faction; and had they not been thus early " closed in endless night," the world, perhaps, would have wanted the *Paradise Lost*, and that master spirit of England have been wasted in more praises of Cromwell and more ribaldry against Salmasius. You, then, who are impatient to take a part in public life, remember, that there is hardly to be found a consummate statesman or warriour in a literary age who was not himself a man of letters. I will not weary you by an enumeration; but you will instantly call to mind Alexander, the accomplished scholar of Aristotle; Caesar, at the head of Rome, the *deliciae literatorum*; Charlemagne, master of all the science that an ignorant age could afford; Alfred, the philosophical translator of Boethius; and Frederick, who gathered around him the great men of his age, not so much as their patron, as their competitor.

On the other hand, there are some finely attempered spirits, who, disgusted at the grossness which belongs to the common contests and occupations of active life, are in danger of entirely relinquishing its real duties in the luxurious leisure of study. In the actual state of the politicks of our country, this opposite temptation has been already felt by many studious minds. The young man, early enamoured of literature, sometimes casts a disdainful glance at the world, and then sinks to repose in the lap of his mistress. He finds it easier to read than to think, and still easier to think than to act. His indisposition increases by indulgence. His learning becomes effeminate. He reads to furnish amusement for his imagination, not to provide materials for intellectual greatness. He passes his time among the muses, it is true; but it is the graces, who mingle in the circle, that engross his attention; and his life, though nominally given to contemplation, is little else than " to sport with Amaryllis in the shade, and play with the tangles of Neaera's Hair." He goes to his books, to enjoy a certain mild delirium of the mind, regardless of the claims of society, and of the account, which he must give at last, of his studies and advantages. Whenever he comes out into the world, he thinks it was not made for him; and soon returns in disgust, to seek relief in that employment which has been admirably called the "invisible riot of the mind, that secret prodigality of being, secure from detection, and fearless of reproach."

The history of letters does not at this moment suggest to me a more fortunate parallel between the effects of active and of inactive learning than in the well known characters of Cicero and Atticus. Let me hold them up to your observation, not because Cicero was faultless, or Atticus always to blame, but because, like you, they were the citizens of a republick. They lived in an age of learning and of dangers, and acted upon opposite principles, when Rome was to be saved, if saved at all, by the virtuous energy of her most accomplished minds. If we look now for Atticus, we find him in the quiet of his library, surrounded with his books; while Cicero was passing through the regular course of publick honours and services, where all the treasures of his mind were at the command of his country. If we follow them, we find Atticus pleasantly wandering among the ruins of Athens, purchasing up statues and antiques; while Cicero was at home blasting the projects of Cataline, and at the head of the senate, like the tutelary spirit of his country as the storm was gathering, secretly watching the doubtful movements of Caesar. If we look to the period of the civil wars, we find Atticus always reputed, indeed, to belong to the party of the friends of liberty, yet originally dear to Sylla, and intimate with Clodius, recommending himself to Caesar by his neutrality, courted by Anthony, and connected with Octavius, poorly concealing the epicureanism of his principles under the ornaments of literature and the splendour of his benefactions; till at last this inoffensive and polished friend of successive usurpers hastens out of life to escape from the pains of a lingering disease. Turn now to Cicero, the only great man at whom Caesar always trembled, the only great man whom falling Rome did *not* fear. Do you tell me, that his hand once offered incense to the dictator? Remember, it was the gift of gratitude only and not of servility; for the same hand launched its indignation against the infamous Anthony, whose power was more to be dreaded, and whose revenge pursued him till this father of his country gave his head to the executioner without a struggle, for he knew that Rome was no longer to be saved! If, my friends, you would feel what learning and genius and virtue should aspire to in a day of peril and depravity, when you are tired of the factions of the city, the battles of Caesar, the crimes of the triumvirate, and the splendid court of Augustus, do not go and repose in the easy chair of Atticus, but refresh your virtues and your spirits with the contemplation of Cicero.

A little observation of the state of knowledge in this country brings to mind the remark of Johnson on the learning of Scotland: " that it is like bread in a besieged town, where every one gets a little, but no man a full meal." So it is among us. There is a diffusion of information widely and thinly spread, which serves to content us, rather than to make us ambitious of more. Our scholars are often employed in loose and undirected studies. They read, it is true, but without an object; and lose their time in superficial and unconnected inquiries. Such is the want of leisure in some of our professions, and the necessity of turning our knowledge to immediate account; so defective in many places are our rudiments of education, and so inadequate the provision made for instructors; so insulated are our men of study in this vast territory, and such is, after all, the genius of our government, that we find few who are willing to pass through the long and severe discipline of early application, and still fewer of whom we can say *geraskousi didaschomenoi*. We have yet to form systems of more effectual instruction, and to assign the departments of literary labour, where exertion shall be encouraged by suitable rewards. In the mean while, in this unsettled state of our studies, let us not weaken our powers by feebly grasping at every thing. We have been long enough flying from novelty to novelty, and regaling upon the flowers of literature, till we begin to know *where* learning may be found; it is time *now* to think of making it our own. The most powerful minds, which the world ever knew, have sometimes dissipated their powers in the multiplicity of their pursuits. Gibbon, in his masterly portrait of Leibnitz, concludes with comparing him to those heroes, "whose empire has been lost in the ambition of universal conquest." If then a mind like his, formed for intellectual supremacy, may suffer by designing more than it can accomplish, or by neglecting to concentrate its powers and pursuits, let us not spend *our* lives in hastily traversing regions of knowledge which we certainly shall never conquer, and which we may never inhabit, but turn to the patient cultivation of some of the provinces of literature.

The moral defects and faults of temper to which scholars are exposed are not peculiar to any country. It is every where the natural tendency of a life of retirement and contemplation to generate the notion of innocence and moral security; but men of letters should remember that, in the eye of reason and of Christianity, simple unprofitableness is always a crime. They should know too that there are solitary diseases of the imagination not less fatal to the mind than the vices of society. He who pollutes his fancy with his books may in fact be more culpable than he who is seduced into the haunts of debauchery by the force of passion or example. He who by his sober studies only feeds his selfishness or his pride of knowledge may be more to blame than the pedant or the coxcomb in literature, though not so ridiculous. That learning, whatever it may be, which lives and dies with the possessor, is more worthless than his wealth, which descends to his posterity; and where the heart remains uncultivated and the affections sluggish, the mere man of curious erudition may stand, indeed, as an object of popular admiration, but he stands like the occasional palaces of ice in the regions of the north, the work of vanity, lighted up with artificial lustre, yet cold, useless, and uninhabited, and soon to fall away without leaving a trace of their existence. You, then, who feel yourselves sinking under the gentle pressure of sloth, or who seek in learned seclusion that moral security, which is the reward of virtuous resolution, remember, you do not escape from temptations, much less from responsibility, by retiring to the repose and silence of your libraries. . . .

—VII (September, 1809), 146-53

From Boeotia to Attica

The task would now be easier to designate our Boeotia than our Attica. It will not always be so.

—William Tudor, Jr. (1810)

Preface

THE ATTEMPT OF the Anthologists to discover the role of the man of letters in their time is a part of their larger effort to explore the condition of literature as it existed at the beginning of the nineteenth century. The next part of this collection of writings from the *Anthology* presents appraisals by the Anthologists of their literary situation and of the state of literature.

The initial group of selections in this part pertain to the institution most of the Anthologists acknowledged as their "literary parent," Harvard University. The first two extracts call attention to a connection more vital than it might seem: the integral relationship existing between "Boston . . . that literary town" and Cambridge, "snug and sleek," to use the words of Alexander H. Everett's *jeu d'esprit*. The whole history of American letters, it is not too much to say, would be different if Harvard had been located an appreciable distance from Boston. The final two selections represent critical events in Harvard's history: the bitter theological controversy that placed Harvard in the domain of religious liberalism and the installation of John Thornton Kirkland as the fourteenth president of the school. Following these are writings concerning the establishment of the Boston Athenaeum.

The bulk of "From Boeotia to Attica" is devoted to a miscellany of essays, addresses, and so forth, in which the Anthologists are seen grasping for critical standards and seeking to open up critical vistas. This group of writings can be read as a debate between the pious defenders of a dogmatic neoclassicism heavily tinged with Anglophilism and the proponents of an incipient romanticism colored by an uncertain nationalism. The quarrel between Buckminster and Gardiner over the merits of Gray has been mentioned in the Introduction. In addition to this exchange of essays, the reader will find aspects of this debate revealed in Walter's essay on Pope, Edmund Trowbridge Dana's attack on the classics, and Benjamin Welles's excursion into the relationship

105

between man and nature. These selections all emphasize a growing romantic bias. Further expositions of the classical bias may be seen, among other places, in Kirkland's statement of the objects and principles of the *Anthology*, in Buckminster's—he was pulled different ways—concept of a rigid literary polity, in Theodore Dehon's Phi Beta Kappa address, and in an anonymous comment (probably by Gardiner) which defends Pope as "the poet of the human species" and dismisses the charge that he was not original with a disdain worthy of a Dr. Johnson, "Originality! Fiddledy diddledy!"

The literary sensibility of the Anthologists, however, can hardly be gauged by their involvement in the debate between classicism and romanticism. Their involvement was superficial. Although Gardiner on one occasion referred to "the whimsical novelties of lyrical ballad-mongers," he and his colleagues were scarcely aware of Wordsworth and Coleridge. What counted was their sense of mission—their awareness of the theme of the historic *translatio studii* and of the lore and legends of the traditional Republic of Letters. (See especially "The Polity of Letters" by Joseph Stevens Buckminster and "The Importance of Literature to Our Country" by Theodore Dehon.) What mattered was their effort to measure the distance from Boeotia to Attica.

"From Boeotia to Attica" represents an endeavor by William Tudor to measure this distance by surveying the state of letters, learning, and the arts in Western civilization from the Renaissance on and by relating America to the broad picture. (Only the section of Tudor's remarks concerning America is printed in this volume.) Typically, his study is more ambitious than successful. But Tudor's address, another Phi Beta Kappa oration, may well serve as a summary statement of cultural aspiration in the Boston-Cambridge world at the dawn of the New England Renaissance.

The pattern of cultural history Tudor follows, as the organization of his address indicates, is fundamentally that of the *translatio studii*. He describes (in the portion of his address which has been omitted) the recovery of the classics after the ages dominated by the "jargon of scholastick philosophy," the transfer of arts and letters to France and England, and the circumstances of their transplanting in America. He concludes with a vision of the continental progress of literary culture in America. This is the most interesting feature of his address. True, he is celebrating the impending spread of a transplanted Anglo-Saxon culture rather than a national one, he appears to believe that this culture represents an ultimate achievement, and he is ambiguous about the future economic and political unity of the continent. But in his vision he breaks through the gloom of Boston's Federalist isolation in 1809 to contemplate the relation between cultural achievement and the conquest of the continent. Note in particular that he prophesies the role of Harvard in the transmission of culture to the vast continental reaches. "Future societies of men that will exist in regions that man has not yet explored will turn their eyes toward this ancient seminary, will be attracted by its fame, and seek for knowledge in its copious fountains." How influential, and complicated, this return to the fountains was to become in the future history of American culture, however, would have amazed even such a devoted son of Harvard as Tudor.

Incidentally, it is interesting to compare Tudor's oration of 1809 with a second Phi Beta Kappa oration he delivered in 1815. This has a decidedly nationalistic tone and explores the possibilities of employing American scenery and the American Indians as poetic subjects.*

The final address of the Anthologists to their readers is printed as the last item in this edition of writings from the *Anthology*. The Society's *Journal* records that at the meeting on May 12, 1811, "Mr. Thacher . . . committed himself for the last words and dying speech . . ." (*J*, 255). This he read to the gentlemen at the meeting on June 11, 1811, when a "full club" was present. George Ticknor, who served as the last secretary of the club, remarks: "It was written in his happiest manner and if on no other account at least on this, the Anthology may boast non *omnis* moriar. We shall indeed perish with a halo of splendour about us. The ironical solemnity of the address was admirably suited to the languor and indifference of the Society and was read amid bursts of laughter" (*J*, 256).

---

* It may be found in the *North American Review*, II (November, 1815), 13-32.

It is doubtful if Ticknor's rendering of the tone and the reception of Thacher's remarks is entirely accurate. Possibly Thacher responded to the mood of the occasion in a way that led the youthful Ticknor to get the impression he entered in the *Journal*. But the farewell address seems completely in keeping with the convictions of the Anthologists. Probably they felt a sincere desire to apologize for their occasional impetuosity. Probably they believed that they had been free from political and theological prejudices, although this was hardly the case. Certainly they were earnest in stating their conviction to " polite letters " and " sound science "—terms which to them were synonymous with civilization.

OUR LITERARY PARENT

Laudes Cantabrigiae

ALEXANDER H. EVERETT

THOSE WHO LIKE me are enamored alike of collegiate scenes and authors will be pleased with an application of

HORACE, Lib. 2, Ode 6
Septimi, Gades aditure mecum, et
Cantabrum indoctum, &c.

To J. B.

Dear Jac.[1] did pence attend my quill,
I'd pass my days in Boston still,
Farfamed for dinners cooked with skill,
    That literary town;
But forced by fate to douse my peak,
I've often wished with thee to seek
A seat in Cambridge snug and sleek
    And set me quiet down.

---

[1] The "J. B." to whom Alexander H. Everett addressed his poem was Jacob Bigelow (1786–1879), physician and botanist. The two were classmates at Harvard, graduating in 1806. Together with Joseph G. Cogswell (1786–1871), they entertained their fellow students at Harvard with what Bigelow described as "a poetic periodical called 'The Jingler,' which was devoted mainly to strictures and facts connected with the social and parietal regulation of the college, and which enjoyed for a time a limited circulation in manuscript within the walls of the institution." See G. E. Ellis, "Memoir of Jacob Bigelow," *Proceedings of the Massachusetts Historical Society*, XVII, 405. For an example of Bigelow's light verse, see "Timothy Tankard, the Scientific Drinker," *Anthology*, VI (January, 1809), 38.

There fair and softly lulled to rest
On Alma Mater's downy breast,
With cares of fame nor pelf distrest,
    Of sleep we'd take our fill;
O'er Greek and Latin gently snore,
Relieve with wine our arid lore,
And try, when streams Parnassian pour
    To drive a mutual quill.

There, haply, loosed from griping claw,
Of physick thou and I of law,
The lot propitious each may draw
    To fill tutorial chair.
No wayward wife shall scold and weep,
No brawling babies break our sleep,
Nor busy female dare to sweep
    The learned cobwebs there.

What though they lure to sad surprize
With rising breasts, and rolling eyes;
Convinced we know the seeming guise,
    And shun the shining woe.
And then, when Clotho cuts my twine,
Thy hand shall weave the serious line,
A drop of ink, and one of brine,
Shall say, in sacred peace, recline
    The student's bones below.

—V (December, 1808), 658

Commencement Day at Harvard

JOSEPH McKEAN

COMMENCEMENT DAY is an attractive festival to all descriptions of our people. The wealthy welcome it as one of the occasions on which they may nobly exercise hospitality, or participate, in turn, of the elegances of a college entertainment. The man of business is pleased with the opportunity of a holiday to take a pleasant excursion into the pleasant villages which surround our metropolis. Persons of various classes and ages unite in its celebration, and with one heart and voice pronounce it a favourite season, and to this vicinity the carnival of the year. But to Harvard's sons this day has a peculiar value. It interests all their social, it delights all their literary attachments. Reason and feeling combine to endear the venerable domes and groves of Cambridge to all who have tenanted those walls and strolled in those woods. The meeting of classmates and cotemporaries revives the loved impressions of former years. The cares and perplexities, disappointments and regrets of vulgar life, are at these precious moments forgotten; and with hearts void of care and vexations, as in old times, they crowd to the chapel of prayer and the hall of refreshment. Here many solemn recollections crowd on the memory of numbers whose faces once gladdened these rooms, now not to be seen there; some detained by indispensable avocations, some remote in foreign climes, some registered in the catalogue of death. By the literary exhibitions they are reminded of their own efforts at eloquence and argument; and probably acknowledge that few if any after attempts have seemed to themselves so successful, or given so much satisfaction. The antique chair, from which is pronounced the classick meed; the academick fraternity in their appropriate garbs; the crowd of spectators, all with smiling countenances and gay attire, agreeably

engage the thoughts and amuse the fancy. The temperate grati-
fications of the festive board succeed; and "commons are remembered with many pleasing & mortifying associations." They
unite in the solemn song,

> "Which our Forefathers' pious care
> To us has handed down,
> And Generations yet to come
> Shall, to their unborn Heirs,
> Religiously transmit the same
> And they again to theirs."

This customary service past, and one tributary glass gone round
to "memory of revered instructors and beloved associates," one
soothing cigar consumed, and a pensive glance taken all around,
under the impression that it may be the last time these joys are
to be tasted, each retires, and returns home, "dragging at each
remove a lengthening chain." [2]

—IV (August, 1807), 429-30

[2] This description of the annual Harvard commencement festival is
restrained. Deriving apparently from an amalgamation of scholastic and
patriotic ceremonial with the gay activities of the English fair, it retained
a vivid carnival atmosphere until at least the end of the first quarter of
the nineteenth century. See "The AD, a Poem in Ten Books by J.
Lowbard," *Harvard Lyceum*, I (August 25, 1810), 94. In this satirical
effort, probably by youthful Edward Everett, the Genius of Cambridge
Common, enraged by the merrymaking at commencement, has Rum
render the crowd helpless. John Holmes, historian of Cambridge, said of
the old time commencement at Harvard, "The atmosphere . . . created in
the interests of literature was to the true devotee of Commencement what
the flavor of the holocaust was to the pious ancient." *Letters of John
Holmes*, ed. William Roscoe Thayer (Boston and New York, 1917), xxii.
An evocative, though possibly somewhat tempered, description of the
carnival spell of commencement can be found in Oliver Wendell Holmes,
"The Seasons," *Writings* (Boston, 1891), VIII, 158-61. Also, see Lewis P.
Simpson, "The Intercommunity of the Learned: Boston and Cambridge
in 1800," *New England Quarterly*, XXIII (December, 1950), 496-97.
    The date of commencement was fixed on the last Wednesday in August
by a vote of the Corporation and Overseers in March, 1802; prior to that
time it had been held on the last Wednesday in July. See Albert Matthews,
"Harvard Commencement Days, 1642-1916," *Publications of the Colonial
Society of Massachusetts*, XVIII, 349, 365.

Notions of Genius at Harvard

DAVID PHINEAS ADAMS (?)

HAPPENING NOT LONG since to attend an Exhibition at Harvard University, I was was highly gratified with the ingenious, correct, and manly performances of several students. Their elocution was appropriate and graceful, considering they have there no established Professor of Oratory. Their compositions were, for the most part, neat and elegant, neither overloaded with ornament, nor deficient in imagination. They greatly exceeded the style of writing in any other American college with which I am acquainted. In most other places it is usual to abound in figurative language and in attempts at wit. Here there were no unnatural efforts after the latter; and the former was managed with accuracy and taste. The writers appeared to consider imagery as the ornament, and not the essence of composition. Indeed from the specimens exhibited, I was not unwilling to acknowledge that this University bears the first rank in respectability, as well as age, among her sister seminaries in this country.

But I cannot forbear to remark that there was one trait in the performances which excited disgust. The orator and poet seemed to conspire which should most ingeniously ridicule the want of genius. As far as such language is calculated to expose the neglect or abuse of talents, it cannot be justly condemned. But, when it equally tends to pour contempt on those who are industrious though unsuccessful in their literary pursuits, it argues both consummate pride and unfeeling cruelty. It is proud; because the speaker implicitly glories in his own conscious superiority. It is cruel; because he wantonly sports with the feelings of those whom he esteems his inferiours.

But what appeared to me the most exceptionable was the contracted notions they entertained of genius. They would allow none to possess it who had not precisely the same taste with themselves. Hence let a student make ever so great proficiency in mathematical or metaphysical sciences, if he be not passionately fond of the belles-lettres, if he have not the talent of writing fine orations and pretty poems, it seemed a fair inference from their remarks that he must be destitute of genius.

This led me to inquire into the true meaning of the term. Examining Johnson's dictionary I found one of its significations to be, " a man endowed with superiour faculties." According to Dr. Blair, " it signifies that talent or aptitude, which we receive from nature, in order to excel in any one thing whatever." As an illustration he proceeds to remark, " a man is said to have a genius for *mathematics* as well as a genius for *poetry*." I should, therefore, be glad to know, by what right these young gentlemen are such literary monopolists. Do they hope by undervaluing other sciences to raise the reputation of their own? Or do they rather act upon the principle of the crafty animal in the fable who affected to despise what he could not attain?

I should not have made these remarks had I not reason to believe that these performers are neither the first nor the last who have delivered similar sentiments. A friend of mine, who is in the habit of attending exhibitions, informs me that it has for several years been fashionable to decry almost every species of genius; and that an oration or poem, in every other respect excellent, let the subject be what it may, is esteemed dry if not seasoned with invectives against the admirers of Newton and Locke.

It may be alleged that these are the mere hyperbolical effusions of youthful imagination, and are intended only to assert the vast superiority of the belles-lettres to the other sciences. But this presents a topic too contested to justify such unequivocal and dogmatical assertions. It may not require great logical talents to show that the learned world is more indebted for utility, if not for enjoyment, to mathematicians and metaphysicians than to orators and poets. However this subject may be decided, it is surely opposed to every just definition of genius to limit it to a few in the large circle of arts and sciences. Who will presume to deny that Sir Isaac Newton possessed this faculty to an eminent

JOHN SYLVESTER JOHN GARDINER from a painting by Gilbert Stuart

Joseph Stevens Buckminster from a painting by Gilbert Stuart

WILLIAM TUDOR, JR. from a painting by Thomas Sully, after Stuart

WILLIAM SMITH SHAW from a painting by Gilbert Stuart

degree? Yet we may readily conceive his awkwardness at a popular harangue. Or who will not allow to the celebrated Mr. Locke, a distinguished genius in metaphysics? Yet he is said to have preferred the dull and barbarous rhymes of Sir Richard Blackmore to the productions of any other poet.

—I (December, 1803), 57-59

A College Rake

JOHN PIERCE

MY DEAR STUDIOSUS,

By this title permit me to address you, though I have forfeited every claim to your friendship by unworthy conduct. When I was under your care at the Academy, you were unwearied in endeavours to inspire me with just sentiments and virtuous behaviour. Happily for me, as my morals were then in a good measure pure, I cautiously observed your directions. . . .

Accordingly, when I first entered College, I firmly resolved to follow your counsels. I treated my instructors with filial affection and respect. I carefully observed the rules they prescribed and studied the tasks they assigned. While many of my classmates were ransacking the library with a view to other studies, my highest ambition was to become a classical scholar. Several private proposals to pilfer watermelons and to rob orchards I resolutely withstood. Nor would I club to go to a tavern for food and drink while they were provided to my satisfaction at my regular meals. In fine, I commenced College life by laying a foundation for virtuous morals and attentive study.

But I soon began to find that I was remarked for my preciseness. Hints were circulated that I was " a dupe to government." My deportment was narrowly watched. Some on seeing me enter a tutor's room for leave of absence swore that I went to inform of the misdemeanors of my fellow-students.

Hence violent prejudices were excited against me. Though I always recited well, it was imputed to excessively hard study. My superiority in the languages, mathematics, and metaphysics was never disputed. But then it was alleged, that

—Such dry " roots are always found
To flourish best in barren ground."

These various aspersions I bore with considerable firmness, till I was charged with want of genius. This, as it was a novel accusation, and I was conscious of its falsehood, I ought to have spurned with contempt. But, I confess, it produced the opposite effect. In endeavouring to refute the charge, I was insensibly led into those unhappy mistakes, which I had most resolutely determined to avoid.

To acquire a popularity, which I had unjustly forfeited, my first step was to adapt myself to the prejudices of my fellow-students. I allowed that the government had faults; and I loudly inveighed against the severity with which some of my classmates were treated at the exhibition of their themes. I took but little pains with these exercises myself, lest I should appear to be anxious for " parts."

By degrees I was led to abjure mathematics; the languages soon followed; nor did I arrive at the summit of College favour till I assumed the right of directing my own studies, and of treating with heedless neglect the stated exercises of my instructors. But what contributed most to this change in my sentiments and conduct was the assignment of a part at Exhibition which I with my flatterers were pleased to consider beneath my merit.

From that moment I swore revenge. On the evening of Exhibition I resorted to a tavern, and, with some rakes from Boston and a few College *bloods*, I got very drunk. When I had so far recovered that I could stagger into College yard, I yelled, and swore, and broke windows, till I was tired, and then finished the night in gambling and carousing.

From this period I remissly attended recitations and prayers.

I was several times fined. Once I was privately admonished, and I narrowly escaped a threatened suspension.

As a natural consequence of neglecting studies, I associated with unprincipled companions and contracted bad habits. I constantly strove by what arts I should oppose and perplex government. Profaneness, although I had been accustomed to consider it beneath a gentleman, I began to employ as my familiar language. As for lying, I thought it not only expedient but commendable when used to deceive my instructors.

But the worst effect I experienced was a love of strong liquors. At first I found them disgustful. I could drink only wine, and that in moderate quantities. This soon became too weak to satisfy my raging appetite, till by degrees I contracted an inveterate habit of intemperance.

What promoted my dissipation was admission into the *Pig Club*. Here I found ample scope for irregular indulgence. I was one of the first to approve an absurd motion, once made by a member, that it should be the established rule before parting for every one to get drunk. I also clamorously applauded a most impious blessing, which was on a certain occasion asked, and which threw the whole Club into a tumultuous shout of praise.

It is true, I sometimes felt rebukes of conscience when I recollected my early instructions and resolutions, and when I accidentally met my virtuous friends. But I was in a great measure relieved from these momentary pangs by having the credit among my companions of an extraordinary genius. They took unwearied pains to proclaim it to the world. But for this purpose they used to mention not so much what I had done, as what I could do. They constantly maintained my great superiority to all those who were obliged to earn their reputation with the government by hard study.

To preserve as well as to gain renown from such friends, I had recourse to some of the methods, which, you my dear Studiosus, in a late communication so very justly exposed. I particularly remember, that when I was to copy a poem, which had cost me much time and exertion, I went to a classmate's room to borrow pen, ink, and paper, under the pretence that I was destitute of these conveniences, and that I wished to compose my talk under a shady tree. In about three hours I returned with my poem completed, and written without blots. By this artifice I attracted general attention and received indiscriminate praise.

I had, indeed, sense enough to feel my real inferiority to several others. But I took care to make myself more celebrated. Thus while my industrious fellow students were poring over Locke, Euclid, and Conic Sections, I was cursorily reading Shakespeare's plays and committing some of his most striking passages to memory that I might employ them as occasion should require. While they were deeply immured in their studies, I was often in company. In this way I acquired a confidence and volubility on popular topics of which they were destitute. I took particular care to familiarize [myself with] the anecdotes contained in Boswell's life of Johnson, and every other circumstance relating to this truly great scholar. Hence, while my plodding classmates were endeavouring in vain to interest parties in their abstruse speculations, I could entertain them whole evenings by agreeable stories respecting the celebrated Doctor.

But since I have received the honours of the University, I have had time for cool reflection. My crimes and my errors stare me in the face. For, though I reconciled myself to indolence at College by resolving to study closely my future profession; yet I find by experience that my resolutions were useless and vain. The habits of indolence contracted at the University I find it next to impossible to reform. My reputation for a great genius affords me no assistance. On the other hand, it excites general indignation that such talents should have been so grossly neglected and perverted. So accustomed have I been to bad company that I find gratification in no other.

—I (February, 1804), 152-56

Religion and Learning:
the Hollis Professorship

WILLIAM WELLS

THE OBJECT OF this pamphlet is not a little singular. It is to prove that it was the intention of Mr. Hollis, the founder of the professorship of divinity in the University of Cambridge, to confide that office solely to one professing Calvinistic sentiments; that in the late choice of a professorship no evidence has been given of his being a Calvinist; and, consequently, that the nomination of the Corporation and the confirmation of the Overseers have been improper, contravening the intent of the founder, and even subversive of the tenure of the bequest.[3]

---

[3] As the Boston-Cambridge community drifted rapidly in the later eighteenth century toward a general, though by no means exclusive, acceptance of liberal Christianity, the religious atmosphere of Harvard became increasingly alarming to the Massachusetts orthodoxy. An open fight did not come until the death of David Tappan, Hollis Professor of Divinity, in 1803. Tappan, a conservative, had come to the Hollis chair in 1793, partly because of the backing of Jedidiah Morse, another conservative. At the time of Tappan's death, the Fellows of the Corporation of Harvard were divided in religious opinion, the majority favoring the liberalism of the Buckminster variety. When the Corporation submitted to the Board of Overseers the nomination of Henry Ware, a known liberal, to fill the vacant Hollis chair, Jedidiah Morse believed the time had come for a genuine display of orthodoxy. A struggle, fought chiefly over the issue of whether or not the Hollis Professor must subscribe to a formal declaration of faith, ensued. But the liberals were in control of the situation at Harvard, and Morse and his cohorts were forced to found Andover Theological Seminary as the training institution for the conservative ministry. See Josiah Quincy, *History of Harvard University* (Cambridge, 1840), II, 284-85; James King Morse, *Jedidiah Morse: Champion of New England Orthodoxy* (New York, 1939), 82-100.

The pamphlet referred to by William Wells is *The True Reasons on Which the Election of a Hollis Professor of Divinity in Harvard College Was Opposed at the Board of Overseers, Feb. 14, 1805* (Charleston, 1805).

The title is not very correct, for though the pamphlet may set forth the "true reasons" upon which Dr. Morse and some others ground their opposition, yet it will not be pretended that *all* the opponents acted under the influence of these reasons; political considerations, if we are not misinformed, were the cause of opposition with the majority.

The design of our fathers in the foundation of the university, it is justly remarked, was to give to religion the aid of learning; *Christo et Ecclesiae* being the motto of the college arms. The principles of the founders were undoubtedly Calvinistick; and of their zeal to perpetuate those principles there is sufficient proof. Mr. Hollis himself appears to have been much in the same sentiments with respect to doctrine; though we can by no means judge decisively upon that point from the extracts given by Dr. Morse. Except a general expression to Dr. Coleman accompanying a present of the works of Calvin, "I imagine they will please you as they do me," of which we say only, *valeat quantum valere potest*, we see no expressions which an Arminian might not have used. . . .

We agree that this is the main point of the controversy, viz. Whether Mr. Hollis, by ordaining that his professor should be "a man of sound or orthodox principles," meant to confine the choice exclusively to a Calvinist; and that, not only in the first instance, but in all future elections. Dr. M. says that affirmative is certain; but this, in our opinion, he has by no means proved.

This was by Morse. A reply to Wells's review was published in the *Anthology*, II (April, 1805), 206-11. Immediately following is an answer to Morse by Wells (*ibid.*, 211-16). See also an earlier communication by Wells in the *Anthology*, II (February, 1805), 78-80, in which he says in part: "Feeling, as I do, most seriously interested in the prosperity of our Alma Mater, I shall lament as deeply injurious to her usefulness and reputation that hour when her present liberal principles shall be exchanged for subscriptions to Articles of Faith; or, what is the same thing, when the belief of a certain speculative system shall be esteemed necessary in him who aspires to the honourable station of an instructor of her sons. The next step, a very short one, is to require such a condition from the youth at their matriculation; to turn the college catalogue into an Index Expurgatorius; and to expel from the shelves of the library all heretical publications. So shall all access to errour be prohibited, and the fountain of knowledge shall flow with an unpolluted stream from generation to generation." The

It appears indeed with sufficient clearness what tenets Mr. Hollis considered as " sound or orthodox," but it does not appear that he was guilty of the egregious folly of determining that all electors of professors through all future time should be of precisely the same opinion with himself. The words, we admit with Dr. M. " were not used without meaning." On the contrary, they appear to us the result of much deliberation, and to have been very happily selected. Mr. Hollis wished to guard against licentiousness and irregularity; he probably wished also to avoid imposing fetters upon the understandings and consciences of his successors; a proceeding which his own observation of the state of religious opinions in the circle of his particular friends must have proved to him both unjust and inefficient. He chose therefore terms of *general signification.* He knew (what Dr. M. seems not to recollect) that all sects of Christians consider themselves as sound or, synonymously, as orthodox; and therefore left the corporation and overseers to elect any person whom they should conscientiously consider as " sound or orthodox."

This we believe was the intent of the founder, and in no other sense can the words be understood. If Mr. Hollis meant to impose upon the college at every election a man of one particular set of opinions, instead of using words admitting such latitude of interpretation, why did he not, as Mr. Henchman has done, make some such article as the following: " The professor of divinity shall profess and teach the principles of the Christian religion according to the well known confession of faith drawn up by the synod of the churches of New England "; or according to the principles of the Westminster confession; or according to the doctrinal articles of the Church of England? The necessity of some such precise mode of expression could not have escaped Mr. Hollis. That he did not use it is very fair proof that he did not mean to tie down the electors to the exclusive choice of a Calvinistick professor.

Our limits do not permit further investigation of this subject. Strong proof, however, if we mistake not, may be produced; and we wish that some son of Harvard, zealous for the honour of his

---

sentiment may seem extreme, but the consequences of an orthodox triumph in the Hollis Professorship fight would have been drastic.

Alma Mater, would vindicate the liberality of her statutes, and rescue the character of this excellent and liberal benefactor of the university from an imputation so disgraceful. We have always understood that Mr. Hollis was a liberal-minded man. It appears that, tho' a Baptist, he did not require his professor should think with him in that particular. The learned Dr. Jeremiah Hunt was his pastor and confidential friend and was particularly consulted upon the establishment of the professorship; Dr. Hunt, who voted against subscribing that article of the Westminster declarative of a belief in the Trinity; who justly thought that the bible *only* ought to be the religion of Protestants, and especially of Protestant dissenters from the established church; and nobly declared that he would sign NO ARTICLES not expressed in scripture language. Is it probable such a man would bind the electors to choose their professor from a particular sect, and that through every age, whatever changes of opinion might take place? It is probable that such a man, a dissenter from the national church, itself dissenting from the religion of its former days, would conceive it reasonable to bind the most worthy and intelligent men of a distant age and country always to choose their instructor of their youth, and the father of their churches, from the narrow limits of his own small sect? The thing is not to be presumed. The professor was to declare it as his belief " that the scriptures of the old and new testament are the only perfect rule of faith and manners, and promise to explain and open the scriptures to his pupils with integrity and faithfulness, acccording "—to what? to the West-minster confession of faith? to the synod of New England? to the articles of the English church? No—"ACCORDING TO THE BEST LIGHT THAT GOD SHALL GIVE HIM."

—II (March, 1805), 152-55

The Inauguration of President Kirkland

ANDREWS NORTON

On Wednesday the 14th of November, John Thornton Kirkland, D.D. was inaugurated at Cambridge, as President of Harvard University. We should think ourselves negligent in our duty if we omitted to give some account of an event of so much public interest and which we feel so much pleasure in announcing.

At 11 o'clock in the forenoon a very long procession was formed, which beginning at Harvard Hall, and making a circuit, proceeded to the meeting house. The order of the procession was as follows:

Students in the University.

Librarian, with the College Seal, Charter, &c.

Regent, with the College Keys.

Members of the Corporation.

Officers of Instruction and Government.

Sheriffs of Suffolk and Middlesex.

His Excellency the Governour and the President elect.

The Governour's Aids.

The Honourable and Reverend Overseers.

Visitors of the Professorship of Natural History.

Committee on the Boylston Prize Questions.

Resident Graduate Students.

Honourable J. Adams, C. Strong, C. Gore, F. Dana, R. T. Paine, T. Pickering, J. Lloyd, and W. N. Boylston, Esquire.

Officers of the Rev. Dr. Kirkland's late Church and Congregation.

Members of the American Academy, and of the Historical Society.

Gentlemen particularly invited.
Judges of the Supreme Judicial Court.
Attorney and Solicitor General, and Reporter of Decisions.
Secretary and Treasurer, Adjutant and Quarter Master
General, of the Commonwealth.
Judges, Attorneys, and Officers of the Federal and State
Courts.
Ministers of the Gospel.
Members of the National and State Legislatures.
Municipal Officers and Instructors of Youth in Cambridge,
Boston, and the neighbouring towns.
Alumni of the College.
Other Gentlemen attending.

When arrived at the meeting-house, the exercises of the day
were opened with an address and prayer by the venerable President pro tempore of the Corporation, Dr. Lathrop. The ceremony
of inauguration immediately followed, which was performed by
his Excellency the Governour; after an address in Latin to the
audience and President elect, he proceeded to invest him with the
robes of his office, and to deliver to him the charter, seal, records,
and keys of the university. The President then made a Latin reply
to his Excellency, in which he paid him the merited compliment
that his name would always be remembered among those of the
patriots who asserted the doubtful liberties of our country. The
ceremony, which was conducted throughout with great dignity
and propriety, was closed by his Excellency's repeating a Latin
prayer of benediction. The ceremony of inauguration was immediately followed by an oration in Latin by Mr. Thacher,[4] the
Librarian of the University. The correctness and purity of the
composition, and the uncommon gracefulness, propriety, and
animation of his manner, were such as his friends ventured to

[4] Samuel Cooper Thacher served as Librarian of Harvard for a period
before he became minister of the New South Church in 1810. He filled the
pulpit vacated by John Thornton Kirkland when Kirkland was elected to
the presidency of Harvard.

expect from so elegant a scholar. The audience were then addressed by the President in English. In the address, among other striking passages, was a mention of the two last Presidents, and particularly a character of President Willard, with whom Dr. Kirkland had formerly been connected in the government of the University. The literary exercises of the forenoon were very agreeably concluded with a poem by a senior sophister of the University, Frothingham,[5] who interested and gratified the audience by the elegance of his poety, and his unusually fine style of speaking. An anthem performed by the students followed, and the whole was closed with prayer by Dr. Elliot. The procession then returned, and his Excellency, with his Honour the Lieutenant Governour, the different branches of the government of the University, and the Clergy who were present on the occasion, together with strangers particularly invited, dined in the commons' hall. After dinner were recited in the hall, a Latin prize ode by Bingaman, a junior sophister, and a Greek prize ode, by Story,[6] a senior sophister. During the day, a vote passed the Board of Overseers, to request copies for publication of the several performances which had been delivered.

The degree of Doctor of Laws was on this occasion conferred on President Dwight of Yale, and Smith of Princeton Colleges, and the degree of Doctor of Divinity on President Appleton of Bowdoin College.

During the evening the college buildings were illuminated, and a ball was given by the students, at which his Excellency and the President were present.

We congratulate the friends of Harvard University on this splendid day for that ancient institution. We do not recollect to have been present on any one of its publick days, when more universal pleasure and satisfaction were expressed. We do not

[5] Nathaniel Langdon Frothingham (1793–1870) graduated from Harvard in 1811. Translator, poet, and hymnologist, he served as pastor of Boston's First Church from 1815 to 1850. Although he was a conservative Unitarian of the Buckminster mold, he was greatly admired by Ralph Waldo Emerson.

[6] Evidently a younger brother of Judge Joseph Story.

know a time when its prospects were brighter than they now are. Before the election of President Kirkland, the immediate government of the University was composed of men in no common degree respectable for their talents, learning, peculiar qualifications for their respective offices of instruction, and the prudence and judgment with which they had managed the internal concerns of the College. With the best wishes and expectations of these men, and of all the friends of the University, the new President is welcomed to his office; and looked up to for all that his abilities, and all that a deep interest in the cause of religion, morality and literature can effect for the benefit of the institution over which he presides.

Harvard University we all of us regard with high respect, and most of us acknowledge with gratitude as our literary parent. On its prosperity we believe that the flourishing state of literature in our country, and consequently the respectability and happiness of our country itself, very essentially depend. Very much must depend upon the tastes here cultivated, the sciences here taught, the principles here inculcated, and the views here opened to those who are to go abroad into society, and be its teachers, guides, and governours. The prosperity of this University and its necessary consequences will tend perhaps more than any thing else to establish our literary character, and to put to silence those wonderfully silly and idle tales which continue to be circulated concerning our manners, customs, and the state of letters among us, even in some respectable publications on the other side of the Atlantick. We felicitate ourselves therefore on the publick interest and regard which have been and continue to be shewn to our Alma Mater. We trust that her flourishing state will continue. We trust that if in aid of any plans of greater usefulness, she should have occasion to call on the munificence of the publick that she will not call in vain. Of the opulent men of our state, and especially of the merchants of Boston, she has never had reason to complain. Their liberality had indeed in seasons of prosperity been open to all who had any claim upon it, and to many whose claims if doubtful were not disputed. It would have been strange therefore if this liberality had been denied to the most venerable of all our literary institutions, and to one whose prosperity should be particularly their care.[7]

—IX (November, 1810), 347-50

[7] The inauguration of Kirkland as President of Harvard did indeed mark a new era in the history of the institution. Unfortunately, however, Kirkland has been associated almost altogether with the troubles at Harvard during the eighteen-twenties, when rampant student rebellion and administrative confusion forced his resignation, even though he was personally popular with the students. James Russell Lowell said of Kirkland, "He was one of those misplaced persons whose misfortune it is that their lives overlap two distinct eras, and are already so impregnated with one that they can never be in healthy sympathy with the other." ("Cambridge Thirty Years Ago," *Works* [Boston and New York, 1890], I, 85.) Yet in Kirkland's administration, especially in its first ten years, the first genuinely new era at Harvard since the presidency of John Leverett (1708–1724) announced itself. More the tool than the creator of change, Kirkland accepted much of the new age and helped to bring it to pass, at the same time trying to retain the paternal quality of the presidential office. This defeated him; Harvard was beginning to require a more complex concept of government. The best study of Kirkland's career is Samuel Eliot Morison, "The Great Rebellion in Harvard College," *Publications of the Colonial Society of Massachusetts*, XXVII, 54-112.

THE BOSTON ATHENAEUM

Literary Institutions in Liverpool

JOSEPH STEVENS BUCKMINSTER

LIVERPOOL, Aug. 12, 1807

GENTLEMEN,

I promised you some literary intelligence, as soon as I could find any in this focus of Guinea ships, and cent. per cent. literati; and I assure you I have found even here more of lettered taste, and sound science, and real, active, habitual literary enthusiasm than I have ever seen in Boston.

The city of Liverpool has now reached that point of wealth at which societies, which have been hitherto merely mercenary and commercial, begin to turn their attention to learning and the fine arts, that is, when they perceive that something more than great riches is necessary to make a place worthy of being visited and interesting enough to be admired. Hence, within ten years, publick institutions of a literary character have increased in Liverpool with incredible rapidity. Their publick reading rooms yield to none in the world, and their botanick garden, though it has been established only six years, is one of the first in England. The first reading room, in my opinion, is the Athenaeum. I send you herewith the regulations and the list of the library. The collection of books is, I think, the most select, I have ever known. O when will the day come when the library of our dearly cherished Athenaeum shall boast of including the labours of Muratori, the *Thesauri* of Graevius and Gronovius, the *Scriptores Byzantini*, the *Memoirs of the Academy of Inscriptions*, the *editiones optimae* of every author of Greece and Rome, the French and English literary journals *ab initio*, and not only possess these books, but have them accessible to every man of letters, who wishes to consult them! By inspecting the catalogue you will see that there

128

is not a library in America which contains so general a collection
in *every* branch of knowledge. Here you may enter at any hour,
and you will invariably find some busy in consulting authors,
others taking notes, and others reading for amusement. If I were
to enumerate the various works which I here saw for the first
time, I should fill this page with a dry catalogue. The modern
works are all bound in the most superb style, and I must acknowledge, that I was never before so much tempted to deprecate the
day which should reduce the luxury of learning.

The Lyceum is a more elegant and convenient reading room,
but its library is nothing better than a common circulating or the
Boston Social Library. The annual subscription to the Lyceum
is only half a guinea, therefore many of its shelves are filled with
wooden books. The Athenaeum is cherished by the choice spirits
of the place, the Roscoes and the Shepherds, while the Lyceum
is rather the resort of the loungers; the repository for books,
which will circulate, rather than for those which remain stationary
to be consulted. Porson would find himself at home among the
folios of the former, while a Cornhill apprentice might spend a
pleasant hour among the miscellanies of the latter. (Cf. p. 79, n. 1.)

I have taken pains to insert all the additions, which have been
made within three years to the class of ancient authors, and of
biography, from which you may judge of the general increase
of the library, which is not less in any of the other departments
of learning. I could not procure a complete list of the periodical
publications which are here taken, and the list of newspapers was
too long to transcribe. One table is entirely covered with new
pamphlets. The collection of maps too is admirable, and among
these are found large plans of London and Liverpool, in which
every house is marked, and a most superb plan of Rome, at least
twelve feet square.

I have met with several ladies of very superiour accomplishments. The institution of the botanick garden has drawn their
attention to botany, and there is hardly a window in Liverpool
which is not decorated with some of the choicest products of
foreign soils; and hardly an evening in this pleasant season, while
the sun sets just before nine, when the walks of the garden are not
crowded with fair forms, who decisively show that the two king-

doms of nature, the vegetable and the animal, cannot be contemplated together, and that the interests of the one will infallibly suffer if the other is present. The little book, which I send you, contains a charming address, written by Roscoe, and delivered by him before the proprietors, at the opening of the garden. It has never been published; I procured the copy by the favour of one of the subscribers, for whom only it was printed. It is worthy of being published in the *Anthology*, in order to promote the interests of the botanical institution at Cambridge.

—IV (November, 1807), 597-99

The Boston Athenaeum:
History, Objects, and Present State

WILLIAM SMITH SHAW (?)

FOR SEVERAL YEARS individuals in this metropolis have expressed their wishes that there might be established here a publick Reading Room; to be kept constantly open, and to contain all the valuable journals, foreign and domestick, periodical publications, books of general reference, and other works adapted to such a place of resort.[8] It has been thought that an establishment

[8] In the reawakening of intellectual life in the Boston-Cambridge community following the Revolution, a number of semi-public libraries were established. Two important ones were associated with learned societies, the American Academy of Arts and Sciences and the Massachusetts Historical Society. Another, the Boston Library Society (not to be confused with the Boston Public Library founded in the next generation), which was incorporated in 1794, was, like the Athenaeum, a proprietary library. During the years 1804–1807, four specialized libraries came into being: the First Social, or the Social Law Library; the Second Social, or the Boston Medical Library; the Third Social, or the Scientific Library; and the Fourth Social, or the Theological Library. These three were eventually absorbed by the Athenaeum. Members of the Anthology group were

of this kind, which is very common both in the large and small cities of Europe, would, if commenced here, receive liberal support, and be regarded as auxiliary to literature and to business; useful to the publick, and honourable to its founders and patrons. Having these impressions of the merit and popularity of the object, a society of gentlemen who conduct a literary publication [the *Anthology*] during the last year issued proposals in which they engaged to provide room of the forementioned description, open at ten dollars annually to each subscriber. The design was so favourably received, and so diligently pursued, that the subscription list was soon filled with a large number of respectable names. In consequence of this success, and in compliance with the wishes of many patrons of the undertaking, it was determined to extend the plan by adding a Library to the foundation. . . .

At this stage of the undertaking, the gentlemen who had commenced and so far conducted it, in order more effectually to secure and diffuse the benefit of their past labour and expense . . . transferred their right and title in the Anthology Reading Room and Library to certain persons denominated Trustees. . . .

The Trustees conceived it expedient, and immediately took measures to procure an act of incorporation for themselves and their future associates. In the act for this purpose . . . they obtained powers to comprehend in the establishment other objects relative to the sciences and the arts, to be provided for in such an extent as may consist with the primary design of founding a Library and Reading Room. By these means, when the whole plan of the institution shall be executed, it will be subservient not only to the acquisition but to the communication of knowledge. . . . In consequence of this enlargement of the plan, a name of more extensive signification than the former one was adopted, and

---

prominent in the direction of all of them. Meanwhile, in Cambridge the Harvard Library, benefited by gifts, was slowly expanding toward the seventy-two-thousand volume collection it possessed in 1850, when it was the largest library in America. One indication of its progress was that in 1812 a new regulation made its facilities available to students six hours every day, Sundays excepted. See Justin Winsor, "Libraries in Boston," *Memorial History of Boston* (Boston, 1881), IV, 281-82, 293; C. K. Bolton, "Social Libraries in Boston," *Publications of the Colonial Society of Massachusetts*, XII, 332-38; "Intelligence," *General Repository and Review*, II (October, 1812), 391.

the Trustees, with their associates, are made a body corporate
by the title of the Proprietors of the BOSTON ATHENAEUM. . . .

That the nature and design of the establishment may fully
appear, having offered a sketch of the *history*, they [the pro-
prietors] will next give a particular account of the

Objects of the Athenaeum

The first department of the Athenaeum is the READING ROOM,
which it is proposed to have large and commodious. It is to
be furnished with seats, tables, pens, ink, and paper; and to
contain all the celebrated gazettes published in any part of the
United States, with the most interesting literary and political
pamphlets in Europe and America, with magazines, reviews, and
scientifick journals in the English, French, and other modern
languages, memoirs of learned societies, London and Paris newspapers, Steele's army and navy list, naval chronicle, London
and Paris bookseller's catalogues, parliamentary debates, bibliographical works, journals of the Congress of the United States,
laws of Congress and of the state legislatures, American state
papers, maps, charts, the latest voyages and travels, and the interesting publications of the day as they appear. . . .

The next branch of the Athenaeum is the LIBRARY, designed
to contain in a separate apartment the works of learning and
sciences in all languages; particularly such rare and expensive
publications as are not generally to be obtained in this country;
the most valuable encyclopedias of the arts and sciences in the
English and French languages; standard dictionaries of the learned
and principal modern languages; also dictionaries, critical and
biographical; books of general reference, useful to the merchant
and the scholar; and, finally, the works of all the best authors,
ancient and modern. . . .

The Reading Room and Library, being considered leading
objects and chief departments of the Athenaeum, it is proposed,
as far as can be done without detriment to them, to join to the
foundation a MUSEUM or CABINET, which shall contain specimens
from the three kingdoms of nature, scientifically arranged; natural
and artificial curiosities, antiques, coins, medals, vases, gems, and

intaglios; also, in the same or different apartment, a REPOSITORY
OF ARTS, in which shall be placed for inspection models of new
and useful machines; likewise drawings, designs, paintings, en-
gravings, statues, and other objects of the fine arts, and especially
the productions of our native artists.

Lastly, the plan of the Athenaeum includes a LABORATORY,
and an APPARATUS for experiments in chemistry and natural
philosophy, for astronomical observations, and geographical improvements, to be used under the direction of the corporation.

The history of this establishment, and a description of its
objects being given, it is proper to exhibit

The means, resources, and present state of the Athenaeum

The Reading Room is largely supplied with the works mentioned above, and is receiving daily additions.

The Library already contains many interesting and important
works. The number of volumes is more than twelve hundred,
and is continually increasing by donations and deposits, as well
as by purchase. There is reason to believe that when the apart-
ments shall be sufficiently capacious to admit them one or more
of the libraries belonging to particular societies or individuals
will be annexed to the Athenaeum, or will be placed on the
shelves of its Library.

The *means* and *resources* now possessed by this institution are:

1st. The annual subscription; that being one hundred and sixty
subscribers at ten dollars a year.

2nd. The American papers and publications, with several
periodical publications from abroad, are furnished by the proprietors of the *Monthly Anthology* free of expense; and the net
funds of the same work are appropriated to the support and
increase of the Reading Room and Library.

3rd. An apparatus of value belonging to a society for the study
of natural philosophy is offered to be incorporated with the
Athenaeum on favourable conditions; so that this part of the
establishment cannot at present require any considerable expense.

4th. It is well to observe that as the institution shall advance
in importance and celebrity, donations and legacies may be ex-

pected to prove a source of continual additions to the various departments of the Athenaeum. . . .

The value of learning, whatever incidental evils it may produce, is admitted by all who are qualified to judge upon the subject. Besides the dignity and satisfaction associated with the cultivation of letters and arts, and which constitute their worth to the individual, they have unlimited uses in respect to the community. Speculative and practical philosophy, history, polite literature, and the arts, bear an important relation to all the conveniences and elegancies of life, to all the good institutions of society, and to all the great interests of man, viewed as a rational and social, a moral and religious being. Not only, however, should those deep investigations of science and exquisite refinements of taste, which are necessarily confined to a few, be held in respect as connected with the general welfare; but that love of intellectual improvement and pleasure, and that propensity to reading and inquiry which are capable of being diffused through considerable portions of the community, should be regarded with interest and promoted with zeal among a civilized and flourishing people. They belong to the regular progress of society. A nation that increases in wealth without any corresponding increase in knowledge and refinement in letters and arts neglects the proper and respectable uses of prosperity. A love of intellectual improvement and of the various objects of literature and taste in a state or society enjoying freedom and affluence is to be coveted and maintained, because it produces the best exercise and application of the faculties; because it strengthens and multiplies the ties that bind men together; because it enhances the value and satisfaction of social intercourse by supplying worthy and interesting topicks of conversation; because it heightens the enjoyment of all the blessings of life, and enables us to derive advantage and pleasure from a multitude of new sources; because, on the whole, it tends to the removal of errour and the discovery of truth, and has a friendly aspect upon the interests and virtue of religion.

—IV (May, 1807), 225-28

The Anthology *and the Athenaeum*

WILLIAM SMITH SHAW (?)

THE EDITORS OF the *Anthology* have so repeatedly solicited the attention of the publick that it not without hesitation that they again ask its indulgence. The circumstance, however, of a change of printers seems to offer a favourable opportunity; and the liberal establishment on which the work is now placed seems to call for some exertions on their part to justify them in accepting it.

It is not our intention to complain of neglected genius, or to accuse the world of want of perspicacity for not discerning our merit. We venture not to say that our patronage has not equalled our deserts. Of this, however, the publick will judge, when it is told that our receipts have never much exceeded the necessary expenses of conducting the work. But this is not our plea. Our patronage, if not extensive enough to flatter our vanity, has been of a kind to content our ambition, and personal remuneration we never required, or would accept. The ground on which we feel justified in making our request is that we do not beg for ourselves, but for the Athenaeum, to which, after the necessary expenses are deducted, all the profits of the work are faithfully devoted. This is a plea, which excuses our request, and would, we think, authorize the importunity of the most sturdy mendicancy. He who gives us his subscription is secure of not throwing away his money; for, however worthless he may find the *Anthology*, he is certain that he will contribute to the prosperity of an institution, which, we venture to foretell, will become the honour and pride of our city.

But we will not affect more humility than we feel. We are not willing to think that the *Anthology* is altogether unworthy the patronage of the publick. The objects to which it is devoted, however imperfectly attained, are all honourable. We have the feelings of men who think themselves not unworthily employed. Our literary chivalry is honest, and, we hope, harmless; if it be not either useful or wise, and if our exploits in the republick of letters have gained us no renown, it is not, we are persuaded because there are no monsters there to be quelled. We seriously think that a work cannot be perfectly contemptible, which is supported by men, certainly above venality, who, if they do not deceive themselves, are desirous of raising the reputation of American literature, and who are pledged to no party in religion or politicks, though, indeed, having their opinions on both, as every man must have, who loves his country and his God. But, after three years labour, the publick have the means of forming a judgment which our representations cannot alter or avert. If the decision is against us, we can appeal to no other tribunal. If we have not yet gained any claim to favour, it is hopeless to attempt to obtain it now by confident assertions or magnificent promises. Without any more observations then, we throw ourselves on the goodness of the publick, and request a larger share of its favour, than we have hitherto received; repeating only that he who subscribes for the *Anthology* may have the feelings of a patron of the Athenaeum.[9]

—V (March, 1808), 121-22

Evils of the Boston Athenaeum

JACOB BIGELOW

IT HAVING BECOME a subject of flagrant notoriety that certain vile abuses and detestable innovations have in these latter days sprung up in this land of simplicity and quietness, to the great annoyance and manifest discomfiture of our uncorrupted and

[9] A study of the financial history of the *Anthology* indicates that this plea had little effect. See the Introduction pp. 20-23.

ignorant citizens, and tending to produce a total subversion of their purity of manners and uprightness of deportment; it hath therefore become the indispensable duty of all pious and influential men to lift up their heads and their hands, yea, their hearts and their voices, in opposition to such crying and unheard of enormities.

At the head of these abominations, and far exceeding the rest by the extensiveness of its influence and the perniciousness of its operations, is the Boston Athenaeum, an open receptacle, intended as a place of accommodation and shelter for the disturbers of the town's peace, a lurking hole for the knowing ones, and a lounging place for the slothful. Now it is the intention of the undertaker of this essay to bring unto light, and to make clearer than the noon of the day, the various designs and tendencies which are implicated and wrapped up in the existence of this pestiferous institution.

And in the first place, it operateth as a wily and a subtle enticement, inducing people to quit and neglect their honest callings and gainful occupations, whereby are amassed both comfortable livings and goodly estates, and to run after the superfluity of nonsense contained in sundry unprofitable and filthy volumes with which the world is much vexed. It induceth people to turn poets, and literati, and other odious characters, so that many an otherwise honest man, who might have tilled the ground, or who might have bought and sold and gotten gain, is now destitute of his daily dinner and weareth a mutilated pair of breeches. . . .

Moreover, instead of that eligible and compendious library, the spelling book, the psalter, and the primer, which was by our worthy and pious ancestors deemed amply sufficient to the completion of a superiour and highly polished education, they have now collected together a cumbersome and unseemly congregation of books on all unprofitable topicks, and in all unintelligible languages, whereby they might subvert and turn topsy turvy the brains of our simple and unwitting citizens. And furthermore, among the monstrosities of the place are certain unlawful books upon the black art, and upon necromancy, written in unknown tongues, and in horribly mysterious characters, the semblance whereof is like unto pothooks and trammels. . . .

Verily it is a grievous thing to observe the multifarious streams of evil which have arisen from this polluted source, and have flowed throughout all the land. Our young men, not content with the use of their mother tongue, do run after divers unknown and barbarous dialects, both reading the same and intermingling them with their common speech, in the guise of puns and quotations, thereby abusing the gift of language, and tending to bring back all the jargon of the tower of Babel. Our young women, instead of looking well to the ways of their household and eating not the bread of idleness, yea, instead of taking hold on the spindle and the distaff with their hands, they do learn to read novels and romances, and other perverse and outlandish books, whereby they become unprofitable housewives, yea, and do not comprehend the getting up of a dinner. Our old men become spendthrifts in their latter days, and squander away much treasure, wherewith to cherish this nest of abominations, together with divers other establishments like unto it in kind, which operate together for the destruction of all upright and sober conversation. And, moreover, persons of all classes do purchase them books and libraries, thereby wasting and destroying much of their useful substance; and withal supporting a numerous and pestilent race of printers and booksellers, a species of men who, like unto mosquitoes and bedbugs, do wax fat upon the blood and vitals of the community.

And now it behoveth all honest and pious men to unite with their whole soul and their whole corporeal strength, to root out from the face of the earth this horrible nuisance and grievous abomination; lest the continuance thereof should draw some signal judgment upon the land, and lest this prudent, flourishing, and penny-getting people should suddenly be transformed into a nation of bookworms and of necromancers.[10]

—IX (October, 1810), 226-28

---

[10] The Anthology Society's *Journal* for September 4, 1810 (p. 237), records that "D^r. Bigelow read an essay against the Athenaeum, which was accepted." Bigelow's somewhat clumsy satire was another way of attracting attention to the infant library.

CRITICAL STANDARDS AND PERSPECTIVES

Our Infant Hope: the Anthology

WILLIAM EMERSON

ALTHOUGH WE HAVE the feelings of a parent for the publication before us, yet it may be proper to declare to the world that it is not indebted to us for its birth, nor was it born in our house. We knew neither its father nor mother, nor hardly of its existence, until, naked, hungry, and helpless, it was brought and laid at our door. Pity for its orphan state bade us for the moment give it shelter and nourishment. In proportion as it engaged our care it won our affections. We began to provide for its maintenance; and what we were unable to afford ourselves was supplied by the contributions of charity. It seemed grateful for the care of its patrons, and tried to reward our beneficence by its smiles and prattle. The older it grew the more it was caressed. We carried it into the parlours of our friends, who praising it as a child of beauty and promise, predicted its eminence in the world.

Whether these predictions will be verified agreeably to our desires is a matter of uncertainty. We still guard our infant hope; and present appearances are very favourable. It is extremely docile; and we have no doubt, under good management, of his being everything we could wish. We continue to solicit for him the various bounties which are usually bestowed on children of his condition and merits. We are daily introducing him to the acquaintance of the wise and good, and laying plans to give him an excellent education. It is our intention to have him instructed in several ancient and modern languages, matriculated in two or three universities, and versed in almost every art and science.

He shall be associated with all our learned and humane societies, and made a corresponding member of some very respectable institutions abroad. To the advantage of a home education he shall enjoy privileges from travelling. He shall inspect the colleges, hospitals, and armies of Europe, take now and then a peep into the cabinets of princes, and get a general acquaintance with the great affairs of the political world.

Though we have principally in view his literary and scientifick attainments, we purpose that he shall not be destitute of the manners of a gentleman, nor a stranger to genteel amusements. He shall attend Theatres, Museums, Assemblies, Balls, &c. and whatever polite diversions the town may furnish; so that whilst he is familiar with the lore of books and the wisdom of sages, his dress and conversation shall borrow mode and graces of the most polished circles in our society. . . .

Indeed it will be strange if the being whom we shall have thus assiduously formed may not mix in good company with as high pretensions as any portable personage of his pursuits in the United States. As he acquires age and importance, therefore, and as long as we retain parental influence, we venture to promise that he shall often reveal his knowledge of natural history and philosophy, of logick and theology, mathematicks and poetry, of law and medicine. As his very liberal education will peculiarly fit him for the task, he shall read and review the most important literary productions of our country, and candidly give his opinion of their worth. He will take an exact note of the works of literature, the progress of the arts, and the state of publick concerns; and be so far a politician as to be a judicious biographer of the great and a persecutor of the ambitious. Versatile without being unprincipled, he will sometimes visit the hall of Congress, record doings of state legislatures, follow the field preacher with the fanatical, attend ordinations, weddings, and funerals, gaze at the stars, keep a diary of the weather, observe whatever is worth observation, relate clearly what he hears, testify boldly what he knows. . . .

—I, i-iii (Preface to Volume I of the *Monthly Anthology*,
dated January 1, 1805)

Courtesy The Boston Athenaeum

WILLIAM EMERSON

The Anthology: *Objects and Principles*

JOHN THORNTON KIRKLAND

ON THE COMMENCEMENT of a new volume of the *Anthology*, it becomes a suitable expression of our regard for its interests for us to pay our compliments to its patrons, and invite the attention of others to its claims. At this stage of publication, it is unnecessary to be particular in pointing out the objects of the work, or explaining the principles on which it is conducted. On these subjects the volumes already issued will afford better evidence for making a decision than our declarations. They will show how far we have accomplished our design of promoting useful knowledge and harmless amusement, sound principles, good morals, and correct taste. In our selections, essays, and reviews, we have wished to aid the cause of classical learning, so extravagantly decried and presumptuously neglected in this age of innovators and sciolists. We have aimed to withstand corruptions in literature; and to establish the authority of those laws of composition which are founded in nature, in reason, and in experience. In proposing our judgment of authors, we have frequently discussed as well doctrines and opinions, as method and style; and in this discussion we trust we have appeared, what we profess to be, in politicks neither worshippers nor contemners of the people, and in religion at once serious in belief and catholick in spirit.

We have conducted the *Review* under the conviction that publick criticism upon writers for the publick does not in itself imply either injustice or malevolence. At the same time we have sought to keep in mind those considerations which should guide and restrain the exercise of literary censure, to make adequate allowance for the general and incurable diversity of taste, and for our own fallibility, and to espouse, with all becoming humanity, the feelings of the candidates for publick approbation. We would be the ministers of that criticism which has been described attending the Muses as an allegorical personage, to whom Justice gives a sceptre and Labour and Truth a torch. To whatever errours or infirmities we may be liable in the execution of the delicate and responsible office of Reviewers, we disdain the imputation of aiming to gratify personal or party animosity under the specious form of a judgment upon a book. If any of our readers wish to know on what grounds we vindicate the liberties taken with some works in the department of our Review, let them peruse again the Remarker, number five on this subject; and they will probably admit the justness of our general rules, though they may differ from us in their particular application. . . .[11]

Perhaps the present state of society tend in a peculiar degree to foster general selfishness of character. A man's intellectual attainments appear to be regarded as the means only of his personal advantage. Doubtless many men of sense ascribe to us a species of fanaticism as the spring of that propensity we discover to enlighten, improve, and entertain a publick, which gives us for our pains neither fame nor money. We suggest to them a solution of our conduct which does not assign us a place greatly below or above the standard of human nature. We are exposed to the influence of that " Esprit de corps " which animates literary association. The pleasures found in composition and in the exercise of the mental powers put some of us upon blotting paper. If the cause still appear inadequate to the effect, we must be supposed to feel a desire to be useful in the way which our pursuits and studies direct; or if this seem too elevated a principle, let our services be deemed symptoms and effects of an impulse of more doubtful value, what a late writer on moral philosophy denominates *the passion for reforming the world*.

We must confess, however, that we have a motive somewhat interested for wishing that the pecuniary receipts of our publication may rise as high as possible above its demands, which is, that all the surplus funds are applied to the support and increase of a *Publick Library*; one of those institutions, of which every scholar in most parts of our country feels the want, which our

[11] See this number of " The Remarker " under the title " The Polity of Letters " pp. 176-82.

government from its nature does not comprise within its cares, and which nothing but the industry and munificence of individuals will establish and supply. . . .[12]

Every judicious effort to promote the love of Letters and Arts is entitled to countenance, for this, among other reasons, that a progress in letters and arts corresponds to the progress of society in other respects in our country. We are becoming familiar with wealth. Out of wealth grows luxury. If those enjoyments that flow from literature and taste are not emulated, we shall be exposed to that enervating and debasing luxury, the object of which is sensual indulgence, its immediate effect, vice, and its ultimate issue, publick degradation and ruin. . . .

—IV (January, 1807), 1-4

The Anthology *and Literary Nationality*

WILLIAM TUDOR, JR.

As WE HAVE only one opportunity in a year of directly addressing the publick in our private capacity, to neglect it would seem churlish, as well as a violation of former custom. It affords us too an occasion to greet heartily our old, tried friends, and to offer our compliments to some new ones that have arisen within the year. Though the number of these may not be so great as either we or our publishers might have expected, we will try to derive consolation from disappointment itself by thinking that our gratitude, which would have been enfeebled in being widely spread, will be quite perceptible when divided among a few.

We have completed the seventh volume; a great age among the literary ephemera of this country. Having arrived at this

---

[12] The reference is to the Athenaeum, although it is not a "public" library except in a restricted sense. The Boston Public Library came into being in the 1850's.

degree of maturity, in spite of innumerable predictions to the contrary, we almost begin to flatter ourselves that our constitution and temperament are more vigorous than those of most others in the class to which we belong; and that this uncommon duration is not accidental or artificial, but is the evidence of something sound in our stamina and pertinacious in our structure. Still the wonder and mystery of our existence, more extraordinary to us than it can be to the world, was so impressed on our minds that when we have been confidently told we were speedily destined to perish, we have assented to the declaration with almost as much humility and conviction as we should to the same truth when applied to us more seriously as individuals. Yet after acquiescing in these predictions of the certitude of our fate, the elasticity of hope or the force of vanity has made us the next moment exclaim, to compare small things with great, like Galileo rising from his recantation before the tribunal of the holy inquisition, *però si muove.*

It must be the lot of all those who have any intercourse with the publick to condescend sometimes to notice accusations palpably absurd. The *Anthology* is conducted by a society of gentlemen who derive no direct emolument from their labour, and persist in it, though many a shrewd, wise countenance may be covered with a smile at their simplicity, in still continuing to "*scribble, scribble.*" This smile, which is really excited more by good-natured wonder than contempt, they can return with one of the same character. Plutus then not being in the number of our household gods, it could hardly be supposed we should be subject to any other reproaches than those of sterility. In this case it would be prudent to be silent, as mediocrity can only hope for toleration, while it is submissive and defenceless. But we have been accused of wishing to depreciate our country, of fostering without discrimination every thing exotick, and depreciating every thing indigenous. Can there be an accusation more opposed to our very existence, more boldly ridiculous?

In all the more liberal and noble branches of science and literature, it would certainly be difficult, perhaps mischievous, to attempt very accurate limits of our *nationality*. Formed as we have been on the English school, as far as the English language is concerned, we can hardly establish a separate one, and if our *esprit de corps* as a nation is as marked as that of the Scotch in the republick of literature, that will be the extent of its force. We have a sensation of delight, which to very enlarged minds may seem founded on narrow feelings, when we see any countryman of ours justly attracting notice in this republick; and if wishing were a suitable employment, we should wish that we could boast of a greater number, who hold conspicuous stations in it; of more men who possess the wit and sagacity of Franklin, or the eloquence of Ames.

It is owing mainly to some glaring faults in our scheme of widespread, superficial education that we are harassed with a class of authors, we are sorry to degrade the name, who are incomparably more numerous here, in proportion, than in any other country. We allude to those who have triumphed over an audience in some species of occasional discourse, orations, sermons, &c., who have occupied the poet's corner, or a column of a newspaper, or whose vanity and attainments are shewn in the meanest manner in eulogies and characters of deceased insignificance. To almost every one of this numerous description, the familiar Latin proverb, that, on occasions, *Socco dignus cothurno incedit*, may be fairly applied. These worthless seeds spring up prematurely, and though it is an irksome, fatiguing employment, we are bound to contribute our efforts to eradicate them, lest they stifle and exhaust the nourishment from the valuable plants that are slower in their growth, but which will be in perfection long after these have perished. To these may be added all who are stirrers up of sedition, in either church or state, and who of course address themselves to the most ignorant of the community; all those well-meaning men who have mistaken virtuous, patriotick sentiments in rhyme for poetick inspiration; the whole class of book-makers, the grand pest in Europe, but who in this country are still covered with their pinfeathers and are just trying their wings, and whose only plausible plea must be founded on the favour due to domestick manufactures. All these classes would naturally accuse us of being deficient in national feeling, or what, in poor imitation of English arrogance, is called *American* feeling; and as we are willing to flatter ourselves that the accusation will come from no one else, we hope our tranquillity on this account is not unreasonable.

We turn eagerly to a more grateful theme, an expression of thanks to those who have at any time been pleased with our labours. Studied praise is always fatiguing; but when we discard all desires and intentions of gain, and wish only to be thought to have "done the state some service," our satisfaction must arise from the satisfaction of others. A word of encouragement, even an exclamation, or a look that denotes sympathy, a degree of excitement, of fellow-feeling; all these tend, and we may be indulged in saying, have tended to animate and encourage us. We have not been in the habit of holding out many promises; we are not going to begin the practice now, but we may be excused for suggesting an obvious remark. It may be reasonably presumed, from the slightest knowledge of human nature, that the care, the animation, the reflection of him who is writing for the publick will be inevitably influenced and modified by the idea that he is to be read by a few, or by many.

We have had the pleasure of recently acquiring as honorary associates, in this, and in other states, individuals, whom if we were to name, we should be accused of inordinate vanity. We expect that some of the fruits of their leisure will enrich our columns.[13]

—VIII (January, 1810), 3-5

[13] Formal provision for the election of corresponding members to the Anthology Society was not made until late in its history. It was obviously a move inspired by the society's search for ways to secure recognition, patronage, and contributions for the *Anthology*. The *Journal* does not record the names of those invited to become corresponding members, but it identifies nineteen persons who apparently accepted the invitation and were elected. Undoubtedly this identification is partial (see *J*, 301-303). Among the prominent corresponding members were Benjamin Silliman, the noted Yale scientist; Chancellor James Kent, the famous lawyer; and Judge Jeremiah Smith, at one time governor of New Hampshire. But if these gentlemen contributed prestige to the Anthology Society, they contributed nothing more substantial, except for one article by Silliman. Some of the corresponding members, especially those in the Boston-Cambridge area, were more active contributors.

The Vanity of American Puffers

JOHN SYLVESTER JOHN GARDINER

Heaven sent us, KNOW THYSELF.—*Gifford.*

WERE WE TO judge of the state of American literature from the conversation of certain enlightened criticks whom we occasionally fall in with, we might reasonably conclude that we had already attained the point of perfection, and that the new world rivals, if it does not surpass the old. The literary adventurers of the day are the theme of every tongue, and their productions, whether in poetry or prose, receive such lavish encomiums from the editors of our publick prints that, were we to adopt the opinions of these gentlemen, we might proudly proclaim that we can write better verses than Pope and more elegant essays than Addison.

But when foreigners, excited by our typographical puffers, interrogate us respecting the literary state of our country and demand the names of our celebrated authors, we are unable to reply as satisfactorily as our vanity would wish. For notwithstanding the laudable partiality which we feel for our native land, we should hesitate in preferring the Muses of New England to those of the Thames or Seine, and justice would hardly allow us to exalt the *Gleaner* above the *Spectator* or *Rambler.*

I am sensible of the danger that I incur of censure for advancing so bold an opinion, since the profoundest criticks of our metropolis have considered the *Gleaner* as a *chef-d'oeuvre* in essay-writing. But though I reluctantly dissent from these great authorities on this subject, yet I most willingly retract an erroneous assertion into which I was inadvertently betrayed. I asserted that the *Gleaner* had departed this life. But as the author has corrected this mis-statement in the newspapers by assuring the publick that she is still living, I think it unfair to insist on the

point, though I might plead the authority of Swift in my favour
in the memorable case of Partridge. Be it known then, however
extraordinary and incredible the intelligence may appear, that
the Gleaner is still living, though, till lately, she had not been
heard of for many years.[14]

If we review our progress in science and literature, we shall
have no reason, I fear, to be greatly elated with our success.
Dr. Franklin by his lucky discovery of the electrick fluid has done
honour to his country, and probably immortalized himself. But
the literary character of the doctor has no claim to admiration.
He writes on useful topicks with good sense, in a style simple
and perspicuous, and though he may have few faults, he displays
no striking beauties.

Mr. Rittenhouse has acquired considerable reputation, which
we believe however is chiefly confined to his own country; nor
can I indeed discover that it has any other foundation than the
execution of an ingenious piece of mechanism.[15]

In poets, however, such as they are, we abound. But where
can we find a single poem of distinguished excellence, or one
which will be read fifty years hence? *McFingal* [*sic*] is a happy
imitation of Butler, but the original is now little read, and fast
hastening to oblivion. Novelty constitutes the chief merit of
hudibrastick verse, which consequently must be confined to the
inventor. Any imitator, then, can expect only temporary fame,
which may arise from the wit and personal satire with which his
performance may abound, and which will terminate with the
interest and memory of the fleeting occurrences it celebrates.

Connecticut has proved the fruitful nurse of epick poets, and
Barlow and Dwight started nearly at the same time for the prize
in the Olympick contest. But what original beauties can be

[14] "The Gleaner" was a periodical essay series by Judith Sargent Stevens
Murray (1751–1820). It appeared in the *Massachusetts Magazine* from
February, 1792, to August, 1794.

[15] David Rittenhouse (1732–1796), the noted American scientist, was
widely known for his orrery, an instrument representing motions of the
bodies of the solar system and illustrating solar and lunar eclipses, and so
forth, over a period of 5,000 years. Gardiner apparently had no conception
of Rittenhouse's achievements. His disparaging remarks seem to indicate
a general antipathy to science.

pointed out in either? What passages can be discovered eminently distinguished by justness of thoughts, liveliness of description, or elegance of language? But the greatet defect in these poems is an entire want of interest. We doze over the *Vision of Columbus*, and if we are kept awake in perusing the *Conquest of Canaan*, we are indebted to the thunder and lightning that roars and flashes in every page, and which, like another JUPITER TONANS, the poet discharges in perpetual rumble and coruscation; so that, as a wit once observed, it is scarcely safe to read this poem without a conductor.

Humphreys will be considered a great poet when the merit of a work shall be determined by its dimensions. But if we can say little in favour of his poetry, and still less of his prose, we may justly praise the type and paper with which they are ornamented; and the striking likeness of the author, which forms the frontispiece of the volume, must be peculiarly interesting to his friends and admirers. We doubt not that his generosity will amply compensate Messrs. Gilbert & Dean for the loss they have sustained by their good nature in undertaking the disposal of so unsaleable an article.[16]

Other poets amongst us, who have not yet risen to the dignity of a volume, have displayed, in some instances, no inconsiderable genius. But they seem to have forgotten, or never known, that genius without judgment is useless or ridiculous and that there can be no good poetry where there is not good sense. Broken metaphors, gorgeous epithets and forced thoughts are the artificial flowers that adorn their gaudy parterres, and are substituted for the simplicity of nature and the justness of truth.

Nor are our prose writers entirely free from these defects. From want of true taste, and a misconception of real elegance, they are forever torturing their faculties for novel expressions,

[16] *M'Fingal* by John Trumbull (1750–1831) was published in its full form in 1782. A poem in Hudibrastic couplets detailing the misfortunes of the Tory squire M'Fingal, it was very popular for over fifty years. Joel Barlow's *Vision of Columbia* was published in 1787; it appeared in revised form as *The Columbiad* in 1807. *The Conquest of Canaan* by Timothy Dwight (1752–1817) was published in 1785. David Humphreys (1752–1818) was, like the others mentioned by Gardiner, a member of the Connecticut Wits. His *Miscellaneous Works* came out in New York in 1804.

and newly invented combinations; so that the dictionary of Webster will be absolutely necessary for the understanding of our own productions. We shall derive however this advantage from these fopperies that our literary goods will be in no danger of exportation in foreign bottoms, and, by debasing our currency, we shall be sure of retaining it in our own country.

Let us, then, follow the advice in the motto of this paper, and endeavour to know ourselves. In the aggregate we are better informed, perhaps, than any nation on earth, and unquestionably possess men in the science of government and in the transaction of political affairs not inferiour to the great statesmen of Europe. But in literature we are yet in our infancy; and to compare our authors, whether in prose or poetry, to those of the old world can proceed only from the grossest ignorance or the most insufferable vanity.

—II (December, 1805), 630-32

Freneau's Poetry in Retrospect

JACOB BIGELOW

IT IS A rule applicable to many subjects that the quality of a thing bears an inverse ratio to its quantity; or that the more it is diffused the less exquisitely does it gratify our sense. A volume of four hundred pages, containing poetry on a hundred different subjects, chiefly newspaper politicks and local events, must be above the rank of mediocrity, did it compensate us for a complete perusal.[17] The reader who inspects the index to Mr. Freneau's poems will recognize all that peculiar variety which

[17] *The Poems of Philip Freneau. Written Chiefly During the Late War* (Philadelphia, 1786). Bigelow's review appears in the series of historical reviews in the *Anthology* entitled "Retrospective Notices of American Literature." See Joseph Stevens Buckminster's inaugural essay for this series which is published herein under the title "American Literary History" (pp. 169-74).

distinguishes the poet's corner in any of our gazettes. He will know how to bound his expectations, and will commence the book with the same composure and equanimity, which its subsequent perusal is so admirably adapted to continue. Indeed, that reader must be "tremblingly alive" whose feelings can be much discomposed by emotions either of pleasure or disgust in turning over the leaves of this monotonous collection. It would be unfair to bestow on the book unqualified censure or applause. It is pretty good for the time and circumstances under which it was written, tolerably good for American poetry, and would be very good if we possessed no better poetry. But in these days of refinement, while the poetical market is glutted with delicacies of every description, a bard of the middling class can hardly expect his produce to be sought after with the greatest avidity, or that the pampered taste of our literary epicures should indulge on a coarse and unsavoury, though perhaps a wholesome morsel.

A large proportion of Mr. F's poems are satirical and invective pieces, aimed at the subjects and partizans of the British government, and calculated to promote the spirit of patriotism so universal among Americans during the revolutionary contest. To this end they were probably subservient as far as passably good poetry, applied to subjects of great moment may be supposed capable of exciting interest. Many of these effusions possess a considerable share both of harmony and humour, blended with more bitterness and sarcasm. . . .

"The Jamaica Funeral" and "The Beauties of Santa Cruz," though very copious subjects for description are not handled with the same ability as many other of the performances. They are too prosaick, and appear to have been "done up by the job." But the most monstrously uncouth piece which the book has to boast is entitled "The House of Night," a poem of four or five hundred lines. The very novel machinery of this piece consists in the personification of Death, who is represented as overtaken with his death sickness, and after consulting physicians, writing his epitaph, and agreeing with an undertaker to entomb his bones, at length dies in a paroxysm of horrour, agony and despair, after which his relations and chaplain make a funeral for him! The poem then concludes with a few remarks on the impropriety of too great an attachment to the present life, and on the importance of those virtues which fit us for a better; a very pious moral, to be sure, but little connected with the fantastick extravagance of the fable. . . .

A general observation will apply to the book, that its serious subjects are no where treated in a strain capable of moving admiration; while the satirical pieces now lose much of their interest from the remoteness of the local circumstances which occasioned them. At the time of their first appearance, however, when their subjects were fresh and interesting, the invectives of Freneau could not fail to command attention. The keenness and asperity which characterize some of his productions, especially the several addresses to "A Foe to Tyrants," are sufficient to make one believe all Billingsgate in rhyme. The poet himself has given a sufficiently faithful character of his writings in his life of Hugh Gaine, who gave some of them publicity.

> " To gain a mere trifle, a shilling or so,
> I printed some treason for Philip F—neau,
> Some damnable poems reflecting on GAGE,
> The KING and his COUNCIL, and writ with such rage,
> So full of invective, and loaded with spleen,
> So pointedly sharp, and so hellishly keen,
> That, at least in the judgment of half our wise men,
> ALECTO herself made the nib to his pen."

—IX (September, 1810), 198-203

An Original American Poetry

SAMUEL COOPER THACHER

THE COMMON CHARGE against us of poverty of genius is least easily eluded when we are told that America has never yet produced a poet of more than second rate excellence. We can account pretty well for not having any rivals to the philosophers and scholars of Europe; but poetry has no necessary alliance with opulence and refinement. Its fullest and richest tones have often been heard where science never raised her voice, and refinement never imprinted her footsteps. The birth place of the original poet has often been where, as in our country, nature appears in all her rudeness, where the mountains rise in their unsubdued and gigantick elevations, the cataracts fall without mechanical precipitation, and the rivers roll without artificial meanders. The only reason that I can think of, without admitting the justice of the charge, is that our writers import the style and imagery of the poets of England, as much as our merchants do its wares. The new appearances of nature in our country, one would think, ought to have extended the limits of an art confessedly imitative. But our poets have been contented with attempting to revive the lilies and roses of Europe, all whose leaves are withered, and all whose fragrance is exhausted by having been so long plucked, and having been transferred to so many possessors. When we are farther advanced in refinement, we shall have poetry of as much beauty as any that has recently appeared in Europe; but whilst we continue to receive our riches by inheritance, and not to produce them by our vigour, we shall not be able to boast of any imperishable name; of one who may sit down with Homer, Milton, and Shakespeare.

—II (September, 1805), 460-61

Noah Webster
and the Confounding of Language

STEADY HABITS [18]

In my former number, I submitted some remarks on Mr. Webster's *manner* of introducing his "Discoveries," and concluded with a promise to investigate the *matter* of the discoveries themselves. On this head I might with propriety be silent; as the Reviewers, who are abundantly more able, have already accomplished that task. Silent indeed I well might be on another account; for in the great acquirements of which Mr. W. can boast, I am deficient in the proportion, as a pigmy child of Lilliput is smaller than the towering Polyphemus; and should I pretend to oppose my powers to his, the attempt will, perhaps, be as destructive to me as was that of the aspiring frog in the fable. But, in truth, an incurable *cacoethes scribendi* has so grievously afflicted me on this occasion, that it will be a wonder if I do not, to use the precision of Mr. Webster, fill " ten or fifteen pages." The great grammarians and refiners of language, who flourished among the Saxons, the Goths, the Celts, the Teutones and the Mohawks, from whom Mr. W. extracts those many flowers to deck the parterre of the "American English " language, have never honoured *me* with their acquaintance.

But, levity apart, I pretend to the possession of no *other* sense for this investigation than common sense; and in the exercise of

[18] " Steady Habits " was the pseudonym of Benjamin Douglass Perkins, a New York bookseller, who was nominated on February 20, 1810, to be a corresponding member of the Anthology Society (see *J*, 224). His election is not recorded, although it would seem likely that he was approved. In any event, his attacks on Noah Webster were congenial to the Anthologists. The first appeared in the *Anthology*, VII (December, 1809), 366-71. The second is the one reprinted. The third and fourth appeared in the *Anthology*, VIII (March, 1810), 147-55; and VIII (April, 1810), 219-27.

this endowment, I have been induced when reflecting on his
recurrence to long forgotten languages with the view of over-
turning rules and systems established in the most enlightened age
of the world, to exclaim, *cui bono?*

At the very threshold of his edifice Mr. W. appears to me to
have woefully stumbled. In the first page of the preface to his
Dictionary, he remarks: "To men who have been accustomed to
repose almost implicit confidence in the authors of our principal
dictionaries and grammars, it may appear, at first, incredible that
such writers as Johnson and Lowth should have mistaken many
of the fundamental principles of our language; but that such is
the fact will appear certain to *any man* who will read a few pages
in a Saxon author." Now I think it will require more ingenuity
than even Mr. W. possesses to explain why those learned men,
Dr. Johnson and Bishop Lowth, themselves, who have given us
such proofs of their having read more than a "few pages in a
Saxon author" should not have discovered that the fundamental
principles of the language had been mistaken, as well as the "any
man" alluded to by him. The truth is that *their* acquaintance
with that language, together with their extensive knowledge and
great judgment, not only satisfied them that present usage was
not inconsistent with the principles of the language, but that
changes and innovations with regard to the division in the parts
of grammar, and to the terms, were unnecessary, and ought not
to be attempted; and Dr. Johnson has left us his opinion on this
subject, conveyed with a force of language which might well
have repressed the ardour of any common man, who panted for
revolutions in grammatical systems. At the very commencement
of his grammar, prefixed to his dictionary, Dr. Johnson has the
following remarks: "In the division and order of the parts of
grammar I follow the common grammarians, without inquiring
whether a fitter distribution might not be found. Experience has
long shown this method to be so distinct as to obviate confusion,
and so comprehensive as to prevent any inconvenient omissions.
I likewise use the term already received, and already understood,
though perhaps others more proper might sometimes be invented.
Sylburgius and other innovators, whose new terms (one could
almost believe that he here spoke prophetically, and meant Noah

Webster) have sunk their learning into neglect, have left sufficient warning against the trifling ambition of teaching arts in a new language."

Dr. Johnson was one of the last men who would have shrunk from the task of altering our grammars, if he had cause to believe that any real utility, and not harm, would result from it. He was possessed of the ability to judge, the courage to attempt, and the power to enforce. His decisions were like the fiat of Jove; for

Criticks "attentive, trembled as he spoke."

He perceived that "though, *perhaps*, terms more proper might *sometimes* be invented," yet he evidently considered this to be uncertain; and as those already in use were well understood, he was decided against such an *injurious* innovation.

The sentiments of Dr. Johnson will be found in unison with those of every reflecting mind which is not tinctured with that restless and dissatisfied spirit, which under the imposing pretence of improvement, produces all the revolutions, or in other words the confusions and disorders which disgrace and disturb mankind.

At this place let me enter my protest against the inference that I would discourage the investigation of etymology, or any other pursuit which really enlarges the boundaries of human knowledge; on the contrary, few would go further in promoting them. Investigations into the origin of languages, like many other pursuits which engage the attention of the learned, are calculated to gratify a rational curiosity; though none can deny that they lay claim rather to the *dulci* than the *utile* of literature. Whether an enlargement of intellect is to be accomplished by researches into the natural or moral world is immaterial: I am in favour of both. On this principle I have viewed with regret the neglect of the study of the learned languages in several of the colleges in this country. I could encourage Spallanzani, Hunter, Lewenhook, Lionet, &c. in all those of their physiological researches which would not be attended with unnecessary cruelty or obscenity. What facts can have a greater tendency to inspire one with emotions of surprise and gratification than Lewenhook's discoveries of the extraordinary organs of vision in beetles? How eminently are they calculated to impress the mind with the wondrous works of the Great Creator! In conformity with these sentiments, I have never been disposed to ridicule Mr. Jefferson for his fondness for natural history; and especially for his exertions to collect and preserve the remains of extraordinary animals, provided this subject did not occupy the mind of the *philosopher* to the exclusion of the more important duties pertaining to the *president*.

But had our philosopher gone the length of Mr. Webster, and issued *one* of his proclamations against the farmers of the United States, interdicting their further intercourse with those useful domestick animals, the horse and the ox, and commanding all the said farmers to pack off beyond Lake Superior to hunt mammoths, for the purpose of training them for domestick uses, I should certainly have joined in a decided opposition to the reasonableness of such a proclamation.[19] The race of mammoths, like the languages which Mr. Webster would revive, is doubtless extinct; but even were those unruly monsters still living, I apprehend that we should not find them more convenient for the purposes of riding or ploughing than we shall find the language of the Goths and Saxons more convenient for our daily discourse. Mr. Jefferson's proclamation never inveighed with more bitterness against Great Britain for violating the " freedom of the seas " than Mr. Webster's phillipicks have done against learned men for contenting themselves with the usages of English writers and grammarians, and for refusing to abandon these usages to wander with him in quest of new lights among Saxon and Gothick barbarians. . . .

I do not deem it necessary to offer many reasons to convince any reflecting mind that the tendency of such innovations on " respectable, national, and present use," is to place us on an ocean that has no shore. To the genuine principles of orthography, grammatical construction, and the interpretation of words,

---

[19] The satirical reference to mammoths is directed at Thomas Jefferson, who held that in the economy of nature no creature can become extinct. This, however, was not a personal eccentricity on Jefferson's part; it was supported by the concept of the chain of being. See Daniel J. Boorstin, *The Lost World of Thomas Jefferson* (New York, 1958), 36-38. Cf. John Quincy Adams' satire on Joel Barlow's " On the Discoveries of Captain Lewis," pp. 56-60.

Mr. W. is in direct hostility. His plans for retracing our steps; or, as he acknowledged that he himself has done, of *unlearning* what he has been taught, is to conduct us back to that huge tower, where " was confounded the language of all the earth. . . ."

English words, whatever may have been their origin, claim now, by prescription, the right of being considered as *English.* If not, why has Mr. Webster deviated from his rule in many of his definitions in his dictionary?—When the mountain, now in the pangs of labour, shall bring forth (not a mouse), but the terrifick volume with which we are threatened, all will doubtless be correct, all will doubtless be consistent. We shall then find that a butterfly is defined to be a chrysalis, and a frog a tadpole, because, forsooth, it is certain that these animals proceeded from a chrysalis and a tadpole.

Now to my second proposition. Mr. Webster is of all men possessed of the fewest qualifications for the great task of *improving* the English language. Should any man doubt this fact, all his skepticism would vanish, could he but take a survey of the scene which the table before me exhibits. It is *loaded* with the literary lumber of Noah Webster; Jun; Esq: " Spelling Books," " Old Grammars," " New Grammars," " First Parts," " Second Parts," " Third Parts," " Elements "; and again, their " First Parts," " Second Parts," " Third Parts," *interumque, interumque*; puffs direct, puffs oblique, puffs collateral, with plans for suppressing all projects but his own in New York *Spectators*, Boston *Centinels*, Albany *Gazettes*, and Hartford *Courants*; octavo volumes of " Fugitiv Peeces ritten at various times as will appeer in the *improved* mode of spelling "; two octavo volumes on Pestilence, another on the English language; one letter on Religion, another to Dr. Ramsay on the " Hottentot " Johnson, and his " wretchedly imperfect " dictionary; a Compendious Dictionary with FIVE THOUSAND WORDS MORE than can be found in the best English Compends; a *little* Dictionary not *so big*; and proposals for another a GREAT DEAL BIGGER!—" confusion worse confounded "!!

The versatility of genius and the volatility of man was never displayed in more enlivening colours than in the *various* lucubrations before me. Here litters a project more dazzling than the

brightest spot in the particoloured coat of a Harlequin; here
shines another ready to accommodate itself to every hue of the
chameleon and here in my imagination approaches the author
himself, bent on *change*, no matter how, and with a facility to
invent changes, which might have roused the envy of even
Proteus himself. . . .

                                    —VII (February, 1810), 80-86

An American Language

WILLIAM SMITH SHAW

THE OFFICE OF the Remarker is not confined to speculations
on morals and literature, but will occasionally be extended to
the delineation of schemes for the whole country. Objects of
national concern ought to employ the most active exertions of
every individual, and the labours of our statesmen ought to be
diminished by the assistance of every citizen who possesses leisure
and ingenuity to devise means of publick safety and private
repose.

Since the liberation of our countrymen from the tuition of a
cruel stepdame, who fondly hoped that in the decrepitude of age
she should be nourished and sustained by our labour and love, our
citizens while engaged in lawful commerce have been exposed to
violence and impressment. The licensed buccaniers and royal
robbers of the ocean have divorced our citizens from their friends
and families, and compelled them to exert, in the service of a king,
every muscle not palsied by fear of the thong and scourge.
Remonstrance only admonishes them of their power of inflicting
still greater injuries, and the specious plea of justification is that
*similarity of language prevents discrimination between English-
men and Americans.*[20] It is now proposed to strike at the root

[20] The impressment of American seamen by the British Navy was one
of the outstanding disputes between the United States and England in the

of the evil, and to construct a language entirely novel. This language must be composed of five-parts, viz. one part Indian, another Irish, and three fifths Negro tongue. These ingredients well mixed will constitute a language unintelligible by any human nation from Gades to Ganges. As drivers of herds of cattle sometimes bind a spat across the horns of a fierce bullock to prevent his escape in the thickets of the forest, so will this language debar us from all intercourse with other nations, and will erect a strong wall of partition between us and our adversaries.

Without doubt this plan will be strenuously opposed by those who are continually declaiming against the subversion of ancient institutions and the destruction of ancient principles. But it is reasonable that man would pursue a course analogical to that of nature, which is a process of continual change, of decay and revival. Flowers, whose existence is brief, and which flourish only for the scythe, are ever most beautiful and fragrant. Besides, a virtuous republican government induces modes of thought and action so different from those produced by a monarchy that many of the terms of the English language are in this country as insignificant and destitute of meaning as the representatives of old Sarum are of constituents, and the bold and original thoughts of Americans perish as would giants in this pigmy land, because they could not be cooped in our cabins, or covered by our garments. On account of this paucity of terms, adapted to our ideas, most of our authors and holiday orators have been compelled to invent new words, and make our language as various as the face of our country.

It will be perceived, that this new language is the result of a spirit of compromise and conciliation, and that those classes of citizens which are most numerous contribute most to its formation. If we inspect the American court calendar, we shall immediately ascertain that in selecting materials for this language due attention has been paid to the origin and descent of those who guide the destinies of our nation: the most eminent of whom are

---

early years of the nineteenth century. England did not claim the right to impress American nationals but did take a good many American citizens from American vessels on the assumption that their Irish or British accents proved them to be subjects of the Empire.

of Irish or Indian blood. We need not the aid of the college of heralds to trace the lineage of our greatest orator, Randolph, to the renowned Pocahontas, for no sachem among the aboriginals could hurl the tomahawk with more unerring aim, or could, with more adroitness, mangle, and scalp, and lacerate the trembling victims of his wrath. His eloquence is of the whooping kind, and his words, "like bullets chewed, rankled where they entered, and, like melted lead, blistered where they lighted. . . ." The fame and glory of our orators in Congress must be attributed wholly to their knowledge of Indian dialects. Those who utter English are fortunately few; otherwise the circumstance of their receiving their tone and language from a foreign court would subject them to punishment, as it now does to suspicion and disgrace.

The excellencies of the proposed dialect will be numerous; it will not possess the quality of harmony, so that it may be congenial to the nature of our government; and as it will be difficult to be uttered, it will counteract tumults and seditions, which are usually the effect of sudden and inconsiderate expressions of anger and indignation. Our countrymen, like the wing-footed horses of Phoebus, need restraint, rather than impulse.

Sponte sua properant; labor est inhibere volentes.

They are not perfect, and no one ought to expect that American citizens should be Gods, till they are nourished by nectar, and breathe aether on Olympus. In forming this language, our great object is to conform to the sacred rights of the majority, and therefore we banish all delicacy and beauty; for he that would move minds that are material, and souls that are sensible, must use instruments ponderous and palpable, otherwise his labour will be as vain and futile as was that of Aeneas, when, in the nether world, he instinctively put his hand to the sword, and would have smote the disembodied spirits, " et frustra ferro diverberet umbras."

Republicans, who seek right and follow reason, ever prefer utility to elegance; they use language as a medium, not as a commodity. The materials which we have selected will compose a currency, cumbrous as the iron money of Sparta and base as the copper coin of Birmingham; but in its clumsiness and relative baseness will consist its intrinsick value; for then the cupidity of our merchants will not be tempted to exhaust our country of its circulating medium, neither will the despot of the world exact from us a tribute so debased. If we wished for a language as a valuable commodity, then indeed our words should resemble "apples of gold set in pictures of silver," which we could use as toys for traffick.

The adoption of this new language will operate very favourably on our foreign relations, and will erect a barrier more powerful than navies, and proclamations, and non-intercourse bills. The policy of our government is not to exhaust the bowels of our country to afford protection to commerce, which infects the manners of republicans with a thirst for lucre and love of luxuries; which imports the elegancies of the East, and yellow fever of the West Indies, and supplies silks for our ladies; and slaves for our lords. Though our ports are thronged with merchantmen, richly laden, they receive no other protection than one gun-boat to each port, "*ut unoculus inter caecos.*"

When this language shall have become common and universal in our country, we shall be a world by ourselves; and will surround our territory by an impregnable wall of brass, and all sit down, each in his whirligig chair, and philosophize. Then our oaks shall not be ravished from our mountains, and compelled to sport in the ocean with mermaids and monsters of the deep; but they shall be permitted still to wear their green honours, and their foliage, instead of quivering through fear of the axe of the shipwright, shall dance and dally with Zephyrus. Our citizens will then enjoy all the happiness of hermits, and all the tranquillity of monks.

—III (August, 1806), 399-401

The Dominion of the Voice

JOHN QUINCY ADAMS

IT IS THE fortune of some opinions, as well as of some individual characters, to have been during a long succession of ages subjects of continual controversy among mankind. In forming an estimate of the moral or intellectual merits of many a person, whose name is recorded in the volumes of history, their virtues and vices are so nearly balanced that their station in the ranks of fame has never been precisely assigned, and their reputation, even after death, vibrates upon the hinges of events with which they have little or no perceptible connexion. Such too has been the destiny of the arts and sciences in general, and of the art of rhetorick in particular. Their advancement and decline have been alternate in the annals of the world. At one period they have been cherished, admired, and cultivated; at another neglected, despised, and oppressed. Like the favourites of princes, they have had their turns of unbounded influence and of excessive degradation. Now the enthusiasm of their votaries has raised them to the pinnacle of greatness; now a turn of the wheel has hurled them prostrate in the dust. Nor have these great and sudden revolutions always resulted from causes seemingly capable of producing such effects. At one period, the barbarian conqueror destroys, at another he adopts the arts of the vanquished people. The Grecian Muses were led captive and in chains to Rome. Once there, they not only burst asunder their own fetters, but soon mounting the triumphal car, rode with supreme ascendancy over their victors. More than once have the Tartars, after carrying conquest and desolation over the empire of China, been subdued in turn by the arts of the nation they had enslaved; as if by a wise and equitable retribution of nature the authors of violence were doomed to be overpowered by their own prosperity, and to find in every victory the seeds of defeat.

On the other hand, the arts and sciences at the hour of their highest exaltation have been often reproached and insulted by those on whom they had bestowed their choicest favours, and most cruelly assaulted by the weapons which themselves had conferred. At the zenith of modern civilization, the palm of unanswered eloquence was awarded to the writer who maintained that the sciences had always promoted rather the misery than the happiness of mankind;[21] and in the age and nation which heard the voices of Demosthenes, Socrates has been represented as triumphantly demonstrating that rhetorick cannot be dignified with the name of an art; that it is but a pernicious practice, the mere counterfeit of jutice. This opinion has had its followers from the days of Socrates to our own, and it still remains an inquiry among men, as in the age of Plato and in that of Cicero, whether eloquence is an art worthy of the cultivation of a wise and virtuous man. To assist us in bringing the mind to a satisfactory result of this inquiry, it is proper to consider the art, as well in its nature, as in its effects; to derive our inferences, not merely from the uses which have made of it, but from the purposes to which it ought to be applied, and the end which it is destined to answer.

The peculiar and highest characteristick which distinguishes man from the rest of the animal creation is *reason*. It is by this attribute that our species is constituted the great link between the physical and intellectual world. By our passions and appetites we are placed on a level with the herds of the forest; by our reason we participate in the divine nature itself; formed of clay, and compounded of dust, we are in the scale of creation little higher than the clod of the valley; endowed with reason, we are little lower than the angels. It is by the gift of reason that the human species enjoys the exclusive and inestimable privilege of progressive improvement, and is enabled to avail itself of the advantages of individual discovery. As the necessary adjunct and vehicle of reason, the faculty of speech was also bestowed as an exclusive privilege upon man: not the mere utterance of articulate sounds; not the mere cries of passion, which he has in common

[21] Adams refers to Rousseau's famous *Discours sur les sciences et les arts* (1750).

with the lower orders of animated nature: but as the conveyance of thought; as the means of rational intercourse with his fellow creature, and of humble communion with his God. It is by the means of reason, clothed with speech, that the most precious blessings of social life are communicated from man to man, and that supplication, thanksgiving, and praise are addressed to the author of the universe, How justly then, with the great dramatick poet may we exclaim,

> "Sure, he that made us with such *large discourse*,
>   Looking before and after, gave us not
>   That capability and God-like reason
>   To rust in us, unus'd."

A faculty thus elevated, given us for so sublime a purpose, and destined to an end so excellent, was not intended by the supreme Creator to be buried in the grave of neglect. As the source of all human improvements it was itself susceptible of improvement by industry and application, by observation and experience. Hence, wherever man has been found in a social state, and wherever he has been sensible of his dependence upon a supreme disposer of events, the value and the power of publick speaking, if not universally acknowledged, has at least been universally felt. . . .

The immeasurable superiority of ancient over modern oratory is one of the most remarkable circumstances which offer themselves to the scrutiny of reflecting minds, and it is in the languages, the institutions, and the manners of modern Europe that the solution of a phenomenon so extraordinary must be sought. The assemblies of the people, of the select councils, or of the senate in Athens and Rome were held for the purpose of real deliberation. The fate of measures was not decided before they were proposed. Eloquence produced a powerful effect, not only upon the minds of the hearers, but upon the issue of the deliberation. In the only countries of modern Europe where the semblance of deliberative assemblies has been preserved, corruption, here in the form of executive influence, there in the guise of party spirit, by introducing a more compendious mode of securing decisions has crippled the sublimest efforts of oratory, and the votes upon questions of magnitude to the interest of nations are all told long before the questions themselves are submitted to discussion. Hence those nations, which for ages have gloried in the devotion to literature, science, and the arts, have never been able to exhibit a specimen of deliberative oratory that can bear a comparison with those transmitted down to us from antiquity.

Religion indeed has opened one new avenue to the career of eloquence. Amidst the sacrifices of paganism to her three hundred thousand gods, amidst her sagacious and solemn consultations in the entrails of slaughtered brutes, in the flight of birds, and the feeding of fowls, it had never entered her imagination to call upon the pontiff, the haruspex, or the augur for discourses to the people upon the nature of their duties to their maker, their fellow-mortals, and themselves. This was an idea too august to be mingled with the absurd and ridiculous, or profligate and barbarous rites of her deplorable superstition. It is an institution for which mankind are indebted to Christianity, introduced by the Founder himself of this divine religion, and in every point of view worthy of its high original. Its effects have been to soften the tempers and purify the morals of mankind; not in so high degree as benevolence could wish, but enough to call forth our strains of warmest gratitude to that good being who provides us with the means of promoting our own felicity, and gives us power to stand, though leaving us free to fall. Here then is an unbounded and inexhaustible field for eloquence, never explored by the ancient orators, and here alone have the modern Europeans cultivated the art with much success. In vain should we enter the halls of justice, in vain should we listen to the debates of senates for strains of oratory worthy of remembrance beyond the duration of the occasion which called them forth. The art of embalming thought by oratory, like that of embalming bodies by aromaticks, would have perished but for the exercises of religion. These alone have in the latter ages furnished discourses which remind us that eloquence is yet a faculty of the human mind.

Among the causes which have contributed thus to depress the oratory of modern times must be numbered the indifference with which it has been treated as an article of education. The ancients had fostered an opinion that this talent was in a more than usual degree the creature of discipline; and it is one of the maxims handed down to us as the result of their experience that men must be born to poetry and bred to eloquence: that the bard is always the child of nature, and the orator always the issue of instruction. This doctrine seems to be not entirely without foundation, but was by them carried in both its parts to an extravagant excess.

The foundations for the oratorical talent, as well as those of the poetical faculty, must be laid in the bounties of nature; and as the Muse in Homer, impartial in her distribution of good and evil, struck the bard with blindness when she gave him the powers of song, her Sister not unfrequently, by a like mixture of tenderness and rigour, bestows the blessing of wisdom while she refuses the readiness of utterance. Without entering, however, into a disquisition which would lead me far beyond the limits of this occasion, I may remark that the modern Europeans have run into the adverse extreme, and appear during a considerable period in their system of public education to have passed upon eloquence a sentence of proscription. Even when they studied *Rhetorick* as a theory, they neglected *Oratory* as an art; and while assiduously unfolding to their pupils the bright displays of Greek and Roman eloquence, they never attempted to make them eloquent themselves. Of the prevailing indifference to this department of human learning, no stronger evidence could be offered than the circumstances under which we are assembled.

Nearly two centuries have elapsed since the foundation of this university. There never existed a people more anxious to bestow upon their children the advantages of education than our venerable forefathers; and the name of Harvard is coeval with the first settlement of New-England. Their immediate and remote descendants down to this day have inherited and transmitted the same laudable ardour, and numerous foundations of various kinds attest their attachment to science and literature: yet so far have rhetorick and oratory been from enjoying pre-eminence in their system of education that they are now, for the first time, made a separate branch of instruction; and I stand here to assume the duties of the first instructor. The establishment of an institution for the purpose was reserved to the name of BOYLSTON: a name, which if publick benefits can impart a title to remembrance, New England will not easily forget; a name, to the benevolence, publick spirit, and genuine patriotism of which, this university, the neighbouring metropolis, and this whole nation have long had, and still have, many reasons to attest: a name, less distinguished by stations of splendour than by deeds of virtue; and better known to this people by blessings enjoyed than by favours granted: a name, in fine, which, if not encircled with the external radiance of popularity, beams, brightly beams, with the inward lustre of beneficence. The institution itself is not of a recent date. One generation of mankind, according to the usual estimates of human life, has gone by since the donation of Nicholas Boylston constituted the fund for the support of this professorship. The misfortunes which befel the university, unavoidably consequent upon our revolution, and various other causes, have concurred in delaying the execution of his intentions until the present time; and even now they have the prospect of little more than honest zeal for their accomplishment.[22]

In reflecting upon the nature of the duties I undertake, a consciousness of deficiency for the task of their performance dwells upon my mind; which, however ungraciously it may come from my lips, after accepting the appointment with which I am honoured, I cannot yet forbear to express. Though the course of my life has led me to witness the practice of this art in various forms, and though its theory has sometimes attracted my attention, yet my acquaintance with both has been of a general nature; and I can presume neither to a profound investigation of the one, nor an extensive experience of the other. The habits of instruction, too, are not familiar to me; and they constitute an art of little less difficulty and delicacy than that of oratory itself: yet as the

[22] The Boylston Professorship of Rhetoric and Oratory was provided for by the will of the Boston merchant Nicholas Boylston in 1771. The fifteen hundred pounds Boylston left was invested and was not employed for the intended purpose until Adams was made the first occupant of the Boylston chair in 1805. See Goodfellow, " The First Boylston Professor of Rhetoric and Oratory," *loc. cit.*, pp. 372-74. Although Goodfellow deals with the favorable reception Adams' inaugural address received, he fails to mention that it was printed in the *Anthology*. Cf. pp. 87-88 n. 4.

career must necessarily be new by whomsoever it should here be explored, and as it leads to a course of pleasing speculations and studies, I shall rely upon the indulgence of the friends and patrons to this seminary towards well-meant endeavours, and assume with diffidence the discharge of the functions allotted to the institution. In the theory of the art and the principles of exposition, novelty will not be expected; nor is it perhaps to be desired. A subject which has exhausted the genius of Aristotle, Cicero, and Quintilian can neither require nor admit much additional illustration. To select, combine, and apply their precepts, is the only duty left for their followers of all succeeding times, and to obtain a perfect familiarity with their instructions, is to arrive at the mastery of the art. For effecting this purpose, the teacher can do little more than second the ardour and assiduity of the scholar. In the generous thirst for useful knowledge, in the honourable emulation of excellence, which distinguishes the students of this university, I trust to find an apology for the deficiencies of the lecturer. The richness of the soil will compensate for the unskilfulness of the tillage.

Sons of Harvard! you who are ascending with painful step and persevering toil the eminence of science to prepare yourselves for the various functions and employments of the world before you, it cannot be necessary to urge upon *you* the importance of the art concerning which I am speaking. Is it the purpose of your future life to minister in the temples of Almighty God, to be the messenger of heaven upon earth, to enlighten with the torch of eternal truth the path of your fellow-mortals to brighter worlds? Remember the reason assigned for the appointment of Aaron to that ministry, which you purpose to assume upon yourself. *I know that he can speak well*; and in this testimonial of Omnipotence receive the injunction of your duty. Is your intention to devote the labours of your maturity to the cause of justice; to defend the persons, the property, and the fame of your fellow citizens from the open assaults of violence, and the secret encroachments of fraud? Fill the fountains of your eloquence from inexhaustible sources, that their streams, when they shall begin to flow, may themselves prove inexhaustible. Is there among you a youth whose bosom burns with the fires of honourable ambition; who aspires to immortalize his name by the extent and importance of his services to his country; whose visions of futurity glow with the hope of presiding in her councils, of directing her affairs, of appearing to future ages on the rolls of fame, as her ornament and pride? Let him catch from the relicks of ancient oratory those unresisted powers which mould the mind of man to the will of the speaker, and yield the guidance of a nation to the dominion of the voice.

Under governments purely republican, where every citizen has a deep interest in the affairs of the nation, and in some form of publick assembly or other has the means and opportunity of delivering his opinions, and of communicating his sentiments by speech; where government itself has no arms but those of persuasion; where prejudice has not acquired an uncontrolled ascendancy, and faction is yet confined within the barriers of peace, the voice of eloquence will not be heard in vain. March then with firm, with steady, with undeviating step to the prize of your high calling. Gather fragrance from the whole paradise of science, and learn to distil from your lips all the honies of persuasion. Consecrate, above all, the faculties of your life to the cause of truth, of freedom, and of humanity. So shall your country ever gladden at the sound of your voice, and every talent added to your accomplishments become another blessing to mankind.

—III (June, 1806), 288-95

American Literary History

JOSEPH STEVENS BUCKMINSTER

Under this head we propose to commence a review of books in American literature which have either been forgotten or have not hitherto received the attention they deserve. Interested as we are in everything which relates to the honour of our country, we are not ashamed to express our conviction that one reason of the low estimation in which our literature is held among ourselves as well as in Europe is that there has yet been no regular survey of this field of letters. It is supposed to be utterly barren because it is so wide and desolate, because there has never been a map of the region. But, as in the highest parts of a mountainous country, which appear at a distance to be covered with eternal snows, you will discover in crevices and little spots some humble and modest plants which sufficiently reward the toilsome ascent of an enthusiastick botanist; so in the extensive, if not copious records of American learning, we hope to detect a few rare and undescribed specimens which may by this means awaken at least the regard of some future historian of literature. It is unfortunately true that, while every country in modern Europe has produced copious annals of its literature, or maintained regular journals of its new works, this country has till within a few years had nothing of the kind. There was indeed a thin quarto volume published in the year 1789, which bears the imposing title of *Bibliotheca Americana*; but it is in the first place a meagre compilation, and is confined, not to works of American authors, as would be imagined from the title, but to books which relate only to the general history of the country. The late Dr. Homer of Oxford, whose death our antiquaries ought to deplore, had projected a complete work of this description, and the proposals for his *Bibliotheca Universalis Americana* have been long before the publick; but how far he had proceeded in the execution of the work, or whether it will ever be given to the world, we have not been able to ascertain. In Miller's retrospect of the last century, there is an interesting sketch of our literature, which is the more valuable, as it is the first attempt to give a general outline of the advances we have made, and the works we have produced. It has shown us, it is true, the pitiable sterility of our literary history, but it has reclaimed also some of our treasures, disclosed others which were hardly suspected, and opened a range of enquiry which we doubt not may yet be pursued, and to which it will be our object in any way to contribute.[23]

[23] Arthur Homer (1758–1806) completed one volume only of his projected *Bibliographica Americana, or a Chronological Catalogue of the Most Curious*

We are afraid it will be found that the further back we go in our history the more monuments and relicks we shall find of what is usually called learning; but the acquisitions of our first emigrants who received their education and laid in their stores before they crossed the Atlantick can hardly be claimed as American. This, however, we have the less reason to regret, as they brought with them chiefly the scholastico-theological knowledge of that age, and the generation which immediately succeeded them inherited little more than the rags of their father's ecclesiastical habiliments. The elegance of Queen Anne's golden age of literature seems to have had little cotemporary influence in this country. The clergy were still the principal writers of the times, and the character of a gentleman author, who wrote for amusement or fame, was almost unknown. In the interval between the commencement of the last century and the establishment of literary journals in Great-Britain may be found a few of the most rare and curious articles which we shall be able to present. Since the establishment of the *Monthly Review* in the year 1747, it has been the good fortune of some of our writers to have their works reprinted, and consequently reviewed in England; and the political complexion of this journal has, since the revolution, given some of our authors an estimation, and procured some of our writers an attention, which others of not inferiour merit have failed to obtain.[24] Still, however, we believe that the connexion of this country with England has been just sufficient to place us in the train of their literature, where, like some of the couples in a long procession, we have been rather overlooked through the weariness of the spectators than distinguished according to our real, tho' not pre-eminent merit. We have received just enough attention to lead us to think too little of ourselves; and it is perhaps a just punishment of our want of national curiosity that we have taken our notions of our own literary wealth from

---

and Interesting Books . . . upon the Subjects of North and South America. It was published in London in 1789. Samuel Miller (1769–1850) published his *A Brief Retrospect of the Eighteenth Century*, Part I, in two volumes (New York, 1803). His contemplated second part was never published, but the first part is an invaluable document for the literary and intellectual historian of the early American Republic.

[24] The *Monthly Review* was published in London from 1749 to 1844.

the partial and scanty hints which we find in the journals of foreigners.

In the notices which we propose to insert in future numbers of the *Anthology* of former American works, there is only one department which we shall entirely disregard, and that is unfortunately the most rich in materials. Theology, or something which has been called so, is the subject upon which much of our genius and learning has been always employed, and not seldom wasted.

It would be an endless task to review even the works of tolerable merit in this class which have issued from the presses of New-England alone. Here we are proud to mention the works of Jonathan Edwards, a man whose powers of mind need not have bowed before the genius of Locke or of Hartley, and whose theological research, in a remote part of an unlettered country, would have been considered creditable to any divine surrounded with learned libraries and aided by the intercourse of men of erudition. But we refuse to enter this field of literary history, because it is perhaps not only the best known, but would be also less generally interesting.

Neither shall we trespass upon the ground of that respectable and industrious society which has already published several volumes of historical collections; for their objects are rather archaeological than literary, and extend to the earliest periods of our history, which are so remote as to furnish little for our review.[25] Still, however, we shall be happy to avail ourselves of their aid, and we especially solicit information and suggestions on the subject of early American authors, which we doubt not their inquiries have abundantly enabled them to give. It is of no small importance to the honour of our literary history that notices and anecdotes should be collected of authors and their works before all their cotemporaries, or their immediate descendants, shall have left the stage. The fame of some men, whose works really deserve not to be forgotten, lives now chiefly in the recollections of their personal acquaintances. It will be our pleasure to revive, guard, and magnify their worth; and if in the

[25] The Massachusetts Historical Society was founded in 1791 and incorporated in 1794.

great republick of letters their dignity should be still thought inconsiderable, it should be remembered that the emoluments of literature also were then inconsiderable, and the prospect of fame, from our intercourse with Europe, exceedingly obscure. Literary men have always in this extensive country been too widely separated to enjoy the advantages of lettered intercourse. There has been little to excite emulation, nothing to generate an *esprit de corps*, and the hope of posthumous fame has, from our remote situation, always been too faint to stimulate to solitary exertions.

It does not come within our plan to review works which have appeared since the revolution, unless they are recommended by some peculiar or hitherto unnoticed excellence. Within the last thirty years many domestick magazines and reviews have taken upon themselves the trouble of giving an account of works as they appeared; but these journals, enjoying only a temporary and local importance, which it was necessary to preserve by not offending, have almost invariably praised without discrimination, and thus, as we think, kept our literature in a state of imbecility, or rather tinctured it with a vain and presumptuous spirit, not unlike that of a young and ignorant pedagogue. Nothing seems at present to be in the way of our gradually taking a rank in the scale of literary nations, but our avarice; and the extraordinary opportunities we have had of making money, as it is termed, are at least some apology for our immoderate love of gain. This is the sin which most easily besets us, and debases much of the native generosity of literature. . . .

From what we have said, it will perhaps be perceived that the inquiries we shall make into former American publications will relate chiefly to works of literature and scholarship. We shall not, however, entirely neglect works relating to this country, though published in Europe, by men who have lived or travelled among us. We are sensible that we shall find much difficulty in procuring many books, whose titles and merit we know; and we particularly solicit printers, antiquaries, and men interested in the literature of this country to furnish us with curious information and with curious works. One of the objects of the Athenaeum, which has been so liberally established in this town, is gradually to collect all the American works of merit into one grand and accessible repository, and we now formally renew the promise, which we have formerly made, that any books sent to us for review, whether old or new, shall be faithfully deposited there. The time we hope is not far distant when this town shall possess an institution, and a library, which need not shrink from a comparison with any in this country, and be worthy of commendation even in Europe. The spirit of literary encouragement seems to be at last awakened among us, and it is not too late to redeem our character. We can never in this country possess many of the luxuries of the fine arts, but we may learn to enjoy the more refined and loftier elegancies of literature and taste. These can never be entirely debased by sensuality, never can be completely pressed into the cause of corruption. God grant that our expectations may not be disappointed, for we think we discern the dawn of better days. *"Novus saeclorum nascitur ordo."*

—V (January, 1808), 54-57

The Reviewer as Executioner

ANONYMOUS

THE NUMEROUS REVOLUTIONS and extensive improvements in the various sciences, the facility of multiplying copies of books by the art of printing, the brevity of life, and its necessary duties and avocations, preclude even the most diligent and laborious student from the perusal but of a small portion of the innumerable books, daily issuing from the press. Knox observes, "There were probably as many books, and perhaps as many bad books, written by the ancients, as the moderns; but the art of printing being unknown, and consequently the multiplication and preservation of books being attended with great trouble and expense, such as were of little intrinsick value were not transcribed, copies of them were not increased, and they consequently soon perished by the depredations of time." [26]

Since books are so excessively multiplied, it is our duty to destroy useless, unnecessary, and pernicious productions, as the ancient Grecians exposed their most puny and imbecile offspring to perish. Therefore the office of a reviewer is in the republick of letters as beneficial and necessary, though as odious and unpleasant, as that of an executioner in the civil state. They are the porters at the gates of the temple of Fame, and should be as blind and inexorable as Justice, which, " in its punishments, rather seems to submit to a necessity, than to make a choice."

Authors who, by plausible professions and false pretensions defraud the publick of money, dissipate valuable time, and insidiously rifle them of their good principles, are enemies of their kind, and merit the thong of chastisement and the knout of criticism; and he that undertakes the task of analyzing their works, displaying their beauties, and exposing their wicked arts, confers a favour on the publick. Harmless and obscure writers in their prefaces frequently supplicate the candour of readers by observing that their hasty productions will not injure, if they do not benefit mankind. But voluntary trifling with the publick is criminal; and lenity to the former is cruelty to the latter. In estimating the merit or demerit of literary productions, the motives and circumstances of the author constitute no justification; they must be considered abstractedly, for the republick of letters is not a state of moral probation. Bloomfield, Phillis Wheatly,[27] and many others in humble life have attracted some attention by their writings, not because they are excellent, but because they are extraordinary; as Dr. Johnson observed that dogs by art and labour taught to dance are noticed, not because they dance with ease and grace, but because they *dance at all.* Sound intellect and real erudition ought not to exempt from the lash of

[26] Vicesimus Knox (1752–1821), scholar, preacher, essayist, imitator of Johnson, was known for his *Elegant Extracts.*

[27] Robert Bloomfield (1766–1823), an English poet of humble origins, gained considerable notoriety for his work entitled *The Farmer's Boy.* Phillis Wheatly (1753?–1784), a Negro poet, was a slave who belonged to the Boston merchant John Wheatly. Her volume entitled *Poems on Various Subjects* (1773) contains poems which are derivate and weak in quality.

severe criticism those who intrude their works on the public; for in the literary commonwealth there is no hospital for the reception of mendicant vagabonds, no Bedlam for insanity and frenzy, no Magdalen for impunity and defilement, and no Lazaretto for lame and hobbling authors. Therefore a large portion of the multitude of publications are at their birth ripe for extinction; and may be sentenced, as Clarence in his troubled dream fancied he was addressed by an angry spirit, " *Seize him, Furies, take him to your torments.*"

—IV (February, 1807), 84-85

The Polity of Letters

JOSEPH STEVENS BUCKMINSTER

Darent operam censores, ne quid respublica (literarum) detrimenti caperet.—Sall. Cat.[28]

So LITTLE HAVE the writers of our country been accustomed to the rigour of a critical tribunal that to secure a comfortable seat in some of the out-houses belonging to the temple of fame nothing has been hitherto necessary but the resolution to write,

---

[28] Buckminster is playing upon a passage from Sallust. The entire passage from Sallust, as translated by J. C. Rolfe in his *Sallust* (London, 1920), 49-50, is as follows: " When these events were reported to Cicero, he was greatly disturbed by the twofold peril, since he could no longer by his unaided efforts protect the city against these plots, nor gain any exact information as to the size and purpose of Manlius's army; he therefore formally called the attention of the senate to the matter, which had already been the subject of popular gossip. Thereupon, as is often done in a dangerous emergency, the senate voted ' that the consuls should take heed that the commonwealth suffer no harm.' The power which according to Roman usage is thus conferred upon a magistrate by the senate is supreme, allowing him to raise an army, wage war, exert any kind of compulsion upon allies and citizens, and exercise unlimited command and jurisdiction at home and in the field; otherwise the consul has none of these privileges except by order of the people." Buckminster's alteration of the Roman

and the folly to publish. While, however, the same models of excellence are accessible, the same laws of taste are promulgated, and the same language is vernacular on both sides of the Atlantick, I know not why the sentences of criticism should not be executed in all their rigour on these western shores; or why the majesty of the republick of letters should be insulted with impunity in the remotest provinces of the empire. Every man of reading, who has watched the jealous spirit of the times, must have observed that whenever an American work is censured in the journals of British criticism, their judgment is attributed to some unextinguished remains of national animosity; and when a critick among ourselves has sometimes ventured to speak in a tone of authority, he has been set down for a conceited imitator of foreign impertinence. So rare have been the instances among us of a manly and unprejudiced criticism that to point out the faults of a living author, instead of making him grateful, only makes him mad; and he discovers all the fury which is felt by an antiquated belle when her little niece unluckily espies a gray hair among the sable honours of her head, and innocently presumes to pull out the intruder.

So imperfectly has the right of criticism been attended to among us that many a sober citizen, I doubt not, is unable to distinguish between the privilege of finding fault with an author, and the wickedness of publishing a defamatory libel. But in truth this right of literary censure is bestowed upon the critick by the author himself. Every man who publishes virtually offers a challenge to the publick, or at least courts their decision. By claiming praise, he runs the hazard of censure; and they, in whose power it is to confer the one, have undoubtedly a right to administer the other. " S'ils veulent avoir en nous des admirateurs, il faut qu'ils nous permettent d'oser etre leurs juges," says the charming La Harpe, in the introduction to his *Lycaeum*. But if we have a right to judge, we must have also a right to laugh;

---

provision conferring dictatorial powers in a time of emergency (" darent operam consules ne quid res publica detrimenti caperet ") reads "that the censors should take heed that the literary commonwealth suffer no harm." In this connection, see Lewis P. Simpson, " Federalism and the Crisis of Literary Order," *American Literature*, XXXII (November, 1960), 253-66.

for nothing can compel us to read with gravity in print what would have convulsed us with merriment if we had heard it in conversation. If indeed we laugh at what is not laughable, or applaud what is not commendable, or hiss at what is not absurd, we run the common hazard of a critick in the pit when he has clapped in the wrong place and is sufficiently disgraced by finding himself alone.

It is plainly no violation of the laws of literary courtesy to hold up dullness and absurdity to the derision of the publick; for it has long since been tacitly agreed that if an author has a right to be dull, the critick has a right to be severe. Common equity declares that one side ought not to claim a monopoly of privileges. Nothing but the immunity of satirical criticism can impose the slightest restraint on the vanity of authorship. By ridicule too, the taste of the publick is insensibly corrected and refined; for many who have no time to listen to a reason are always ready to join in a laugh; and thousands who understand nothing of the principles of taste can see an absurdity when exposed by another. How far it is lawful to distress an author by ridicule or censure without transgressing the laws of Christian benevolence, I am not casuist enough to determine. I will give you the opinion of the greatest master of moral science, as well of literary discussion, which the last age produced. "As it very seldom happens, that the rage of extemporary criticism inflicts fatal or lasting wounds, I know not that the laws of benevolence entitle this distress to much sympathy. The diversion of baiting an author has the sanction of all ages and nations, and is more lawful than the sport of teizing other animals, because, for the most part, he comes voluntarily to the stake, furnished, as he imagines, by the patron powers of literature, with resistless weapons and impenetrable armour, with the mail of the boar of Erymanth, and the paws of the lion of Nemea." (Johnson's *Rambler*, No. 176.)

Authors boldly encounter the silent neglect of the publick, and at the same time complain of the opinion of an individual, and imagine themselves outraged by the censure of a reviewer. While they see with much composure their favourite productions quietly devoured by the moths, those merciless reviewers, who have no more respect for a polished than for a clumsy period, and make as hearty a meal upon a genius as upon a dunce; they will take instant offence at a critick, who presumes to separate in their works the dry from the nutritious, who accidentally makes a wry face at what is nauseous, or involuntarily rejects what is insipid. It is a common trick of incensed authors to rail against reviewers as men who have impudently set themselves up as guardians of publick taste, or rather as a band of literary executioners. Indeed there is some show of reason in the complaint that anonymous reviews are an unjust assumption of authority, because they in some measure include the power of punishing, as well as of judging; which powers in every free state should be kept perfectly distinct. To explain this anomaly I will attempt to give you some hints which I have gathered from Bayle, who was long a dictator in the republick of letters.

The commonwealth of learning is the only permanent example of pure and original democracy. In this state, under the protection of truth and reason, whose authority alone is acknowledged, wars may be carried on with the utmost innocence, though not always with impunity; for here every man is sovereign, and every man also under the jurisdiction of every other. The laws of *civil society* have in no degree abridged the independence of the state of nature as to errour and ignorance. No man can be excluded by the social compact from his unalienable right to be a fool; and, on the other side, every man retains the right of the sword and may exercise it without a commission. "If it is asked," says Bayle, "why the civil authority should leave every one at liberty to expose the mistakes and follies of authors, it may be answered that to criticise a book tends only to show that the author does not possess a certain degree of knowledge or of talent. Now, as an author may enjoy all the rights and privileges of the community in which he lives, notwithstanding this defect of knowledge and of talent; and as his reputation as an honest man and a good subject of the commonwealth does not receive by it the least blemish, it is evident no usurpation is made on the majesty of the state by showing to the publick the faults of a book." (Bayle's Dict. art. *Catius*. Note D.)[29]

[29] The reference is to Pierre Bayle's *Dictionnaire historique et critique*,

If then the correlative rights of publishing and of censuring nonsense remain alike unimpaired by the conventions and established by the immemorial customs of society, it follows that if every writer of a book may publish anonymously, the writer of a review cannot be compelled to declare himself; and as the object of criticism is not persons, but works, there is no cowardice in this concealment. There is nothing dishonourable in firing at a senseless mark out of an ambush, or from behind a tree.

It will perhaps be esteemed a more difficult task to maintain the expediency than to establish the right of critical severity in the present state of American literature. It will be said that our country is young, and therefore her infantile productions in the field of letters deserve rather to be cherished by the gentle and perfumed gales of flattery than to be checked by the chills of neglect, or beaten down by the blasts of angry criticism. It will be said that our most able minds will continue to shun the dangers of authorship if every thing which issues from the press must be subjected to the unrelenting severity of anonymous remark. But is he a friend to the literature of his country who wishes to excuse it from examination? Does he think that the easy multiplication of feeble works will eventually establish a solid basis for our future fame? No: the everlasting oaks of our forests were not raised in a hot-house. The indulgent remarks of candid friends, the simpering smiles of kitchen-criticks, the puffing advertisements of newspapers, and the lullaby strains of poetasters, will never patronize the growth of solid learning, nor confer immortality on the authors of our country. We have yet to

---

the article on Catius, footnote D. Apparently the translation is Buckminster's. At least it does not follow the one in the English translation of the *Dictionnaire*. According to the auction catalogue of his library (Boston, 1812), Buckminster possessed the English version (London, 1734) but not the French. He did have in French the *Oeuvres de P. Bayle, contenant tout ce qu'il a publié en théologie, philosophie, critique, histoire et littérature, excepte son Dictionnaire* (The Hague, 1727). It seems odd that he did not purchase the famous *Dictionnaire* in the French version when he was buying his library during a journey abroad in 1807. His command of French was excellent, and he purchased many French works in the original. Of course the auction catalogue is not an infallible guide to the books he possessed in what was one of the largest personal libraries in New England at the time.

learn that to write correctly and to think sensibly ought to be made inseparable habits; if then when a poet is a dunce, we say that he is a genius; when an orator talks fustian, we say that he is eloquent; when a writer is solecistical, we say that he is a little inaccurate; or when a book is composed in a Babylonish dialect, we excuse it because it is American, we are only feeding children with sweetmeats, or wrapping them up warm against the cold, and thus laying the foundations of perpetual vanity, imbecility, and idiotism.

The earliest reviews which appeared in Europe were undoubtedly the most gentle in their animadversions. It is true also that they were recommended by some of the most celebrated names, which the annals of literature can furnish. Bayle, LeClerc, Basnage, and S'Gravesande did not disdain to be editors of literary journals. But the first has always been censured for the encomiastick strain of his remarks and the others commonly restricted themselves, except where their peculiar prejudices were concerned, to bare analyses of the works, which they announced.[30] Since that time the state of the republick of letters has essentially altered. Then the literature of Europe was just awaking from its long repose in the cloisters of monks, and the legends of popish superstition. The liberty to think and the disposition to write demanded every stimulus and every encouragement. Now the licentiousness of the press has become a greater evil than its inactivity, and instances of superfetation are more frequent than of sterility. Then the laws of fine writing were imperfectly established, and rarely understood; now they are or ought to be familiar to school boys and abecedarians. Then the method of conducting literary journals was to be ascertained by experiment, and an author was to be flattered into a quiet acknowledgment of their privileges; now every candidate for fame has it in his power to consult innumerable precedents,

[30] The vogue of the European literary and learned journals began with Pierre Bayle's *Nouvelles de la république des lettres* (Amsterdam, 1684–1687). Henri Basnage (1665–1710) continued Bayle's work in the *Histoire des ouvrages des savans* (Amsterdam, 1687–1709). Meanwhile Jean Le Clerc (1657–1736) got out the *Bibliothèque universelle et historique* (Amsterdam, 1686–1693). Willem Jacob Van S'Gravesande (1688–1742) had a hand in the *Bibliothèque raisonnée des ouvrages des savans de l'Europe* (The Hague, 1728–1751).

statutes, and declarations of criticism by which the verdict of the publick and the sentence of the reviewer may be previously and probably conjectured. Then authorship had not become a trade; plagiarism was not practised with unblushing effrontery; nor were the scraps of every author's scrutoire swept out upon the publick; now every starvling pedant writes for bread, and all that is necessary to constitute an author is the industry to borrow or to steal materials till he is able to swell out a volume. In such a state of things it is not enough that a review contains an analysis of a work, for some works defy analysis; neither is it enough correctly to state the subjects of a book, for that might be done by transcribing the table of contents; but the faithful reviewer is daily called upon to detect literary thefts, to expose absurdities, to correct blunders, to check the contagion of false taste, to rescue the publick from the impositions of dullness, and to assert the majesty of learning and of truth.

In stating these lofty pretensions of the critick, we had almost forgotten the claims of the author. If I am asked, what redress can an author obtain who has been ignorantly criticised, or unmercifully castigated, I answer the redress of an author, who deserves any, will always be found in the ultimate decision of the publick. " The satire of Pope," says Johnson, " which brought Theobald and Moore into contempt, dropped impotent from Bentley, like the javelin of Priam." Besides, the name of an author will always command more intrinsick respect than that of a critick. The former naturally takes rank of the latter in the ceremonial of literature. It requires less ability to detect faults than to avoid them; but even if it were not so, the author should remember that he forever retains the right of primogeniture, and the advantage of pre-occupying the attention of the publick; and while authors may exist without criticks, the latter cannot maintain themselves a moment if writers should withhold the customary prey.

As to the herd of vain and disappointed authors I have long perplexed myself to find a remedy for their chagrin. I can recommend no better mode of avenging themselves on the criticks and on the publick than by obstinately refusing to publish any more. . . .

—III (January, 1806), 19-23

With Literature as with Government

THEODORE DEHON

It has been remarked, and we fear there is too much foundation for the remark, that the passion for wealth, and the ardour of political contention, which are, perhaps, the predominant traits in the character of our countrymen, have retarded the ascendancy of genius, and obstructed the progress of letters.[31] Wealth, which gives leisure and which procures the finest models of art, and the best copies of ancient authors; which promotes the intercourse and facilitates the researches of the learned, is unquestionably favourable to the interests of literature. But when it is the absorbing passion of a people, when it is pursued only for itself, and the extent of possessions is the measure both of merit and influence, there will be little emulation of superiour attainments. The soul, intent upon the acquisition of sordid wealth, as the only means of power and distinction, will have for intellectual pursuits neither time or regard.

"Fervet avaritia miseroque cupidine pectus."

In like manner, that open discussion of publick measures, and equal access to publick honours, which are the privileges of a free people, are not unfriendly to the development of genius, and interests of learning. But there is a warmth of contention in which the just claims of talents and wisdom are disregarded; and confidence, honour, and publick employment are bestowed, not upon the sage and hero, not upon the ingenious and learned, but upon the subtle leaders of the successful party, or the wretched minions of unprincipled power. In each of these cases there is a deadly chill upon the exertions of superiour minds.

[31] Theodore Dehon delivered this address at the annual Phi Beta Kappa exercises at Harvard on August 27, 1807.

The Muses in disgust retire to their groves, and their votaries, disheartened, hang up their harps upon the trees that are therein.

Shall we be pardoned the expression, if we further observe, that through the innovating spirit of the times the *republick* of letters may have its dignity and prosperity endangered by sliding inadvertently into a *democracy?* We have heard the time lamented as lost which students, who would attain to legitimate honours, are compelled to spend in the retired walks of ancient learning. In this sagacious and prolifick age men have discovered better models than the Iliad and the Aeneid, and better instructors than Cicero and Quinctilian. A Bloomfield has sung from his bench, and what is the advantage of a toilsome acquaintance with languages, that are dead! The Indian is eloquent by the force of nature, and where is the necessity of models and laws! Much to be deprecated is the spread of these wild sentiments which, like the irruption of the barbarians upon the civil world, would overturn all that is great and beautiful in the walks of literature, and leave in their stead the barrenness of desolation, or the uncouth productions of ignorance and rudeness. Let it be remembered that whatever there is of correct criticism and taste in the world is to be traced to the recovery of the classicks from obscurity and corruption. In the study of these commenced the revival of letters and the liberation and improvement of the human mind. These masters of antiquity were conducted to the Castalian fount by the Goddesses of the spring themselves. Let us discourse with them of the way; and not disdain to follow their steps, when we are witnesses of their immortality. It is with literature as with government. Neither is a subject of perpetual experiment. The principles of both are fixed. They spring from sources and have relations which are unchangeable and eternal. If men will despise the principles and rules which are founded in nature, if they will disregard the models which time has proved and hallowed, if they will be irregular in their literary appetites, and arrogant in their designs, what wonder if they should be often left by the justice of Olympus to delight themselves on the bosom of a cloud, and the world of letters should be overrun with Centaurs?

Ignorance, or corruption, in the very important tribunals of criticism, would unquestionably impede the progress and diminish the reputation of American literature. If those should be permitted to erect themselves into literary censors whom the divinities of Helicon have not anointed, nor deep and thorough acquaintance with ancient authorities and established principles prepared; if indolence, friendship, or political partiality should pervert the judgment of our literary courts, and affix the seal of unqualified approbation to works of small or questionable merit; if proficients in the arts, and professors of learning, in giving their opinion upon the productions of the day, suffer their minds to be prejudiced by the clamour of the moment, and learn of the multitude what to admire, instead of teaching them what is admirable, who can anticipate all the consequences? The publick taste would be vitiated. There would be herds of imitators of the false excellencies to which corrupt criticism had given currency. And instead of having our admiration excited, and our attention fixed by distinct and splendid greatness, we should be obligated to turn away, wearied and confused, from the multifarious glitter of countless ephemeral productions.

Here let us be permitted to remark the importance of an able and judicious management of periodical publications. These miscellanies may undoubtedly have a considerable influence upon the literature of a people. In the hands of such men as Addison and Johnson, Goldsmith and Steele, they confounded absurdity and rectified opinion; they roused attention and engaged it in the service of the Muses; and formed and refined the publick taste. Very great, we are persuaded, would be the advantage to the literature of our country, if the meritorious editors of these works were enabled by the generous patronage of the rich, and the liberal contributions of the learned, so to conduct them that Minerva would not blush to find her image in the frontispiece; and the streams, which are conveyed by them into the circles of the fashionable and the closets of the studious, might be brought, under her direction, from the fountains of Ilyssus.

America in the freedom of her government, the face of her territory, the native powers of her citizens, the toleration, which subjects no reasonable efforts of the mind to penalty or dismay, and the rich capital of England's learning, which community of language enables her with facility to use as her own, has certainly opportunity and inducements to vie with any nation upon the earth in the pursuit of literary distinction. . . .

—IV (September, 1807), 471-73

Greek Literature: Criterion of Learning

JOHN SYLVESTER JOHN GARDINER (?)

EVERY MAN, SAYS Dr. Johnson, now-a-days gets as much Greek as he can. In this country, I fear, we are less skilled in ancient lore than before the revolution. The death of George II was mourned, and George III congratulated on his accession in Greek odes, of which, it is feared, we now hardly know the construction. The war not only interrupted the studies of the learned, but in some degree unfitted the nation for such pursuits. *Inter arma silent leges, inter arma vacat academia.* We have indeed reasons for hoping that the incapacity is only temporary, yet sad would be the task to expose to foreigners the whole state of literature among us. Our colleges, to be sure, are crowded; but the number of them is prejudicial to real learning, for their endowments are too niggardly to support instructors: academick honours are too easily acquired, and our youth learn to despise them: and of all our commodities, scholarship, though the most rare, bears the lowest price in the market.

In so little repute was the study of Greek literature not long since holden that the boys at one of our universities by glorying in their ignorance of it have disgraced the proud name of their mother, from whom they expected a rank and title in the world of letters; and at another have erased, as far as their power could go, every vestige of that unsightly alphabet.[32]

---

[32] The author, undoubtedly John Sylvester John Gardiner, refers apparently in one instance to the anti-classical rebellion staged at Yale by the

But within a few years we have exhibited some signs of awaking from our long trance. The language of Rome is now considered with respect, if not studied with fervour; and the nation, to whom Rome owed her letters and her arts, will, we hope, ere long vindicate her intellectual supremacy in our country. Let us remember, that, as the use of gold and silver coin are the surest criterion of civilization, Greek literature supplies the best proof of a people's advancement in learning.

—IV (December, 1807), 656

George Crabbe, Arcadians, and Quinnabaugs

ALEXANDER H. EVERETT

THE FIRST OFFICE of poetry was to dress natural objects in alluring colours; to heighten the charm of truth and virtue by a pleasing representation. The natural tendency of this powerful machine is to abuse and perversion. . . . To the shame of man it must be confessed that poetry has been employed to inflame passion and blind understanding, at least as many times as for purposes of innocent delight and manly inspiration. . . .

The false representations of real life, which the author of these poems has endeavoured to overthrow, are, it must be allowed, apparently among the most harmless. There have always been those that pleased themselves with the descriptions of Arcadias, and the amours of Phillises and Strephons; in whom it argues an admirable wakefulness and vivacity that they were able to endure the influence of such powerful opiates. Now and then such a man as Florian or Gesner undertakes to revive the thing at the present

---

Connecticut Wits. The other instance is uncertain. Among the Anthologists the most vigorous opponent of the classical curriculum was Edmund Trowbridge Dana. See "The Winter of Criticism," pp. 206-10.

day; and by throwing it into a new light, and mingling with it a large share of known facts and interesting circumstances, gives it some interest; but of late years, generally speaking, more especially among us of English blood, who were always an up and down people, not given to loquaciousness, or fond of frippery, the pastoral writing has been altogether on the wane. It is possible, that, as commerce is at present very unpopular, this country may be the theatre where Tityrus is destined to uplift his drooping head. It has long been by implication, and perhaps may in time be directly a plan of our publick policy, to people our interiour woods and mountains with shepherds and shepherdesses, and they will probably call for a new edition of Sir Philip Sidney's *Arcadia*, and the *Gentle Shepherd*. The present names of our rivers and mountains will be a great obstacle to the application of these ideas to our native scenes. The aborigines of this country were a very unpastoral people; they made their dear Dulcineas plant maize and grind it for them; and they did not value it a beaver's tongue whether the name they gave their village was a dactyl, or a spondee, or neither. Horace found one name so unwieldy that he could not manage it; and a rural poet would here meet the Connecticuts and Quinnabaugs at every turn, not to mention now and then a Chargoggagogmanchoggagog. To return from this short digression, mistaken pictures of rural life are originally harmless; but they connect themselves in the issue with many other kinds of deception. Besides, the infection is spread perhaps further than we are aware. We observe and ridicule the extreme absurdities of the picture; but associated as they are with the classick authors of youth, we do not perhaps all know, till we reflect, how strongly the general notions of rural quiet and felicity are fixed in our minds.

Nothing can be better adapted to remove any favourable bias for these sylvan scenes than Mr. Crabbe's representations. All the principal poems in this collection exhibit pictures of village manners, of village loves and enjoyments, that certainly, applied to this country, surpass the real misery of natural low life. Hence their tenor is cheerless and mournful. Rejecting all petty ornaments, and even disregarding in some measure, the sing song mellifluous chime that is the boast of the meanest poetaster, the author aims at strong thought and nervous expression. These are beauties that will last beyond the passing fashion, or even the changing dialect. . . .

—VI (January, 1809), 57-58

Pope: Poet of the Human Species

JOHN SYLVESTER JOHN GARDINER (?)

IT HAS BEEN the fashion of late years to depreciate the poetical merit of Pope, and to exalt, in strains of lavish encomium, the mushroom poetasters of the day. A writer, who with the rapidity of a Blackmore, shall finish an epick in six weeks, attracts the admiration of many, who consider celerity in writing as a proof of extraordinary genius. The reverse of this however is true; and the greatest masterpieces of writing, far from being dashed off at a hit, have consumed a very considerable portion of time in their composition. Perfection is the reward of great labour, united with great genius. The co-operation of both can alone ensure success. Without genius, labour would be dull and insipid; without labour, genius would be absurd and extravagant. Had the *Alcander* of Pope, an epick poem which he wrote at sixteen, been preserved, he would probably have been deemed a great poet by those who now dispute his claims to that character. These gentlemen require originality at the expense of whatever absurdity. They prefer the wilderness to the garden, though the latter may possess all the beauties of nature, without her deformities. But true taste admires nature only in her charms, not in the gross. Neither poet nor painter would describe a quagmire, nor expose to view those parts of the person which decency clothes. Yet nature has claims as equal to what is concealed, as to what is exhibited.

True wit is nature to advantage drest,

not a ragged gypsy, nor a tawdry strumpet. High, masterly execution is what constitutes a preeminent writer. He exhibits the best thoughts, exprest in the best manner. When he borrows, he improves; what he imitates, he excels. He commands a certain felicity of style, which, though simple, is highly figurative, which convinces by its energy, and charms by its beauty. Of all the ancient poets Pope most resembles Virgil. He has the same correctness, the same majesty of numbers, allowing for the inferiority of a modern language. There is scarcely a page of Virgil, his *Georgics* excepted, in which we cannot trace him imitating or translating whole passages from other writers, so that he has fewer pretensions to originality than almost any poet ancient or modern. And yet what ancient author is so universally read, or affords so much pleasure, Horace perhaps excepted? Pope has more originality than Virgil, but less than Dryden. Yet who reads more of Dryden than a single satire and a single ode? Pope is the poet of the human species, the favourite of all ages, the oracle of all professions. Originality! Fiddledy diddledy! [33]

—III (January, 1806), 15-16

Pope and Natural Genius

ARTHUR MAYNARD WALTER

ORIGINAL GENIUS IS seldom discoverable in the compositions of Pope. His page is irradiated by little of that mysterious light, which is generated by this unknown power. Taste, judgment, and sense, predominate in his works; but in vain do we seek for

[33] Agnes Marie Sibley in *Alexander Pope's Prestige in America, 1725–1835* (New York, 1949), 101, ascribes this comment unqualifiedly to John Sylvester John Gardiner but does not cite the source of her ascription. The marked files used in compiling the list of authors appended to the Anthology Society's *Journal* do not show the authorship of this particular selection. However, it is almost certainly Gardiner's work.

the creative energies of invention, the sublime soarings of thought, and the audacious struggles of imagination, bursting from the confinement of reason. In the translation of Homer, there is splendour of verse; in his satires, acuteness of remark; in the art of criticism, ingenuity and knowledge; in the "Rape of the Lock," playfulness and delicacy of fancy; in the "Windsor Forest," beauty of just description; and in the epistle of "Eloïsa to Abelard," a dignity of diction, a selection of images, and a gloominess of thought, which render it one of the most attractive, and therefore most dangerously licentious poems in the circle of literature.

From the manner in which Dr. Johnson closes the life of Pope, it is reasonably believed, that there had been a serious doubt, whether the latter was a poet. Johnson indeed, in his usual and admirable tone of decision, scoffs at the doubt and pronounces in the affirmative. But if I reverence Johnson, I love truth more. . . . If the word "poet" be taken in its usually accepted sense, the English criticks, Warburton, Warton, and Wakefield, after great diligence of examination and extensive aggregation of commentary, assisted by taste and guided by judgment, have decided the question; and it may be now a source of surprise, that it should ever have been agitated. But if to the ordinary qualities of a poet it be essential that genius should be added, such as Longinus felt, but could not define; if this power be the essence of poetry, without which it cannot exist, as caloric is the substratum of animal life, on which its nature depends; a short examination may shew, that Pope's writings are not impressed with this character; and therefore he must lose part of the renown which he has too long enjoyed, and the blaze of glory, which encircles his name, will be diminshed in extent and efflulgence.

I need not refer to the Greek original of "poet" to prove that it signifies a maker; not merely a constructor of verses, but an inventor; and thus Dryden says, "If a poet is not a maker, he has little right to the title." He must be endowed with a power of creation: and though he may arrange his words in symphony and his syllables in cadence, yet if they are not alive with imagination, there is no more real poetry in them than there was musick in Memnon's statue when the morning rays of the god of fire darted not their mystick potency. Genius is derived primarily from another Greek word, which signifies to generate, to beget, to cause to be; and it is itself that inventive ability, that creative power, which is the establishing criterion of poetry. The Greeks and Romans believed, that it must be natural; that it could not be acquired; that it in fact was, or at least possessed as evidence of its existence, a divine spirit, a kind of fury, a madness, and enthusiasm. . . .

It appears then from etymology and from the determinations of great authorities that in the country of Aeschylus and Pindar, of Lucretius and Lucan, a poet, to be great, must be endowed with a creative power, must be animated by a holy inspiration, and roused to "words that burn, by thoughts that breathe." Genius rejoices in nothing vulgar or common. It is exercised about novelty and invention. It is ever attended by a bold and ardent imagination. It delights to discover new properties in mind and to form new arrangements in matter. The intellectual world is a complete slave to its dominion. . . .

If Pope be considered as possessing original genius, the evidence of his creative energy is to be found in "The Rape of the Lock." His advocates point out this from among his numerous works, as demonstrating the greatest powers of imagination. No one can deny the singular beauties of description and the gloomy scenes of cloistered love exhibited in the epistle of Eloisa, and I should be sorry not to feel the tenderness of the "Elegy to the Memory of an Unfortunate Lady." Yet neither on these, nor on any other of his poems, does the candid defender of Pope lay the solid foundation of his claim to originality, but rests it on the machinery and modes of acting, displayed in the "Rape of the Lock." As to the machinery, Johnson acknowledges that it is not Pope's invention and Warton shews that he found it in the Compte de Gabalis. Indeed the same aerial beings, with different names and characters, may be observed in Shakespeare's *Midsummer Night's Dream*; they existed traditionally in the days of Spenser, and are mentioned in various poets of that age, now not generally known. A little race of similar beings, who sleep on the airspider's web and travel on moon-beams, is still said to exist among them by the inhabitants of a certain English county, remote from the capital, the name of which I do not recollect; and there is little doubt that a curious inquirer by the aid of poetical archaeology might trace the history of these diminutive intelligences back to the age of chivalry; and, together with the dragons, enchanters, and griffins of Ariosto and king Arthur, their numerous and perplexed migrations might be tracked through Europe, and part of Africa and of Asia, till the travelling searcher arrives in Persia, where the Farries, under the eastern name of Peris, Paris, or Perses, have long had their aerial courts and gambolled in invisible diversions. The machinery of the "Rape of the Lock" is not therefore of Pope's invention. He found the beings already existing and only gave them new occupations in a humorous scene of domestick life. Before they lurked in flowers or roved in woods, but now Pope has introduced them into the parlours and assigned them the care of the toilet or card table. This discovers ingenuity. Their names, their duties, their conduct, and sentiments, are testimonies of delicate thought and mature judgment. He has thus, on a trivial incident, with appropriate materials made a most agreeable mock epick. Throughout the whole poem fine taste, pleasant satire, and nice humour predominate. It is therefore one of the most exquisite little productions in the English language, and certainly equals and perhaps surpasses the celebrated "Lutrin" of Boileau, notwithstanding the criticism of La Harpe to the contrary. Yet after admiring its excellence, it seems to me the effort of taste and delicacy, and not of strong, operative imagination. It appears an easy task for a mind, like Pope's, to write a composition of this nature after the materials were prepared. He commanded the whole flock of English words; his judgment was able to combine them in harmonious diction, and his taste was eminent in embellishing the effect of his judgment. The machinery was ready and the incidents were known. His playful mood delicately suggested that the facts should be superintended by fairies, with new names and new modes of operation. From this short analysis it seems to me, that the peculiar and acknowledged faculties of Pope's mind under such circumstances might easily have produced such a performance without the intervention of original genius. In the whole work a creator and true inventor are not discovered; there is little of real generative power, and nothing of poetick enthusiasm. The appellations of the Sylphs and Gnomes were new and appropriate, but the making of simple names is the work of ordinary minds; the conduct of the beings is new, but was fancied without much difficulty, and performed without much labour.

Such are the reasons for a belief that Pope was not endowed with great natural genius. I know not that they are good or satisfactory, but they are impartially written, as they were impartially acquired after considerable reflection. I know not that the publick will care for them, for I know not that the publick will read. But if any arguments are to convince us, that for the " Rape of the Lock," as a whole, however remarkable for taste, humour, and diction, Pope is to be considered as having a mind, fertile of invention and bursting with greatness of thought, the same process of ratiocination must decide that Homer would have been honoured with the same titles if he had shewn no other evidence of superiority than making his divinities superintend the operations of war; and similar reasons must immortalize the cold and creeping enthusiasm of Darwin, who, in verse of " sounding brass and tinkling cymbal," has caused the gnomes and sylphs of Rosicrusian mystery to guide the tender loves of the plants and direct the course and influence of the principles and elements of nature.[34]

—II (May, 1805), 235-38

Poetry Above Reason: the Case of Gray

JOSEPH STEVENS BUCKMINSTER

IT HAS BEEN the fortune of Gray, as well as of other poets of the first order, to suffer by the ignorance and the envy of

---

[34] Among other works, Erasmus Darwin (1731–1802), grandfather of Charles Darwin, composed two poetic treatises: *The Botanic Garden* and *The Temple of Nature, or the Origin of Society.* The reference here is to " The Loves of the Plants," the second part of *The Botanic Garden.*

contemporaries, and at last to obtain from posterity, amid the clamours of discordant criticism, only a divided suffrage. The coldness of his first reception by the public has, however, been more than compensated by the warmth of his real admirers; for he is one of those poets who at every new reading recompenses you double for every encomium by disclosing some new charm of sentiment or of diction. The many who have ignorantly or reluctantly praised may learn as they study him that they have nothing to retract; and those who have delighted to depreciate his excellence will understand, if they ever learn to admire him, that their former insensibility was pardonable. . . . Gray was not destitute of these anticipations of future fame which God has sometimes granted to neglected genius. . . . He knew that it was not of much consequence to be neglected by that publick . . . which had to be told by Addison at the expiration of half a century of the merit of the *Paradise Lost*. Still less could his fame be endangered by Colman's exquisitely humorous parody of his odes. . .; and at the present day, I know not whether it would add anything to the final reputation of a lyrick poet to have been praised by that great man who could pronounce Dryden's ode on Mrs. Killigrew the finest in our language, and who could find nothing in Collins' but "clusters of consonants."

It appears to the Remarker that the whole controversy upon the subject of Gray's twin odes, which have been received with so much disdain, and so much enthusiasm, rests upon this single question, is there such a description of poetry as the lyrick? [35] There are many whose taste in one kind of composition is highly polished who yet remain entirely insensible to the merit of any other. One man is bigotted to didactick poetry, another to descriptive; one likes nothing but reason, another admires nothing but wit; one looks out for the colours of a picturesque fancy, another can never dispense with the melody of versification. Thousands can be made to feel no perfection, but such as

[35] The controversy over Gray's twin odes began shortly after the publication of the "Progress of Poesy" and "The Bard" in 1757 in a single volume containing no other works. Those who condemned the poems charged that they contained obscure passages. Both Buckminster's argument and Gardiner's reply to it (pp. 201-205) appeared in the *Anthology*'s "Remarker" series.

they have been accustomed to admire in their favourite poets, and innumerable are the " word-catchers who live on syllables," men whom nothing but the grace of Apollo can exalt into the unaffected admirers of the enthusiasm and inspiration of his bards.

But if Gray has any claim to the character of a poet, he must hold an elevated rank or none. If he is not excellent he is supremely ridiculous; if he has not the living spirit of verse, he is only besotted and bewildered with the fumes of a vulgar and stupifying draught, which he found in some stagnant pool at the foot of Parnassus, and which he mistook for the Castalian spring. But if Pindar and Horace were poets, so too was Gray. The finest notes of their lyre were elicited by the breath of inspiration breathing on the strings; and he who cannot enter into the spirit which animates the first Pythian of Pindar, or the " *Quem virum aut heroa* " of Horace, must be content to be *shown* beauties in Gray, which it is not yet granted to him to feel, or spontaneously to discern. The Remarker is willing to rest the merit of Gray on Horace's definition of a poet—

> ingenium cui sit, cui mens divinior, atque es,
> Magna sonaturum, des nominis hujus honorem.

This comprehensive definition, even Pope, with all his good sense and satire, has not ventured to disdain; for " Eloïsa to Abelard " is an immortal commentary on these lines, and Horace is propitiated. Whoever will ponder well the meaning of this definition must acknowledge that there is a higher species of poetry than the mere language of reason. Spenser, Milton, and even Dryden knew this, and they studied successfully the Italian poets; but after the time of Dryden, our English poetry began to be formed too exclusively upon that of the French. The authority of Pope has been eminently useful; but the world is not yet persuaded that to be a poet it is always indispensable to write like Pope. Since his time, however, the lyrick powers of *our* language have been retrieved by Gray, Collins, Mason, and Warton; we have been saved from the elegant perfection of the school of Boileau, while the French poetry yet continues barren of the higher beauties of verse, correct without enthusiasm, and sensible without inspiration. When a man like Boileau, of a mind merely didactick, attempts the ode, he falls as he has done in that on the taking of Namur, into frigidity and bombast; or like Pope, when he contended with Dryden in the ode on St. Cecilia's day, " how do the tuneful *echoes* languish! " Racine, and Racine only, could have united that classical polish and spirit of exquisite combination, that touching pathos, and mysterious musick of verse which are requisite to the perfection of lyrick composition. But he has left us little of this kind, except the choruses in his tragedies, and in the judgment of Voltaire, he holds the first rank among their lyrick poets, surpassing even J. B. Rousseau, whom those, who understand French better than the Remarker, are content to admire.

We shall be more ready to admit that the sole perfection of poetry consists not merely in faithful description, fine sense, or pointed sentiment in polished verse, if we attend to some curious remarks of Burke, in the last part of his *Essay on the Sublime and Beautiful.* He has there sufficiently shown that many fine passages, which produce the most powerful effect on a sensible mind, present no ideas to the fancy which can be strictly marked or embodied. The most thrilling touches of sublimity and beauty are consistent with great indistinctness of images and conceptions. Indeed it is hardly to be believed, before making the experiment, that we should be so much affected as we are by passages which convey no definite picture to the mind. To those who are insensible to Gray's curious junction of phrases and hardy personifications, we recommend the study of this chapter of Burke. There they will see that the effect of poetical expression depends more upon particular and indefinable associations than upon the precise images which the words convey. Thus, of Gray's poetry the effect, like that of Milton's finest passages in the "Allegro" and " Penseroso," is to raise a glow, which it is not easy to describe; but the beauty of a passage, when we attempt to analyze it, seems to consist in a certain felicity of terms, fraught with pictures, which it is impossible to transfer with perfect exactness to the canvas. The following instance which occurs to me at present in the poetry of Gray, may explain my meaning. In describing the queen of the loves and graces, he says,

O'er her warm cheek and rising bosom move
The bloom of young desire, and purple light of love.

Here, we feel that no other expressions could have excited in the mind an emotion so vivid, though they might have conveyed an image more distinct.

The dissatisfaction with the poetry of Gray, arising from notions of poetry too confined, is not so common perhaps as that which results from the irregularity of the compositions. Many after reading them are tempted to ask, what is the subject of the piece or what the object of the writer? We have received an indistinct impression of something poetically beautiful but we want the regularity of the drama, the coherence of a canto, the bearings and dependencies of an epick leading to some definite conclusion; in short we want a beginning, a middle, and an end. But this results from the same insensibility to different forms of perfection in writing that suggested the criticism of the mathematician, who, after reading Homer, exclaimed "all this is very fine, but I do not find that he has proved anything!" If the perfection of poetry consists, as Aiken has defined it, in imparting every impression to the mind in the most exquisite degree; and the ode has by the consent of criticks in all ages been indulged in irregularities, which are not pardonable in other kinds of verse, because it is supposed to follow the rapid and unrestrained passage of images through the mind, it is surely enough to satisfy even Aristotle himself that in Gray's odes the subject is never entirely deserted, and that a continued succession of sublime or beautiful impressions is conveyed to the mind in language the most grateful to the ear, which our English tongue can furnish.[36] For my own part I take as much delight in contemplating the rich hues that succeed one another without order in a deep cloud in the west, which has no prescribed shape, as in viewing the seven colours of the rainbow disposed in a form exactly semi-circular. The truth is, that after having read any poem once, we recur to it afterwards not as a whole, but for the beauty of particular passages.

[36] John Aikin (1747–1822), physician and author, was the editor of an edition of British poets with critical and biographical prefaces.

It would be easy to reply in order to the invidious and contemptible criticisms of Johnson on particular passages in these odes, and to show their captious futility. This however has been frequently and successfully done. . . .

The obscurity, however, which is said to attend the whole of his two odes, is of more consequence than the difficulty of particular passages. In "The Bard," it may certainly be justified from the very nature of the subject. The language of prophecy is always indistinct, and the terrour of predictions is heightened by the half uttered intent of the prophet. If Gray in this ode presumed too much upon his readers' familiarity with English history, it is a misfortune which has retarded, but not prevented the perception of his excellence. As to the "Progress of Poesy," if you except the union of the simile and subject in the first stanza, I know of nothing which can long perplex an attentive and poetical reader. It should not be forgotten that every species of poetry has its peculiar character, and obviousness of meaning is not always an indispensable excellence.

The staleness of his morality, also, is an objection with those who forget that there are no discoveries to be made in ethicks. The truth is, that the most impressive maxims in common life are the most indisputable. They have always been the common property of poets, who have sufficiently attained their purpose, when they have given these common sentiments all the force and beauty of poetical expression. . . .

The distinguishing excellence of Gray's poetry, is, I think, to be found in the astonishing force and beauty of his epithets. In other poets, if you are endeavouring to recollect a passage, and find that a single word still eludes you, it is not impossible to supply it occasionally with something equivalent or superiour. But let any man attempt this in Gray's poetry, and he will find that he does not even approach the beauty of the original. Like the single window in Aladdin's palace, which the grand vizier undertook to finish with diamonds, equal to the rest, but found after a long trial, that he was not rich enough to furnish the jewels, nor ingenious enough to dispose them, so there are lines in Gray, which criticks and poets might labour forever to supply, and without success. . . .

Another characteristick of Gray, which, while it detracts something from his originality, increases the charm of his verse, is the
classical raciness of his diction. Milton is the only English poet
who rivals him in the remote learning of his allusions, and this
has greatly restrained the number of their admirers. . . .

The last perfection of verse in which Gray is unrivalled, is the
power of his numbers. These have an irresistible charm even
with those who understand not his meaning, and without this
musical enchantment, it is doubtful whether he would have sur-
mounted the ignorance and insensibility with which he was first
received. His rhythm and cadences afford a perpetual pleasure,
which, in the full contemplation of his other charms we sometimes forget to acknowledge. There is nothing surely in the
whole compass of English versification to be compared in musical
structure with the third stanza of his ode on the "Progress of
Poesy." The change of movement in the six last lines is inexpres-
sibly fine. The effect of these varied cadences and measures is,
to my ear at least, full as great as that of an Adagio in musick
immediately following a Rondo; and I admire in silent rapture
the genius of that man who could so mould our untractable
language as to produce all the effect of the great masters of
musical composition. If the ancient lyricks contain many specimens of numerous verse equal to this, we need no longer wonder
that they were always accompanied with musick. Poetry never
approached nearer to painting than verse does in this stanza to
the most ravishing melody.

                                        —V (July, 1808), 367-72

The Case of Gray: a Reply

JOHN SYLVESTER JOHN GARDINER

Sir,

Whatever credit your defence of Gray may reflect on your talents as a writer, it will never convince reasonable incredulity that "he is one of those few poets, who, at every new reading, recompenses you double for every encomium, by disclosing some new charm of sentiment or of diction." I have perused and re-perused him since the publication of your panegyrick, but I am still unable to discover those beauties which seem to have charmed you. The result of repeated readings has more thoroughly convinced me of the justness of Johnson's criticism, whom you misrepresent when you say that "he could find nothing in Collins but 'clusters of consonants.'" On the contrary, the Doctor affirms that "his poems are the productions of a mind not deficient in fire," that "his efforts produced, in happier moments, sublimity and splendour," though he observes, at the same time, that "his lines are commonly of slow motion, clogged and impeded with clusters of consonants." This surely is very different from saying, as you assert, that he could find "*nothing* in Collins but clusters of consonants"; nor was it necessary, Sir, in praising Gray, to misrepresent Johnson.

Your remarks on the difference of taste in poetry are perfectly just, but your inference, "if Pindar and Horace were poets, so was Gray too," cannot be admitted, because the merit of the two former, consecrated by the applause of ages, has never been disputed, whilst the lyrick fame of the latter still remains unsettled in the minds of many competent judges. I might, with equal propriety affirm, if Dryden and Pope were poets, so is Humphreys too.[37]

[37] On David Humphreys see p. 148 n. 16.

Your quotation from Horace will not prove Gray a poet; for though we grant that he possesses the *es magna sonaturum* in common with Blackmore and many others, yet whether in lyrick poetry he has any claim to the *mens divinior* is still the disputed point, which, with all your ingenuity, you have not settled to our satisfaction.

In reply to your authority from Burke, I will transcribe a sentence from the reviewer of his celebrated treatise, which you will find in the tenth volume of Johnson's works, by Hawkins, though the review has by some been attributed to Murphy. "Obscurity," our author observes, "increases the sublime, which is certainly very just; but from *thence erroneously infers, that clearness of imagery is unnecessary to affect the passions. But surely nothing can move but what gives ideas to the mind.*"

If this remark be just, which I think cannot reasonably be disputed, all your defence of Gray's obscurity falls to the ground. If obscurity increases the sublime, it must be the obscurity arising from the ambiguous meaning of one or two expressions, where something is left to the imagination, not from a whole passage, which in that case would not be sublime but corrupt. The obscurest of all poets is Lycophron, but no critick has yet contended for his superiour sublimity.[38] I know of no sublime passage in Homer, Virgil, or Milton, but what is perfectly intelligible, and scarcely a description which would not make a good picture. Indeed I lay it down as a general maxim, that WHATEVER IMAGERY A GOOD PAINTER CANNOT EXECUTE ON THE CANVASS, MUST NECESSARILY BE INCORRECT. If there be any exception to this rule, it can only be, where images are presented to the mind, which are not subjects of the eye. . . .

I do not recollect, Sir, any ode, either in Pindar or Horace, which is not perfectly clear, with the exception of a few passages, where the obscurity may arise from our imperfect knowledge of the language, or from the carelessness of transcribers. But Gray in those odes which you think sublime is perpetually obscure, and even should you find his meaning, I am far from certain that it will repay the labour of the search. I should be

[38] Lycophron, who was employed in the library at Alexandria, was one of the Pleiad of Alexandrian tragedians.

glad to know what is the meaning of *purple light of loves* in the passage which you quote with so much delight and enthusiasm? The Greek poet, from whom he borrows says intelligibly enough, "*The light of love shines on her purple cheeks.*" But Gray, determined to write like no one but himself, transfers the epithet, "purple," from the cheeks, to which it was appropriate, to "love," which almost any other epithet would have suited as well. And this is the man, who, you would persuade us, is distinguished for the astonishing force and beauty of his epithets.

In his "Ode for Musick" (an odd title by the way) he has these lines:

> And thus they speak in soft accord
> The *liquid* language of the skies.

Now I should be happy if you would inform me, in what consists the *astonishing force and beauty* of this epithet? If he had written, "the language of the liquid skies," we might have supposed that he meant thunder in the fine weather. But, I presume, the beauty of this epithet arises from that inimitable obscurity which is the great source of Gray's sublimity.

I equally dissent from you as to the unrivalled power of his numbers. What do you think of such numbers as these?

> What cat's averse to fish?
> Let us go, let us fly!
> She tumbled headlong in.

In *unrivalled* numbers, we might reasonably expect correct rhymes. But even of this mechanical excellence Gray cannot boast; his inaccuracy is aggravated by the extreme brevity of his performances. If you run your eye along his first odes, you will find *stretch* and *beech*, *noon* and *sun*, *low* and *thou*, *flown* and *gone*, *declared* and *heard*, *between* and *in*, *flood* and *God*, *towers* and *adores*, *wave* and *cleave*, *bent* and *constraint*, *descry* and *joy*, *doom* and *come*, *train* and *men*, *paradise* and *bliss*, *fly* and *joy*, *heard* and *clad*.

Would a poet unrivalled in the power of his numbers employ so low a word as *take* in the following line?

> A thousand rills their mazy progress *take*.

Or the word *goes* in this line of " The Bard "?

> In gallant trim the gilded vessel *goes*.

The third stanza of the ode on the "Progress of Poesy," to
the musical structure of which you say that there is nothing in
the whole compass of English versification to be compared, is,
to my ear, degraded by its double rhymes to the language of a
ballad-monger. I will take the liberty of quoting the passage:

> Oh! lyre divine, what daring spirit
> Wakes thee now? Though he inherit
> Nor the pride, nor ample pinion
>   That the Theban eagle bear,
> Sailing with supreme dominion
>   Through the azure deep of air.

Now, Sir, these lines, in my judgment, are far beneath the
dignity of lyrick poetry, and much in the style of

> Cease, rude Boreas, blustering railer.
> Cupid wave thy purple pinion.

The *azure deep of air* is one of those sublime obscurities,
I suppose, which *overpower* the admirers of Gray *with the blaze
of embellishment*, but which fifty interpreters would probably
explain each in a different manner.

The successful manner in which he has lately been imitated is
a sufficient proof that there is little difficulty in writing like Gray.
The ode on " Summer " published in the last " Sylva," is superiour
to Gray's on the "Spring," and without borrowing a thought or
an expression from him, exhibits all his peculiarities, his quaint-
ness of epithet, his affected alliterations, and the general glitter
and tinsel of his style.[39] I hope that the same gentleman will
shortly gratify the publick by imitations of the sublime obscurities
of the " Progress of Poesy " and " The Bard," and then the
admirers of Gray, if not silenced, must at least submit to be

[39] Gardiner refers to his own poem which appeared in " Silva, No 41,"
Anthology, V (July, 1808), 357.

laughed at. But let the same person attempt to imitate Horace, or Dryden, or any writer distinguished by classick simplicity (from which no one can be more distant than Gray) and he will find it no easy task. The lyrick fame of Gray, like the epick reputation of Ossian, will probably continue to obtain a " *divided suffrage* "; and those who feel no enthusiasm in reading his odes, but are disgusted with his affected refinements, his studied obscurity, and his trite morality, will endeavour to bear the imputation of *ignorance* and *envy* rather than sacrifice their judgment to the whimsical enthusiasm of his admirers. The authority of Warton, who wrote a long essay to prove that Pope was no poet, and of Gilbert Wakefield, who affirms that David Hume could not write prose, can have weight only with the incorrigible admirers of Gray, whilst those who question his lyrick superiority and deny that the mantle either of Pindar or of Horace graces his shoulders feel justified in their opinions by the superiour authority of the mighty Johnson. " These odes (says the doctor) are marked by glittering accumulations of ungraceful ornaments. They strike rather than please. The images are magnified by affectation; the language is laboured into harshness. The mind of the writer seems to work with unnatural violence, *Double, double, toil and trouble.* His art and his struggle are too visible, and there is too little appearance of ease and nature."

Sincerely wishing that you will, in future, employ your acknowledged talents as a writer more usefully than in defence of absurdity,

I remain, Sir,

With due respect, &c. &c.

An Admirer Of Simplicity.

—V (August, 1808), 416-19

The Winter of Criticism

EDMUND TROWBRIDGE DANA

NATURE IS BEAUTY; and her most peculiar feature, variety. The character of man is as various as his species is numerous, and, since the creation of waters, the form of a wave was never repeated. Though we hourly discover parallels amongst our associates, there is an exquisite distinction in the very exactness of likeness; a certain inexpressible something eminently our own; a happiness derivative, as it were, from heaven. Colleges may impair what learning cannot compensate!

Should the frequent failures of modern poesy be attributed to the neglect of this peculiar characteristick of our nature, we beg not to be considered irretrievably gothick. It is difficult to conjecture wherefore, but it has latterly become the vogue to imitate any thing but nature; to filter through the pericranium the fancies of other people in preference to cultivating our own. If, now a days, you take up a communication from a correspondent, you are either enveloped in the voluminous curl of the Johnsonian peruke, or pierced through the sensorium by the tart laconism of Lavater. "Seneca cannot be too heavy, nor Plautus too light: for the law of writ these are the only men." It is not our inclination to cavil at the singularities of established writers, but we wish it always recollected that those who follow can necessarily never come up; and that the peculiarities which are interesting with their originator may be preposterous in his imitator. The oaten stop of rural poesy is surely soothing; but because Rogers, for instance, has written prettily on a ringdove, is it indispensably necessary that our masters and misses should be descriptively ridiculous for a century to come? [40]

The superiority of the ancients in painting, architecture, and

[40] Samuel Rogers (1763–1855) wrote the popular *Pleasures of Memory* (1792) and enjoyed a considerable reputation in his day.

sculpture, might possibly persuade us to conjecture, with Milton, a degeneracy in human nature. But beside the defender of so whimsical a position, the recenter dates of Cowper and of Southey leave us little to question the capability of the period. Inferiority to antiquity, that scarecrow of moderns, like others of the brotherhood of frightful demeanour, is a mere imposition of stubble and straw; and it will be discovered, when children have courage for reflection, that it is rather erected to frighten praise from our neighbours than facilitate by caution the advancement of mind. Yet nothing now, too, is admired by many, but the *hoary*; and the mouldiness of manuscript, like the wall-flowers and mosses of ruins, affords sentiment by barrenness and material from decay. One is hagridden, as it were,

> Over hill, over dale
> Through brush, through briar,
> Over park, over pale,
> Through flood, through fire,

with nothing but the classicks, the classicks, the classicks! A smooth gentleman from Alma mater tutors you, forsooth, that this performance is classical and that is not classical; that this metaphor is disjointed, or that metaphor articulates, and so on to the conclusion of the chapter; when, probably, the sphere of your acquirements is no otherwise expanded than by the interesting disclosure, that to write classically is to write accurately.

> There's not a villain dwelling in all Denmark
> But he's an arrant knave.

Had the classicks squandered themselves on the manufacture of facsimile, the conclusion of their lives, like those of their copyists, had been the period of their fame: but nature was the fountain from which they drank of immortality, nature, pure and unadulterated by frosty infusions of literary empiricks. Their bodies are with the Capulets, but genius is eternal. Numerous are the flowers that bloom on the slopes of Parnassus, various of complexion and shifting in perfume, like the proffers of Ophelia. There are daisies, fennel, and columbines; there are rosemaries, pansies, and rue.

" There's some for you, and here's some for me." But our posies
are all senseless; forced exoticks nourished by foreign fire, painted
leaves of tiffany wound on formal wire. When, oh when, shall
the winter of criticism be passed and the springtide of passion
return! when shall the library be deserted for the fields, and
poetry ruminate in the shades she loves to depicture! when, oh
when, shall the idolatry of learning be superseded by the worship
of truth! We are surfeited with the repetition of repetitions, and
want opportunity for reflection; for thought is as necessary to the
soul as exercise to the body; and the intellect incessantly in arms
is rickety for life.

Furthermore, in essaying to imitate the chastity of the ancients
we have unaccountably neglected their vigour. Singularity of
sentiment and audacity of figure, though sometimes perhaps more
violent than fortunate, are the gifted characteristicks of the bard.
The listlessness of human nature is better gratified with even the
eccentricity of hyperbole than the frigidity of correctness. We
must be awakened before we are persuaded to feel. It is a hard
portion for the delicate palate of connoisseurship, yet compounded by experience and observation, belles-lettres, to be
interesting, must be popular. Poetry and painting were not
intended merely for the retirement of the student. They are
universal appellants to the sentiments and passions of mankind,
and you may calculate with tolerable accuracy upon their deserts
by the extensiveness of their circulation. Yet, in our day of
refinement, very little is directed to the fancy or heart; for, from
some cogency or other, it is unfashionable to be moved. Should
an author in the interest of his subject unfortunately be animated
to an ebullition of the moment, his introduction of the costume
of his grandsire's (square-toes, bag-sleeves, buckram, and so on)
could not more completely expose him for the purposes of
ridicule. Style must be equable and level as water at rest (the
only superficies in nature, mechanically straight); smooth & ton-
sored as the forehead of a friar; no pleasing sallies of cadence
or thought must occur, but members of sentences be inter-
married with members, tediously constituting, like the links in a
chain, a series of polished monotonies. But, in so doing, our
copyists of antiquity, as it generally happens with imitation, have

not only departed from truth, but omitted the spirit of their
original. Variety, that miracle of nature and genius, is endlessly
exemplified in the father of epick. His verse, like some of the
rivers of our country, accomplishes its journey over the abrupt-
ness of precipices, as well as through the tranquillity of vallies;
along the cultivated confines of population, or through the soli-
tudes of the wilderness. We alternately climb with him to be
sublime, or condescend to the simple; struggle with the irregular,
or relapse on the proportional; the imagination is sometimes permitted to subside, that it may endure to be agitated; entertained
with the plaintive, to be contrasted by the tremendous.

But the times of inspiration are departed; and nature, the only
muse of the poet, is unfeelingly forgotten. We have substituted
rhetorick in her room, and degenerated to a race of manufac-
turers. We have striven to be faultless, and neglected to be
natural; criticism is satisfied, but sensibility frozen. The passions
that hung on the lyres of old are long since buried with their
masters, or prostituted on the vulgar intercourses of a day.
Establishment has crowded out sentiment; luxury and refinement
have enervated virility. But posterity will do justice to nature
and genius; and thousands will daily devour Shakespeare for one
that reads Pope; thousands shall prefer playing with a dried leaf
and a switch in the simple retirements of Weston and Cowper
for one that sits primly with Addison and propriety, on a visit of
ceremony in the parlour of the muses. Truth to nature will be
the test by which poetry is tried; and as she approaches or retires
in her analogies, her merits to consideration or neglect will be
eventually determined. The various character of her theme
indulges a multiplicity of styles; but style, without character
appropriate, will perish with its mannerist. Sir Joshua Reynolds
supposes that perfection of his art originates at the point of its
concealment; or, in other words, when the painter and his tools
are forgotten in the truth of effect. With so high an authority
to support our position, permit us farther to quote the pertinent
assertion " that deformity commences with the dancing-master."
But little evidence is necessary where the fact is perspicuous. The
superiority of nature over art is the superiority of the works of
heaven over those of man; and he who neglects the performances

of the former for the second hand imitations of the latter does
certainly little credit to his heart, and still less to his fancy.
Nature is brimful of character; and to genuine taste and philosophy, the untutored gestures of children are more exquisite
than the accomplished ceremony of courts. In the adjustment
of their little etiquettes of first meeting, there is sweeter food for
contemplation than my lord Chesterfield or yourself would
imagine. Nay, there is an interesting character about my great
grandmother, smoking in the chimney corner, or even in the
playsomeness of kittens through the broken straw-bottoms of the
old family furniture. We are environed with articles of delicacy
and daintiness, yet murmur at the narrowness of materials; we
starve upon copying in the centre of originals!

> To me more dear, congenial to my heart,
> One native charm, than all the gloss of art. . . .

—II (October, 1805), 530-33

The Love of Nature

BENJAMIN WELLES

THE LOVE OF nature is a passion of the soul, pure and intellectual. Its energy is sublime, without the violence of animal
impulse, and its enjoyment fine and exquisite, without the riot
and confusion of mental and physical indulgence. It is purely
spiritual, because it is produced by the perceptions of the mind
of what is abstractly beautiful, and it is rapturous in that sympathy which rebounds from the coincidence of natural and ideal
beauty. This sympathy, however, is not merely confined to such
a harmony of beauties; it mingles also with what is tranquil in
nature, and it extends with what is sublime. The softness of the
landscape at sun-setting breathes itself to the bosom with the
tenderest melancholy, and the stillness of the lake under moon-

light soothes the soul into sweetest repose. In the terror of the mighty evolutions of nature, man is also prepared for ruin. His genius bounds at the approach of the whirlwind; it rushes with the swiftness of its fury, and tracks it through its rustling path to the boundaries of the heavens. It is transcendent amid the horrours of the tempest, and, as the lightning breaks from the thunder cloud, it leaps with sublimity, and moves on its blazing line into the profoundity of darkness.

Man thus appears to hold an intimate connexion and grand alliance with nature. But the enjoyment of this blessing seems negative by habitual experience, though the consciousness of it is necessarily deduced from the supremacy of his power, and the sublimity of his position over all surrounding existence. Still, however, must he remain contented with the certainty of its possession, though it be in some measure unaccountable to himself. He must learn to satisfy his mind with the resemblance of facts on subjects too subtle for their operation, and he must not sicken at the disappointment of defining what is infinite. The brightness of beauty should enlighten the mistiness of its existence, and that sublimity which is not instantaneous and universal may be produced by elevation of thought and combination of magnitudes. His mind may, for a moment, stand and gaze on the very borders of its own perfection; but before it can even catch a glimpse of what rolls beyond, it perceives light and vision blended, and is lost in the deep void of boundless space.

There is, moreover, the sweetest union of the pleasures of sense and intellect in the delight of nature. Through this bright medium the vision of fancy has an infinite series of delightful views, sometimes breaking into the opening of rapture, and sometimes lengthening and expanding into the luxuriant extent of enjoyment. Every pleasurable impulse of sense urges incipient action into the execution of delight; and every great passion riots in indulgence, more rapturous by progression, and more vacant by excess; not forbidden by reason, nor tainted by disgust. He, who thus gives himself up to nature, is in the brightness and purity of his existence, his mind philosophizes with itself in the loneliness of meditation, and his passions receive ordinance from the solemn convention of philosophy and religion.

Human nature, thus ennobled with powers so sublime, and softened with sensibilities so delicate, each qualified with capacities of enjoyment, extensive as the subjects are exhaustless, must indeed be inveterate against its own happiness by renouncing the experience of it. We too niggardly encroach on the rights of intellect in the vain enterprize of meliorating that which is already essentially below the standard of human dignity. Few are even aware of the freedom and range of nature, for half mankind come into the world with manacles and fetters. With the smile of slaves, they are pleased and exult with the freedom of breath and the liberty of life. They sicken and rot within the impalement of a city, without once brightening their eye wth a gleam of pure light, or refreshing their lungs with the balmy inhalations of pure expanse. There is a feebleness about them, which is not the relaxation of strength, and a languor, which is not the repose of enjoyment. At death their eye shuts blankly on the walls of their prison, while the vision of him who has communed with nature slowly fades with the melancholy dimness of things and vanishes with their departure.

How truly inglorious is existence, thus drawn out by the continual motives of business, and fretted away by the vain anxieties of city life. How vacant the mind, without the intelligence of nature, and how spiritless the brain, without the thrills of her emotions. He, who is thus kennelled in the city, prefers the bustle of noisy nothingness to the soothing serenity of country life; an atmosphere darkened with the dust of drudgery and labour to the blue expanse over the fresh landscape; the jargon of brokers, and the brawlings and heavings of " fat and greasy citizens " to the sound of the spring bird at evening, or the broken song of the peasant on his doorstone. To all the exquisite niceties and delicacies of cultured product, even his senses are blunt. He had rather sit, of a dog-day, with four and twenty trencher-men, " big and burly," at the head of a table, whose loaded extent presents the perspective of a market place, than to retire to the cool cell in the grove, to regale himself amid the freshness of fruit, and the raciness of vegetables.

On the contrary, how pleasantly and how naturally flows the life of him, who breathes it in the cool shades of silent retirement, his soul expanding with the pure sentiments which rural imagery inspires; who loves to stretch himself, at noon day, in the deep shade of the mountain brow, and follow the huge shadow of the dark cloud as it sails over the plain, deepening the luxuriance of the vallies, and reflecting bright and glaring light on the edges of the cliffs and precipices; or in the stillness of a summer's evening, aside the old oak that sighs in the night breeze, to catch the bright forms of departed friends in the white clouds which wave over the moon.

The constant action of thought in retirement adds another charm to it. The mind here is not left merely to its own opera-tion, reasoning on subjects of its own suggestion, without the standard of perceptible truth for the conclusion of such abstrac-tions. But it has the constant presentation of the sublime experi-ment of universal cause and effect, free from the anxieties of chance, and unincumbered with the ponderous mass of human follies, prejudices, and absurdities. Its acquisition is the wisdom of nature, and its truth is that certainty of conclusion, which is deduced from determinate causes, invariably efficient of conse-quential effects.

There is yet another charm in this retreat from the town, and the throng, which is beyond even the fascination of poetry. We here feel that description is only imitative of nature, and we turn from the transcription, however charming and exact, to the raptures of the original. We are no longer content with the ideal sympathy of visionary existence, but we extend all the pleasures of fiction into the emotions of sensible truth. In the presence of nature, even the minuteness and exactitude of Cowper is indis-criminate and unsatisfactory; the mellow luxuriance of Thomson barren and wasteful. In the bright expanse, which surrounds her, even the sublime and transcendent genius of Milton flutters with dark and heavy wings, near the earth, but faintly tinged with the celestial light, and rests on objects blasted or deformed. Let him then whose soul is pure and holy with the love of nature take his position in the midst of creation and commence the mighty work of the eternal perfection of thought.[41]

—III (June, 1806), 285-88

From Boeotia to Attica[42]

WILLIAM TUDOR, JR.

THERE ARE SOME obstacles to our progress in the cultivation of learning and the arts which are peculiar to our situation and institutions. The first of these is the want of libraries, of galleries of painting and statues, of foundations for the support of learned men and eminent artists. Will not the accumulating wealth of an enlightened community remedy this evil? Will they not take

[41] This essay indicates that its young author had definitely come into contact with romantic and perhaps even transcendental notions not generally expounded in the Anthology circle. Although the attack on the classics by Edmund Trowbridge Dana suggests some of the same ideas, as do some of the other comments in the *Anthology*, this essay ascribed to Benjamin Welles in James Savage's marked file obviously goes farther in its conclusion than would be expected. Apparently the essay was not read to the Society before its publication; at least it is not mentioned in the *Journal*. The reaction of someone like John Sylvester John Gardiner to it would certainly have been unfavorable.

[42] Tudor prepared his remarks as an address to be delivered before the annual meeting of the Harvard Phi Beta Kappa Society. The address was published in the *Anthology* under the following title: "A Discourse, Intended to Have Been Delivered before the Society of Phi Beta Kappa on their Anniversary, the Day after Commencement at Cambridge, August 30, 1810." A prefatory note by the editor of the *Anthology* reads as follows: "Mr. William Tudor, unexpectedly called to embark for England just before the anniversary of the society, was induced by his respect for those who appointed him to leave his discourse at their disposal. They have consented to its publication in the *Anthology*; and thus have expressed their regard for the author, and a sense of the merit of the performance, which we presume no one who reads it will think undeserved." The final

something from the heap, ere it be scattered by their death, to erect permanent foundations for learning? Will they not appropriate what will not be missed by their heirs, but will be felt by their country, and attach recollection to their names, long after all other traces of them shall be lost? In a country animated by commerce, ennobled by freedom, the reputation of the Medici will not be handed down with increasing honours from age to age without provoking generous emulation! Very respectable institutions are in existence, that are worthy to be fostered. This university has long benefited the country; let her sons be grateful for what they have received. Let them add to her respectability by exertions of their talents, or the munificence of their endowments. A university should not only be a place of instruction for youth; it should be a home to the cultivators of learning. In her shades they should find a shelter, in whose calm retreats they may devote their lives to the active pursuits of science and literature, unharassed by the cares of the world.

Galleries of paintings, and collections of statues, for the double purpose of exciting taste in the publick, and furnishing models to the artist are yet to be created. The common excuse for this neglect is, that we are not rich enough. Alas! the poverty is not in our purse, it is in our taste. Many countries are now as superiour to ours, in this respect, as we are superiour to them in riches. Let us hope that this spirit may be awakened; that the time is not remote when we shall cease to drive our artists to seek protection in other countries on which they confer honour. Let us hope that the day will soon come, when sculpture shall have an existence among us, when publick gratitude shall despise paying its obligations by a vote, when the statues of our illustrious dead shall excite the living to emulate their virtues. If each of our cities possessed a statue of him, "who was first in war, first in peace, and first in the hearts of his countrymen," it could never be passed without awakening a love of country. It would

---

part of Tudor's lengthy address is reprinted. In the first part he offers " a few general remarks on the state of learning in some countries of Europe," in the last he makes " some, observations on its condition among ourselves and on the circumstances peculiar to our situation that excite our fears and our hopes for the future."

call into action the proud feelings of national dignity. It would tend to soothe animosity. If parties should ever become so envenomed, so exasperated, that they could not even unite in the ceremonies of a national festival, at least one act of unanimity might be celebrated; they might go in solemn procession to decorate this monument with votive wreaths of laurel, might enjoy for a few moments the delicious feelings of filial gratitude. They could then retire; and when out of its sight, when the statue of Washington was lost to their view, they might separate, stifle the generous, social affections awakened in their breasts towards a common country, and perform the unhallowed rites, the foul, malignant sacrifices of faction.

Another obstacle is the relative importance of wealth. The progress of society for three or four centuries has been gradually producing this effect in every other nation, which is on the whole advantageous to mankind. But in this country, avarice and ambition are more nearly identified than in any other. Wealth is power. Do not let me be misunderstood. I am not degrading my country. Mere wealth has not a very powerful influence. But the absence of all political distinctions, of all privileged orders, gives wealth, in the hands of talent, accumulated weight. Hence the desire of distinction, in many minds capable of feeling it, is enticed into this as a primary pursuit, and commonly persisted in, till the taste or the capacity for other employments is weakened or extinguished.

The equal division of property among children is a considerable disadvantage, though of a negative kind. Whatever value it may possess in perpetuating republican forms of government, or claim upon the feelings as doing justice towards offspring, for whom equal affection is felt, it has doubtless a pernicious effect in regard to literature and the arts. An individual with only a moderate independence may enjoy the innocent luxuries and refinements of life; but his property, when divided into several portions, is insufficient to procure for his children the same enjoyments. He passes through life toiling to accumulate; and leaves his children to begin their career where he started, and to pursue the same course, urged and restrained by the same motives. It is seldom that any family retains affluence through four generations. No family is perpetuated, no man comes into life free from the solicitude attending the acquisition of property. No one inherits independence in this respect, and, with it, that species of fame, of taste, and inclination, for which many families in Europe have been celebrated age after age. A splendid gallery of paintings, a magnificent library, descend to the inheritor, with the virtual obligation to cheer genius, to support science, to protect art. The fame of a family is entailed with its estate. The lot is enviable to an elevated mind, but obnoxious to our institutions; yet, looking at the succession of ages, such establishments are the property of the publick, of which the apparent possessor, is only the hereditary keeper.

Another impediment is produced by the incessant occurrence of elections. The chance of success being continually renewed, the activity of demagogues is always encouraged, and the Cleons of the day will use their utmost efforts to be carried by the obliquity of publick sentiment into power. In a free country, it is every man's duty to take an interest in publick affairs. The good man, the clear-sighted politician, the ardent thinker, is drawn out to warn, to protect, to animate his fellow citizens. Having once taken the oar in his hand, publick expectation chains him to the bench, and life is passed in forcing the vessel against the current of popular delusion. Yet such is the blindness of prejudice that he who might have directed the cabinet of a nation, or poured conviction on a divided, distracted senate, has less political influence in the very district that is honoured by his talents, and blessed with his virtues, than the rankest, the mere stall-fed creature of faction. The talents which should have been employed in the execution of duties to be remembered by posterity are frittered away in guiding temporary perverseness, in conciliating fleeting animosity, in opposing the errours of the passing day—Why do I affect to dwell on a general picture? Why do I linger to mention the name of Ames? Of him, who, in the incessant exertion of political watchfulness, in opposing all the rancour and malignity of faction, never had a foe. When we reflect on the purity of his character, the vivacity, the clearness, the fertility of his mind, how must we regret, that he whom we see at every turn of the political avenue, should only once be met in the walks of literature. I have hung this simple wreath on his tomb in passing; but do not, my friends, betray me to the politicians of the world; they would never forgive the wish that would have deprived them of one of their brightest ornaments.

Having thus noticed some of the evils that are peculiar to our situation, it is doubly grateful to consider some of the circumstances that excite our hopes for the future. It is an inestimable advantage to science and learning that there are no arbitrary laws to restrain their exertions, no inquisitorial college of either politicks or religion, to watch their progress, to keep them in the narrow path that is hemmed in by ecclesiastical intolerance on one side, or political tyranny on the other. Our establishments permit investigation, and do not demand conformity. Truth may be sought in every science, and when found, proclaimed to the world. The physician may practise on his own system; the divine may preach after his own belief; the scientifick investigator may publish whatever he can prove, or even conjecture; the civilian may blame, commend, or expound every code.

The universal diffusion of the first rudiments of education must be thought a favourable circumstance. Every man can read and write. The great superiourity we may claim in this respect over most other nations, while it is productive of great benefit, will be attended by some evils, slight indeed when compared with the former. The exercise given to weak minds may create a degree of fever, and the patient will be apt to mistake his disorder. Many occupations will thus lose valuable labourers. Those who were meant to creep will attempt to soar, and very few will get high enough to meet with the fate of Icarus. Few will lose their pinions by approaching too near the sun; few will rise to a sufficient height to become illustrious even by their fall.

The hasty opening of the faculties, the rude *clearing* of ignorance by the general diffusion of simple, elementary education, though it be only the precursor of cultivation, without which no valuable harvest can be reaped, still it opens the field to the sun and air, and thus gives a chance to some vigorous plants to expand, and become *bearers* from their own native force. A knowledge of reading and writing may here give occasion to the discovery of talents, that with this advantage will be enabled to show their strength and make themselves known, which else might have remained unheeded, and perished with the crowd.

The neighbourhood of a number of free states, speaking the same language, is a very prominent advantage. Emulation will naturally be provoked; men of genius will be valued as shedding a lustre on their native state; and perhaps in the fulness of time we may be inclined to encourage and reward those exertions of which we shall be eager to boast. The time will arrive when the contention will be, not which state has the best soil, which has the largest city, and which city has the best market; but which state has made the most eminent discoveries in science, which has produced the most eloquent divines and orators, which the ablest statesmen; where have the Muses been propitiated to shed inspiration; which cherishes the artists, whose names are to be enrolled with those of Phidias and Apelles, of Michael Angelo and Raphael.

The task would now be easier to designate our Boeotia than our Attica. It will not always be so. There are symptoms of the dawn of taste and love of learning in our country. Some of the states are beginning to rouse themselves. Perhaps the period is not very remote, when this emulation of mental glory will be awakened; when, with the liberty, we shall possess the enthusiasm of Greece; when Demosthenes shall have more power than Philip; when the possession of Plato or Socrates shall be more valued than all the splendour of the great king, supported by his millions of slaves. Fortunate those states which obtain the start in this career, the noblest path of ambition, a career of glory! The sound of applause increasing in strength, the approaching hurrying step of a rival, will stimulate to greater speed; and the reward of victory will be influence, power, publick prosperity, and the admiration of mankind.

The great extent of country governed by the same laws, moving in the same system, and speaking the same language, is a magnificent subject of contemplation. From the Mississippi to the St. Lawrence, from the Atlantick to the Pacifick, we may foresee a population, under many governments perhaps, by whom that language will be spoken which has been so long the favourite dialect of civil liberty, of independent thought, of philosophick discussion, of elevated, pure morality, of rational, mild religion, that while it exists, these can never be forgotten by the world. We may look forward to see nations, between these rivers and these oceans, numerous as the half civilized hordes of China, and other barbarous people of Asia, enjoying, by inheritance and education, the institutions of the most enlightened nation of Europe, the consciousness of independence, the love of order, the intelligence, the activity and security of free governments.

How must these considerations animate genius in its efforts! The historian will feel that he is narrating events, that he is clearing the character of his actors from the distortions of enmity, that he is teaching philosophy by example, not to a city, not to a narrow state, but to unnumbered millions! How will the poet kindle into rapture, when he reflects that the lyrick, which chants the glory of his country, which animates to liberty and virtue, will rouse the latent feelings, will excite a generous sympathy over a continent! How will the orator rise in the impetuosity of his feelings, soar in the grandeur of his subject, overwhelm opposition with irresistible eloquence, when the justice he demands, when the applause he confers, when the rights he defends, shall rouse correspondent emotions in listening states! shall be carried from the ocean to the mountains, from the mountains to the ocean, till the remotest valley shall resound with his theme!

What incitement to our exertions, my friends, to honour this seat of learning, to pay it the homage of our gratitude, to point out to opulence its wants, to ambition its influence: to shew to the friends of science and virtue, that it is not only the smiling landscape around us, the dear homes we cherish, which will be benefited; but that future societies of men that will exist in regions which man has not yet explored will turn their eyes towards this ancient seminary, will be attracted by its fame, and seek for knowledge in its copious fountains. May we, as each returning year renews our pilgrimage to its annual festival, find our Alma Mater contemplating with delight a rising progeny, enjoying additional honours, receiving increased veneration.

—IX (September, 1810), 156-61

To What Purpose We Have Toiled

SAMUEL COOPER THACHER

As we have never laid claim to any extraordinary measure of sensibility, it may be supposed that they who have so long wielded the scourge of criticism, and bathed their hands in the blood of so many ill-fated candidates for fame, must have extinguished the usual feelings and weakness of our nature. Yet, incredible as it may seem, we do confess, with all our obduracy, that we cannot remain wholly unaffected, when we announce, that with the present number, our labours in the *Anthology* are brought to a close. After having for so many years found in preparing materials for this work the amusement and solace of our leisure hours, and in the little circle, which interest in its welfare has weekly brought together, an innocent and cheerful, if not always very philosophick relaxation, we feel, in finally dismissing it from our hands, something of that sadness steal over us, which is experienced in losing a good-natured and long-tried, though not perhaps very valuable friend.

Farewell!
I could have better spared a better man.
O! I shall have a heavy miss of thee.

We do not suppose that the intention we have thus announced will spread much consternation, or that the absence of the *Anthology* will create any very alarming vacuum in the literary world. There may be some who will remember us with kindness, and a few with regret; but on the whole we are inclined to think that the waves will roll as peacefully, and the skies appear as blue, and the sun shine as gaily, on the day of our departure, as though we still existed. Such is the fate which, from the nature of our work, we have always expected to be heirs to. He who writes for a journal must not be disappointed, though his fame should moulder a good deal sooner than the pyramids of Egypt.

In arriving at the termination of labours, which, if not very important, have at least been long continued, it is natural to inquire to what purpose we have toiled. In looking back on our pages we find, as in every fair review of human life, some things to regret; some things of no very positive character; and some, *pace omnium bonorum*, be it said, which we are disposed to regard as not wholly vain and unprofitable. We do confess, for in our last moments it becomes us to be honest, that in reviewing our labours, we find some criticisms on our conscience in which a juvenile love of point and smartness may have betrayed us into asperity and want of candour and in which we may seem to have thought too much of the reputation of the reviewer, and too little of the rights and feelings of the author. We must in fairness also own that it has been incident to our lucubrations to be sometimes crude and indigested, and sometimes meagre and weak; and our remarks have been usually delivered in quite as oracular a tone as was justified either by the authority of the criticks, or the intrinsick weight of their judgments. We make these frank acknowledgments of our faults, because we would willingly go out of the world in charity with all mankind. They are the faults of youth; and young men, we know, are always dogmatical and usually vain.

But we will not affect more humility than we feel. The *Anthology*, though never what we or its friends could have wished to see it, has yet some claims on the regard of the publick. The leading objects to which it has been devoted are such as we can never be ashamed to have pursued, however we may regret the imperfection of our approaches to them. To cultivate and gratify the taste of the lovers of polite letters has been the principal design of our Miscellany, though we have rejected nothing which might appear to aid the general cause of sound science. In pursuing this design we have endeavoured always to feel and to recognize the obligation which is laid on every writer to regulate and sanctify all his speculations by a supreme regard to the interests of virtue and religion. In conducting our critical

SAMUEL COOPER THACHER

department we have had a task of more delicacy, in executing which from its very nature we could not hope for universal approbation. With whatever faults, however, it may have been chargeable, of this at least we are sure; that we have never knowingly suffered any sentiment of *personal* hostility to mingle with any of our criticisms; nor have we ever used the immunities of invisibility to shelter us in launching the "firebrands, arrows and death" of slander and malignity. We claim also this merit, that we have never lent ourselves the services of any party, political or theological; we have never courted the suffrages of the great vulgar, nor attempted to enlist the prejudices of the small; have never felt, in any discussion in which we have been engaged, that we have had any other cause to serve than that of truth and good learning. On this subject we speak confidently. Of the soundness of the great principles in politics and religion which we have advanced, we can deliberately re-affirm our honest conviction. We claim the praise of having been uniformly true to them; and on this ground it is, that in going off the scene, we do not fear to say to the spectators: *Plaudite, omnes.*

There may be some who, in taking their last leave of the *Anthology,* may be prompted by kindness, or curiosity, or both, to inquire why we are now induced to discontinue it. We answer that we are influenced not by one, but many reasons; the weight of which we have long felt, though we have hesitated to obey them. At the commencement of the year we hinted at some of the inconveniences which arise from the manner in which the *Anthology* has been conducted, and suggested our hopes that we should be relieved from them by giving the principal care of the publication to a permanent editor. In this we have been disappointed, from the inadequacy of the receipts of the *Anthology* to repay the labour of any gentleman to whom we should be willing to confide it. Our auxiliaries also, at no time numerous, though always valuable, have lately been diminished. Our own ranks too have been thinned by desertion and death, and many of us feel the claims of professional duties to all the time we can command. Upon the whole, too, the *Anthology* has perhaps lived long enough, and its future existence, at least for the present, would be forced and unnatural. It may be, however, that at some future day we shall attempt to revive it, and possibly in a new form and under brighter auspices. With this mysterious and prophetick intimation any of our readers, who may find themselves disconsolate at its loss, may endeavour to comfort themselves.

It now only remains that we should offer our thanks to the friends who have aided us by their contributions, and rewarded us by their approbation. The assistance we have received, though not frequent nor great, has been from sources to which any one might be proud to owe an obligation. If we felt at liberty, we might flatter ourselves very agreeably by enumerating the names of those who have occasionally condescended to grace the pages of the *Anthology* with their writings. We regret that we have not been able to secure to them a less perishable existence. In returning our thanks for the patronage we have received, our gratitude may be the more valuable as it is not to be very widely distributed. Yet though we have never been in danger of being intoxicated by universal applause, we have been animated by the praises and support of those from whom they are most grateful. We must content ourselves with a general acknowledgment of our obligation. We cannot, however, refuse ourselves the gratification of an expression of thanks to our friend Dennie of the *Port Folio*, who so often cheered us by his kind and generous encouragement. We offer him our cordial wishes for the success of his labours, and hope they may receive a more solid compensation than the feeble whispers of our praise.[43]

In taking our final leave of the publick, we yet linger awhile. It is because we have a mournful duty to perform. It would be unjust that the pages of the *Anthology* should be closed without

[43] The relations between the *Anthology* and the *Port Folio* were cordial but not close. Dennie greeted the Boston publication in the *Port Folio* of August 2, 1805 (V, 238) "with applause." The Anthologists commended Dennie for "his perseverance in the ungrateful task of disciplining the taste of a money-getting age" in the *Anthology* of April, 1806 (III, 174, misnumbered 176). When the *Port Folio* published a satirical "Picture of Boston" which asserted "Gold is thy GOD, on that thy soul relies," the *Anthology* made a spirited rejoinder. See *Anthology*, IV (June, 1807), 289-95.

at least a passing tribute to the memory of a man to whose zeal and activity we owe it that our work did not perish at its birth. Though the pressure of other cares had prevented him from giving much direct assistance to us during the last years of his life; yet we were always sure of his smiles and good wishes. His short and active course is now ended; but his bright example still remains, and "marshals us on" in the path of virtue and piety.

> Peace to the memory of a man of worth
> A man of letters and of manners too.[44]

—X (June, 1811), 361-65

[44] The reference is to William Emerson.

Contributors to the Anthology

THE FOLLOWING BIOGRAPHICAL notes pertain only to contributors to the *Anthology* represented by a by-line in this edition. There were numerous others. The identification of authorship is based on the list appended to the *Journal of the Proceedings of the Anthology Society* (pp. 317-28). This list follows identifications to be found in a set of the *Anthology* owned by James Savage, who wrote the name of the author at the conclusion of each article. Additional information was obtained by the compilers of this list from notations in the Boston Athenaeum's set and from an annotated copy of the second volume in the Williams College Library.

DAVID PHINEAS ADAMS (d. 1823), hopeful first editor of the *Anthology*, joined the American Navy in 1811 as teacher of mathematics and chaplain. He died while serving in an expedition against the pirates of the West Indies.

JOHN QUINCY ADAMS (1767-1848), Harvard, class of 1787, sixth President of the United States and man of letters, was nominated by William Smith Shaw for membership in the Anthology Society on November 14, 1809 (see *J*, 212). What action was taken on this nomination, if any, is not recorded. It was undoubtedly an embarrassing situation. Shaw was a relation as well as a friend of the Adams family. As one can tell from the attack on Adams by Samuel Cooper Thacher (see pp. 88-93), the Anthologists had come to look unfavorably on Adams after his alienation from the Federalist cause in 1808. It would appear that the nomination was simply never acted upon and that when Adams became the American ambassador to Russia the Anthologists were relieved of the situation in which Shaw had placed them.

FISHER AMES (1758-1808) was a contributor to the *Anthology* but was not a member of the Society, and according to the *Journal*, was never nominated for membership; this was probably because of his chronic illness and his retirement to Dedham.

229

JACOB BIGELOW (1787-1879), Harvard, class of 1806, was a regular member of the Anthology Society. He was professor of Materia Medica at Harvard from 1815 to 1855 and had a distinguished scientific career.

JOSEPH STEVENS BUCKMINSTER (1784-1812) was the central figure in the literary and religious history of Boston during the first decade of the nineteenth century. Following his early death he became a legend of piety and learning. And the facts of his life give substance to the legend. The son of the Reverend Joseph Buckminster of Portsmouth, New Hampshire, his inheritance made him, as James Russell Lowell observes, a "member of the academic races." His precocious intellect, shaped by the growing liberalism of Harvard, rejected his father's Calvinism and led to a period of near estrangement between him and his parent, but in the end Joseph Buckminster preached his son's ordination sermon at Boston's fashionable Brattle Street Church, where the youthful minister spent his brief career. Even before this event, his life was clouded by epileptic attacks. A journey to Europe seems to have improved his health somewhat, but it remained precarious. When he died, Boston was greatly stricken.

EDMUND TROWBRIDGE DANA (1779-1859), a charter member of the Anthology Society, was a close friend of Washington Allston, who painted Dana's portrait. He was something of a rebel and something of a dilettante. Possibly because of his aversion to the classics (see the essay by Dana pp. 208-12), he left Harvard without taking his degree. In 1879 he was posthumously awarded the A. B. degree by Harvard as of the class of 1799.

THEODORE DEHON (1776-1817), during the era of the *Anthology*, was pastor of Trinity Church, Newport, Rhode Island. A graduate of Harvard, class of 1795, he was not a member of the Anthology Society but shared in its interests, as can be seen in his Phi Beta Kappa address (see pp. 185-88). He subsequently became the Episcopal Bishop of the Diocese of South Carolina.

WILLIAM EMERSON (1769-1811), Harvard, class of 1789, who took over the *Anthology* from David Phineas Adams, became minister of Boston's First Church in 1799. Identified with numerous religious and intellectual activities in Boston, he was a hard-working, conscientious clergyman and man of letters but neither a brilliant writer nor speaker. Ralph Waldo Emerson was the fourth child of William Emerson's marriage to Ruth Haskins.

ALEXANDER HILL EVERETT (1790-1847), Harvard, class of 1806, was one of the youngest members of the Anthology Society. In later years he had a public career of considerable importance, serving as minister to Spain and United States Commissioner to China, where he died. At one time he was president of Jefferson College in Louisiana; at another period he was editor of the *North American Review*.

JOHN SYLVESTER JOHN GARDINER (1765-1830), president of the Anthology Society during most of its existence, is discussed in the Introduction to this edition (pp. 24-28). Following his defection from the society he seems not to have taken much part in Boston's literary life. He died while in England on a journey for his health.

ROBERT HALLOWELL GARDINER (1782-1864) was a regular member of the Anthology Society. Born in Bristol, England, his surname was Hallowell. He added Gardiner in 1802. He eventually made his home in Gardiner, Maine, and was president of the Maine Historical Society from 1846 to 1855. He held an honorary membership in the Massachusetts Historical Society.

JOHN THORNTON KIRKLAND (1770-1840), Harvard, class of 1789, served as the president of the Anthology Society during its fading months. He was president of Harvard from 1810 to 1828.

JOSEPH McKEAN (1776-1818), Harvard, class of 1794, was pastor of the Congregational Church in Milton, Massachusetts. He succeeded John Quincy Adams to the Boylston chair, which he occupied until his death. He died in Cuba, where he had gone for his health.

ANDREWS NORTON (1786-1853), Harvard, class of 1804, was a corresponding member of the Anthology Society. At one time an effort was made to secure his services as its full-time editor. Norton subsequently founded the *General Repository and Review*, a magazine of high intellectual quality, published for two years in Cambridge. Later he became Dexter Professor of Sacred Literature at Harvard and an influential biblical scholar. Today he is unfortunately remembered only for his part in the quarrel

between the older generation of religious liberals and the Transcendentalists.

JOHN PIERCE (1773-1849), Harvard, class of 1793, was for fifty
years pastor of the church in Brookline, Massachusetts. He was
the secretary of the Harvard Board of Overseers for thirty-three
years. His notes on commencements at Harvard cover a span of
many years. He was present at sixty-three commencements and
led the singing of the tune of "St. Martin's" at fifty-four commencement dinners.

WINTHROP SARGENT (1783-1808), Harvard, class of 1803, was
the author of a satirical poem entitled *Boston*. He was a regular
member of the Anthology Society. His early death was caused
by tuberculosis.

JAMES SAVAGE (1784-1873), Harvard, class of 1803, a regular
member of the Anthology Society, was its vice-president in its
last period of existence. He was also the "Superintending Committee," or managing editor, of the *Anthology* for several years.
Later he became a well-known businessman and New England
antiquarian.

WILLIAM SMITH SHAW (1778-1826) was the son of the Reverend John Shaw and Elizabeth Smith, a sister of Abigail Adams.
Even more persecuted by poverty than the usual village minister's
son—his father was a minister at Haverhill, Massachusetts—he did
not enter Harvard until he was sixteen, a late age in his time.
When he was awarded his degree in 1798, he became private
secretary to President John Adams, serving in this capacity first
in Philadelphia and later, when the seat of government was
removed, in crude, half-improvised Washington. During these
years he began what was to grow into a large collection of rare
American pamphlets. After the election of 1800, Shaw studied
for the bar and was admitted to practice in 1804. Two years later
he was appointed a clerk of the District Court of Massachusetts,
and from then on he found the literary leisure he, like Walter,
preferred to the law. His connection with the founding and
nourishing of the Boston Athenaeum was singular. He became
known, in fact, as "Athenaeum Shaw."

SAMUEL COOPER THACHER (1785-1818), Harvard, class of 1804,

became minister of Boston's New South Church when Kirkland left it to become president of Harvard. His career cut short by tuberculosis, he died at Moulins, France, where he had gone for the climate. In *Anthology* days he was the magazine's first "Superintending Committee."

WILLIAM TUDOR, JR. (1779-1830), Harvard, class of 1796, belonged to one of Boston's most cosmopolitan families. He was a charter member of the Anthology Society and later the first editor of the *North American Review*. He died in Rio de Janeiro while serving under President John Quincy Adams as Charge d'Affaires of the United States.

ARTHUR MAYNARD WALTER (1780-1807), a great great-grandson of Increase Mather, was the son of the Reverend William Walter, loyalist rector of Trinity Church in Boston. After distinguishing himself at the Boston Latin School, he entered Harvard in 1794 at the age of fourteen. His college work earned high honors for him, but when the parts for the commencement of 1798 were distributed, he was so dissatisfied with his assignment that he refused it, thereby losing claim to his degree. He subsequently was awarded a degree with highest honors from Columbia College in New York City after a year in residence there. When he returned to Boston, he became a law student in the office of Samuel Dexter. In 1802 he began a European tour that lasted for two years. When he came back to Boston, he sought to establish a double career for himself in law and literature, but his legal interests were always secondary to his literary aspirations. An intimate friend of Joseph Stevens Buckminster, Walter was one of the few thoroughly faithful members of the Anthology Society. Had he lived he might well have become a scholar of George Ticknor's caliber.

BENJAMIN WELLES (1781-1860), a regular member of the Anthology Society, was a member of the Suffolk bar. Information about him is scanty.

WILLIAM WELLS (1773-1860), a charter member of the Anthology Society, was a bookseller and schoolmaster. Born in Broomsgrove, England, he emigrated to America and was graduated from Harvard in 1796.

The Era of the Anthology Society:

A Selected Bibliography

Primary Sources

Adams, John Quincy. *Lectures on Rhetoric and Oratory*. 2 vols. Cambridge, Mass., 1809.

Adams, John Quincy. *Memoirs . . . Comprising Portions of His Diary from 1795 to 1848*, ed. Charles Francis Adams. 12 vols. Philadelphia, 1874–1877.

Adams, John Quincy. *Writings*, ed. Worthington Chauncy Ford. 7 vols. New York: Macmillan Co., 1913–1917.

Adams, Thomas Boylston. "Letters of Thomas Boylston Adams to William Smith Shaw, 1799–1823," ed. Charles Grenfill Washburn, *Proceedings of the American Antiquarian Society*, n. s., XXVII, 85-176.

Ames, Fisher. *Works*. Boston, 1809.

Bentley, William. *Diary*. 4 vols. Salem, Mass.: The Essex Institute, 1905–1914. Gives a considerable amount of information about literary and religious life in Boston.

Buckminster, Joseph Stevens. *Works . . . with Memoir of His Life*, ed. Henry Ware, Jr. 2 vols. Boston, 1839.

Cameron, Kenneth Walter. *Emerson the Essayist*. 2 vols. Raleigh, N. C.: The Thistle Press, 1945. Reprints list of books in the Reverend William Emerson's library as this appeared in an auction catalogue. See Vol. II, 135-37

Catalogue of the Library of the Late Joseph Stevens Buckminster. Boston, 1812. For the time a large and elegant library that provides a useful index to the interests and tastes of the age.

Channing, William Ellery. "Rev. S. C. Thacher," *North American Review*, VII (May, 1818), 106-11.

Channing, William Henry. *Memoir of William Ellery Channing*. 3 vols. Boston, 1854. Although he was well known in Boston and had strong literary interests, Channing was not a member of the Anthology Society, nor was he one of the founders of the Athenaeum. He made a few contributions to the *Anthology*, but in the early years of his ministry he tended to avoid involvement in cultural enterprises of this kind.

Dwight, Timothy. *Travels in New England and New York.* 4 vols. New Haven, 1821–1822.

Felt, Joseph B. *Memorials of William Smith Shaw.* Boston, 1852. Very useful for miscellaneous information.

The General Repository and Review. 4 vols. Cambridge, Mass., 1812–1813. An interesting, short-lived quarterly edited by Andrews Norton; notable for the editor's effort to make it truly learned, especially in biblical criticism.

The Harvard Lyceum. 18 numbers. Cambridge, Mass., 1810–1811. A rather lively student publication in which Edward Everett had a part.

Howe, M. A. DeWolfe, ed. *Journal of the Proceedings of the Society Which Conducts The Monthly Anthology & Boston Review.* Boston: The Boston Athenaeum, 1910. A carefully edited volume, to which is appended a list of books mentioned in the *Journal*, a list of the officers of the Anthology Society, brief biographical notices of its regular members and corresponding members, a collation of the *Anthology* by Albert Matthews, a list identifying contributors to the magazine by volume and page number, and a thorough index.

Lee, Eliza Buckminster. *Memoirs of Rev. Joseph Buckminster, D. D., and of His Son, Rev. Joseph Stevens Buckminster.* Boston, 1849. A basic source for the study of the culture of early nineteenth-century Boston.

The Literary Miscellany, Including Dissertations and Essays on Subjects of Literature, Science, and Morals; Biographical and Historical Sketches; Critical Remarks on Language; with Occasional Reviews. 2 vols. 8 numbers. Cambridge, Mass., 1804–1806. Affiliated wtih the Phi Beta Kappa Society. Ambitious but undistinguished.

The Monthly Anthology, and Boston Review, Containing Sketches and Reports of Philosophy, Religion, History, Arts and Manners. 10 vols. Boston, 1803–1811.

Newell, W. E. "Andrews Norton," *Christian Examiner*, LV (November, 1853), 425-52.

Norton, Andrews. "Character of Rev. Joseph Stevens Buckminster," *General Repository and Review*, II (October, 1812), 306-14.

Norton, Andrews. "Letter of Mr. Norton to Mr. Ticknor," *Christian Examiner*, XLVII (September, 1849), 196-203.

Pierce, John. "Some Notes on the Anniversary Meetings of Phi Beta Kappa, Alpha of Massachusetts, 1803–1848," *Proceedings of the Massachusetts Historical Society*, ser. 2, IX, 110-43.

Quincy, Josiah. *History of the Boston Athenaeum, with Biographical Notices of Its Deceased Founders*. Cambridge, Mass., 1851. An indispensable work.

Sargent, Winthrop. *Boston: A Poem*. Boston, 1803. An immature but amusing and informative satire.

Smith, C. C. "Notice of William Tudor, Jr.," *Proceedings of the Massachusetts Historical Society, 1791–1835*, I, 429-33.

Sprague, William B. *Annals of the American Pulpit; or Commemorative Notices of Distinguished Clergymen of Various Denominations*. 9 vols. New York, 1857–1869. See Vols. II, V, VIII.

Thacher, Samuel Cooper. "Memoir of the Life and Character of the Late Rev. William Emerson," *Collections of the Massachusetts Historical Society*, ser. 2, I, 254-58.

Ticknor, George. "Memoirs of the Buckminsters," *Christian Examiner*, XLVII (September, 1849), 169-95. Review of Mrs. Lee's *Memoirs*.

Ticknor, George. *Life, Letters, and Journals*, eds. G. S. Hillard, Mrs. Anna Ticknor, and Miss Anna Eliot Ticknor. 2 vols. Boston, 1877. A central work in the literary history of New England.

Tudor, William. "The Monthly Anthology," in *Miscellanies* (Boston, 1821), 1-7. The only account of the magazine by a charter member of the Anthology Society.

Tudor, William. *Letters on the Eastern States*. Boston, 1821. Not very penetrating but suggestive.

Warren, Charles. *Jacobin and Junto: or, Early American Politics as Viewed in the Diary of Dr. Nathaniel Ames*. Cambridge, Mass.: Harvard University Press, 1931.

Willard, Sidney. *Memories of Youth and Manhood.* 2 vols. Cambridge, Mass., 1855. A prime source of information about some of the Anthologists.

Secondary Sources

Adams, Henry. *History of the United States, 1801–1817.* 9 vols. New York, 1889–1891.

Almy, Robert F. "The Role of the Club in American Literary History, 1700–1812." Unpublished Ph. D. dissertation, Harvard Universtity, 1934. An excellent survey of a neglected subject.

Bolton, Charles K., ed. *The Influence and History of the Boston Athenaeum.* Boston: The Boston Athenaeum, 1907. Contains two essays of particular interest: Barrett Wendell, "The Influence of the Athenaeum on Literature in America" and Charles K. Bolton, "The First One Hundred Years of Athenaeum History."

Bolton, Charles K., ed. "Social Libraries in Boston," *Publications of the Colonial Society of Massachusetts*, XII, 332-38.

Brooks, Van Wyck. *The Flowering of New England, 1815–1865.* Rev. ed. New York: E. P. Dutton and Co., 1940.

Bulfinch, Ellen Susan. *Life and Letters of Charles Bulfinch, Architect.* Boston and New York, 1896.

Charvat, William. *The Origins of American Critical Thought, 1810–1835.* Philadelphia: University of Pennsylvania Press, 1936.

Cooke, George Willis. *Unitarianism in America.* Boston: American Unitarian Association, 1902.

Curti, Merle. *The Growth of American Thought.* New York: Harper and Brothers, 1951.

East, Robert A. "Economic Development of New England Federalism," *New England Quarterly*, X (September, 1937), 430-46.

Ford, Worthington Chauncy. "The Recall of John Quincy Adams in 1808," *Proceedings of the Massachusetts Historical Society*, XLV, 354-73.

Goodfellow, Donald M. "The First Boylston Professor of

Goodfellow, Donald M. (*cont.*)
Rhetoric and Oratory," *New England Quarterly*, XIX (September, 1946), 372-89.

Haroutunian, Joseph. *Piety Versus Moralism: the Passing of the New England Theology*. New York: Henry Holt and Co., 1932. The best study of the development of religious liberalism in New England.

Holmes, Oliver Wendell. "Ralph Waldo Emerson," in *Works*. 15 vols. Boston and New York, 1892. XI, 1-28.

Lowell, James Russell. "Cambridge Thirty Years Ago," in *Works*. 11 vols. Boston and New York, 1899. I, 43-99.

Mott, Frank Luther. *A History of American Magazines, 1741–1850*. Cambridge, Mass.: Harvard University Press, 1939.

Palfrey, John Gorham. "Periodical Literature of the United States," *North American Review*, XXXIX (October, 1834), 277-301.

Parrington, Vernon L. *Main Currents in American Thought*. New York: Harcourt Brace and Co., 1927, 1930.

Quincy, Josiah. *History of Harvard University*. 2 vols. Cambridge, Mass., 1840.

Rusk, Ralph L. *The Life of Ralph Waldo Emerson*. New York: Charles Scribner's Sons, 1949.

Simpson, Lewis P. "The Era of Joseph Stevens Buckminster: Life and Letters in the Boston-Cambridge Community, 1800-1815." Unpublished Ph. D. dissertation, University of Texas, 1948. Contains much biographical and bibliographical information concerning the period of the Anthology Society.

Simpson, Lewis P. "*The Literary Miscellany* and *The General Repository:* Two Cambridge Periodicals of the Early Republic," *Library Chronicle of the University of Texas*, III (Spring, 1950), 177-90.

Simpson, Lewis P. "The Intercommunity of the Learned: Boston and Cambridge in 1800," *New England Quarterly*, XXIII (December, 1950), 491-503.

Simpson, Lewis P. "Not Men, But Books," *Boston Public Library Quarterly*, IV (October, 1952), 167-84. Significance of the first European journey of Ticknor and Everett.

Simpson, Lewis P. "A Literary Adventure of the Early Republic:

the Anthology Society and the *Monthly Anthology*," *New England Quarterly*, XXVII (June, 1954), 168-90.

Simpson, Lewis P. "Emerson and the Myth of New England's Intellectual Lapse," *Emerson Society Quarterly*, No. 10 (I Quarter, 1958), 28-31.

Simpson, Lewis P. "Federalism and the Crisis of Literary Order," *American Literature*, XXXII (November, 1960), 253-66. The way in which the Federalist defense of literary standards reflects the larger crisis of literature in Western society.

Simpson, Lewis P. "The City and the Symbolism of Literary Community in the United States," *Texas Quarterly*, III (Autumn, 1960), 97-111. An exploration of the literary sensibility that shaped Boston into a symbolic city of letters.

Tuckerman, Henry T. "Joseph Stevens Buckminster," *Southern Literary Messenger*, XXIV (January, 1857), 50-57.

Ware, William. *American Unitarian Biography*. 2 vols. Cambridge, Mass., 1851.

Winsor, Justin, ed. *The Memorial History of Boston*. 4 vols. Boston, 1881.

Whitehill, Walter Muir. *Boston: A Topographical History*. Cambridge, Mass.: Belknap Press of Harvard University Press, 1959.

Index